SEDONA HIKES

and MOUNTAIN BIKE RIDES

by
Richard K. Mangum
and Sherry G. Mangum

HEXAGON
PRESS
FLAGSTAFF, ARIZONA

NONLIABILITY STATEMENT:
While we have expended considerable effort to guarantee accuracy and have personally taken every one of these hikes, errors in field notes, transcription and typesetting can occur. Changes also occur on the land and some descriptions that were accurate when written may be inaccurate at press time. One storm, for example, can block a road or the Forest Service can change a trail. In addition to the problems of accuracy, there is the problem of injury. It is always possible that hikers may sustain harm while on a hike. The authors, publishers and all those associated with this book, directly or indirectly, disclaim any liability for accidents, injuries, damages or losses that may occur to anyone using this book. The responsibility for good health and safety while hiking is that of the user.

Printed on recycled paper

Printed by Northland Printing, Flagstaff, Arizona

Cover Design by Joan Carstensen, Northland Printing

TABLE OF CONTENTS

Nonliability Statement 2

Table of Contents 3

About the Authors 4

Tips on Sedona Hiking 5

How to Use This Book 6

Location Map 7

Mountain Bike Rides 8-9

The Hikes, A-Z 10-251

Index 252-254

Vortex Information 255

Scenic Drives 255

Rules of the Trail 256

ABOUT THE AUTHORS

RICHARD K. (DICK) MANGUM

Dick was born in Flagstaff and has lived there all his life. When his family acquired a second home in Back O' Beyond south of Sedona in 1951, he began his love affair with the Sedona area. He learned that by driving 25 miles, the distance between Flagstaff and Sedona, one can hike year around: in cool Flagstaff in summer and warm Sedona in winter.

After graduating from Flagstaff High School, he attended the University of Arizona, where he obtained his law degree. He returned to Flagstaff and engaged in the general practice of law for fifteen years, then became a Superior Court Judge for Coconino County in 1976, a position he still holds.

SHERRY G. MANGUM

Although Sherry was not born in Flagstaff, she has lived there since she was seven years old. Like Dick, she enjoyed getting into the outdoors from the time she was a toddler. She loves the scenic beauties of Sedona.

Inheriting her love of photography from her parents, both professionals, she has refined her skills to produce the photographs used in this book.

Adept at all aspects of photography, she prefers landscapes. Her work has been published in books and periodicals since 1978. Sherry's camera of choice is a Nikon F4.

TIPS ON SEDONA HIKING

ACCESS

Many of these hikes can be reached on paved roads. For those hikes on unpaved roads, you need to pay attention to conditions. Some of the roads when wet become slippery and impassable. Some, such as the upper part of the Schnebly Hill Road, are officially closed during the winter by locked gates.

ROCK CLIMBING

We do not provide any rock climbing information. If you want to go rock climbing, you are on your own. Much of the rock around Sedona is sandstone, a notoriously unstable surface.

THORNS

It seems sometimes that every plant along the hiking paths in the Sedona area contains thorns, spines or sharp-edged leaves. Pay attention. Learn to identify the fanged plants and avoid them.

VARMINTS

Sedona is in a life zone favorable to rattlesnakes. Even so, we have only seen one on all our hikes and he was just warning us from several feet away. There are also some scorpions and black widow spiders in the area, though we have never seen either. Pests like mosquitoes are scarce. There are no chiggers nor swarming insects like black flies. Our advice about varmints is: *Be watchful but not paranoid.*

WATER

Do not count on finding water anywhere. Take your water with you. In Sedona's hot dry climate you will need plenty of it.

WEATHER

Sedona is in a high desert, at an altitude of 4000 feet. Its finest weather is from October to May. During the summer it can be quite hot, with many days over 100°F. Some of the strenuous hikes can be exhausting in this kind of heat, so be prepared.

HOW TO USE THIS BOOK

Alphabetical arrangement. The 121 hikes in this book are arranged from A-Z starting on page 10 and running to page 251.

Index. The index starts at page 252. It groups the hikes by geographical areas and by special features.

Layout. The text describing a hike and the map of the hike are on facing pages so that you can take in everything at once. You don't have to hunt to find maps.

Maps. The maps are not to scale but their proportions are generally correct except for a few that are schematic. **The main purpose of the maps is to get you to the trailhead.** The maps show mileage point-to-point, while the text gives cumulative totals, so you have both.

Larger scale maps. For the big picture buy a Forest Service map or "Experience Sedona."

Map Symbols. Shields and striped lines indicate paved roads. Boxes and solid lines indicate unpaved roads.

Bold type. When you see a trail name in **bold** type it means that the hike is described in this book.

Ratings. We show hikes rated as easy, moderate and hard. These ratings are based on our own reactions. We are middle-aged deskbound types, not highly conditioned athletes who never tire.

Adjust our ratings for your own fitness level. The **hike-in-a-box** included with each map may be the best indicator of how hard a hike is.

Mileage. Driving distance was measured from the Sedona Y located at the junction of Highways 89A and 179. All hikes start from this point and were clocked in our 1986 Toyota Tercel. Milepost locations are also shown on the maps (by MP) on highways that have them. Hike mileage was measured by a pedometer.

Altitude. We measured altitude with a pocket altimeter. These are not perfectly accurate, but the span of distance between the high and low points on a hike should be accurate.

Access roads. To reach many of these hikes you will have to travel unpaved roads, some of them rough. Our Tercel has 4-wheel drive but not much clearance. Our access ratings were based on how well the Tercel handled the roads. Some drives require a high clearance vehicle.

Safety. We avoid taking risks on hikes. None of these hikes requires risky climbing.

Wilderness Areas. The Sedona area is blessed by having much of its public lands in desirable hiking places included within federally designated Wilderness Areas. This is great for the hiker, but please read the **Rules of the Trail** about them, page 256.

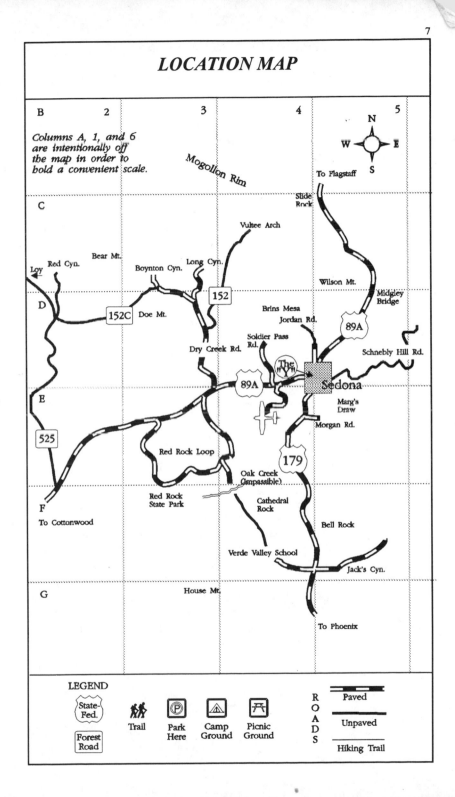

LOCATION MAP

MOUNTAIN BIKE RIDES

NOTE: See the hike descriptions for directions, descriptions and maps

Airport Hill
Follow instructions for the hike, and check out the Vortex on foot. Then ride to the top of the hill, turning left at the top. Go over to the large cross you will see. Dismount and walk to the viewpoint. It is one of Sedona's best views. An easy ride on paved roads. Page 12.

Black Mountain
This is a steep climb, but once on top you will have some fun exploring the little used roads on top of the mountain. There are many interesting viewpoints there. Page 34.

Black Mountain Mystery House
This is a good ride. The pitch is not terribly steep. You will enjoy some interesting sights along the way to the house. You can bike out past the house all the way to the end of the road and walk to an excellent viewpoint. Page 36.

Chicken Point
This is an easy ride that you will share with jeep tours. Nice colorful country. You will probably want to do the whole "collection" of sites along this road on one trip: Chicken Point, **Devils Dining Room** and **Submarine Rock**. Page 68.

Cockscomb
A superior ride. When you get to the Cockscomb, make the effort to hike to the top. You can keep biking on the road after that. It loops around the Cockscomb, about 1.5 miles, and joins FR 152A, on which you can swing northwest and rejoin the main road, another 1.5 miles. Then you loop back to the Northeast on FR 152C to rejoin the trailhead, about 1.4 miles, for a total of 6.4 miles. There is an interesting abandoned ranch to explore on the east face of the Cockscomb. The problem with the full loop is that the road is cut by several deep arroyos near the south face of the Cockscomb. Page 76.

Devils Kitchen
This is a short trip to an interesting site. You can keep biking out the old road to the Wilderness Area boundary to make it a fuller trip. Page 94.

House Mountain
After the fairly strenuous climb, you can explore the roads on the top. They run all over the place. Page 116.

Merry-Go-Round

This is fun and not very strenuous. You ride a portion of the old Schnebly Hill Road, which is washed out in spots but generally passable. You might want to keep going up the hill on the main road, to the Vista. Page 142.

Munds Mountain North

This ride follows old jeep roads along the rim of Schnebly Hill, providing some good views, then goes through the woods to emerge at Jacks Point. We recommend that you follow instructions for the hike all the way, parking your bike at the corner of the fence where the Wilderness Area starts and making the hike on foot. There are roads in this area outside the Wilderness Area that make good exploring. Page 150.

Oak Creek and Verde River Confluence

This has real potential. You travel over good unpaved roads to two places of interest, an Indian ruin (on private land; no trespassing) and the meeting of the rivers. Page 156.

Old Highway 79

This is a good ride. The old road is still perfectly usable by bikes. Watch out for some washouts. There is water in Dry Creek at times. Otherwise the road is suitable. Page 160.

Old Jim Thompson Road

A standout. The beginning of this ride is easy to find and the road thereafter is easy to follow. When you come around Steamboat Rock so that you can see down to Midgley Bridge, take note of Wilson Canyon, which is spanned by the bridge. You will ride up the canyon to a point where it narrows so that you can get across it. Then you come downhill, cross the canyon and go back to the bridge on the other side of the canyon. Page 162.

Robbers Roost

Ride up to the point where the hiking trail starts, dismount, and make the hike. You can then keep on biking on the road, which will climb part way up Casner Mountain. Page 182.

Turkey Creek

Bike to the hike trailhead from the Verde Valley School road. Don't try to ride the hiking trail. Instead, you will see a number of interesting roads in the area that are fun to explore. Page 224.

Van Deren Cabin

This is a point along FR 152. The entire length of that road, up to the Vultee Arch trailhead, makes a nice 9.6 mile ride. There is Wilderness Area at the end. Make a detour to Van Deren Cabin along the way. Page 230.

NOTE: You can't ride a bike in a Wilderness Area, and many of the hikes are located in Wilderness Areas. For this reason, there are fewer bike rides around Sedona than one might suppose.

A. B. YOUNG TRAIL

General Information
Location Map B5
Munds Park and Wilson Mt. USGS Maps
Coconino Forest Service Map

Driving Distance One Way: 8.8 miles (Time 20 minutes)
Access Road: All cars, Paved all the way
Hiking Distance One Way: 1.6 miles (Time 80 minutes)
How Strenuous: Hard
Features: Views

NUTSHELL: This is a steep trail up the west wall of Upper Oak Creek Canyon near Bootlegger Campground, 8.8 miles north of Sedona.

DIRECTIONS:
From the Sedona Y Go:
North on Highway 89A for 8.8 miles (MP 383). There is no official parking area for the trail. Sometimes you can park in the Bootlegger campground, but don't count on it. Look for a place on the shoulder of the highway.

TRAILHEAD: Walk through Bootlegger Campground, where you will see a trail going down to the creek. You must wade the creek or try to hop across it on boulders. There is a marked trailhead on the other shore. This is a maintained trail. You will see a rusty sign reading, "A B Young #100."

DESCRIPTION: Once you get across the creek you will see an old road running parallel to the creek. This old road was formerly the main road through Oak Creek Canyon and it is not what you want. Your trail goes uphill.
　　　　The trail is a broad one at the beginning. It started its life as a cattle trail, but it was improved during the 1930s with CCC labor, so it is better engineered than many of the old cattle trails that are now hiking trails. It was widened and the grades were moderated so it is not as vertical as it was originally.
　　　　An interesting thing about the hike is that you experience three conspicuous life zones. Down at the creek, there is the lush riparian life zone. As you begin to climb, you get into a high desert life zone. At the top, you are in a pine forest. Once you rise above the trees at creekside, you are on an exposed face with no shade. This can be a very hot hike in the summer though it is in the cool upper canyon.
　　　　The hike is steep, so although the trail is a good one, it is a hard climb.

You get some fine views as you go. At the top, you will notice that the trail continues. For the purposes of this book, we have ended the trail at the top, but you can continue southwest about 1.25 miles to a fire lookout tower. If this tower is occupied, the ranger may be willing to have you come up and share the tremendous views. The tower is the East Pocket Fire Lookout Tower, as this part of the rim is called East Pocket.

From many vantage points both above and below the A. B. Young Trail you can see it zigzagging up the face of the west canyon wall. It makes sharp diagonal turns at the end of each zag and is so obviously a passageway cut into the face of the canyon that some people mistake it for Highway 89A when they see it from a distance.

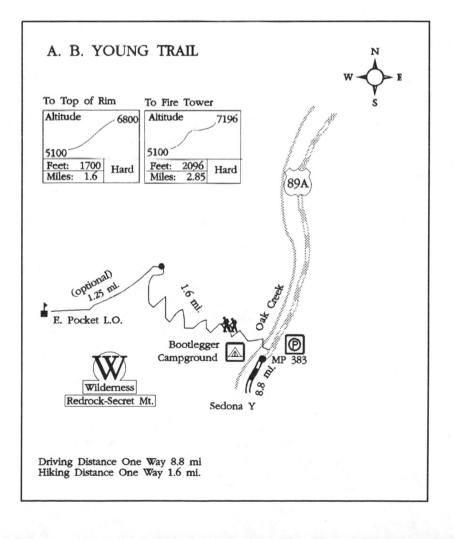

AIRPORT HILL VORTEX

General Information
Location Map E4
Sedona USGS Map
Coconino Forest Service Map

Driving Distance One Way: 1.3 miles (Time 10 minutes)
Access Road: All cars, Paved all the way
Hiking Distance One Way: 0.5 miles (Time 30 minutes)
How Strenuous: Easy
Features: Vortex Spot

NUTSHELL: This is the easiest and most accessible Sedona Vortex spot.

DIRECTIONS:
From the Sedona Y Go:
Southwest on Highway 89A for 1 mile, to Airport Road. Turn left onto Airport Road and drive uphill to the 1.3 miles spot. Here you will see a wide apron on the right side of the road. Park there.

TRAILHEAD: Unmarked, but you will see a path across the road to your left.

DESCRIPTION: There are a couple of access points to the vortex spot on the Airport Road. This is the easier one.
After walking 0.1 miles, you will reach a saddle where the trail forks up to the right, and down to the left. If you want to go directly to the place generally regarded as *the* vortex spot, go downhill to the left, where you will come to a flat spot on a ledge. There is usually a medicine wheel made of stones here. This trail goes on for about 0.5 miles, descending and getting fainter as it goes. It terminates at an interesting old stone water tank, and is probably not worth taking beyond the vortex spot unless you just want to stretch your legs.
After experiencing what you can at the vortex spot, climb back up and take the path to the top of the knoll. It is easy to climb and is a great viewpoint. You will see another knoll to the south, with a path connecting it to the knoll on which you are standing. It's fun to go over there and explore too.
The other vortex spots in this book are: **Bell Rock, Boynton Canyon, Boynton Spires, Cathedral Rock from Back O' Beyond, Cathedral Rock from Verde Valley School Road** and **Cow Pies.**
People want to know what will happen at a Vortex. Books have been written about Sedona's vortexes (vortices?) and you will find these books in Sedona book stores. Experts claim that each vortex spot is different: some have negative energy, some positive; some are male, some are female; some are

magnetic, some electric, and on and on. People come from great distances to visit these power spots and some are taken to the vortexes on guided tours. We have been at a couple of the spots when tours came along. Our preference is to enjoy these places quietly and in solitude.

Each person will have a unique experience, ranging from negative to neutral to positive. Some people have a really cosmic experience, while others feel nothing. The best advice we can give you is just to let yourself be open to get what you can.

Because this vortex is so easy to reach, it is often crowded, which may detract from the spiritual feeling you are seeking at a vortex. Our personal favorite vortex spot is at Boynton Canyon, but to each his own.

From the farthest south knoll you can see a distinct trail running horizontally across the face of Airport Mesa and there is clear access to it from the knoll. We have hiked this trail. It started out promisingly but then dwindled down to nothing in about a half mile.

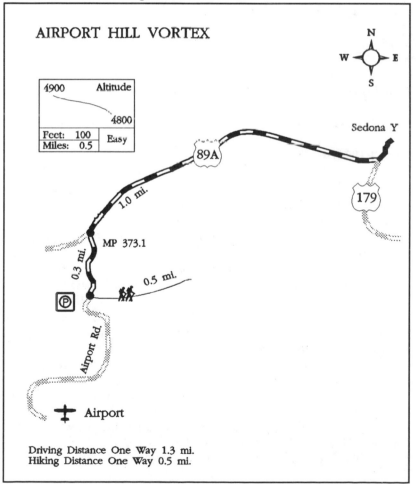

AIRPORT HILL VORTEX

Sedona Y

89A

179

MP 373.1

0.5 mi.

1.0 mi.

0.3 mi.

P

Airport Rd.

Airport

4900	Altitude
	4800

Feet:	100	Easy
Miles:	0.5	

N
W — E
S

Driving Distance One Way 1.3 mi.
Hiking Distance One Way 0.5 mi.

ALLENS BEND

General Information
Location Map D5
Munds Park USGS Map
Coconino Forest Service Map

Driving Distance One Way: 2.3 miles (Time 10 minutes)
Access Road: All cars, Paved all the way
Hiking Distance One Way: 0.5 miles (Time 30 minutes)
How Strenuous: Easy
Features: Creekside walk, Small Indian ruin

NUTSHELL: This trail, located 2.3 miles north of Sedona, provides an easy, yet delightful creekside ramble.

DIRECTIONS:
From the Sedona Y Go:
    North on Highway 89A 2.3 Miles (MP 376.5) to the Grasshopper Point Picnic Area. Park at the lot on Highway 89A or drive to the bottom lot.

TRAILHEAD: Rusty sign at north end of creek-level parking lot.

DESCRIPTION: The picnic area is open only during the summer season, roughly May 1-November 1. If it is open, you can drive down a paved road to a loop parking lot that has capacity for a couple of dozen cars. It also has a toilet. If the gate is closed, then you can park in the upper lot, next to the highway. It's about 0.33 miles to walk to the trailhead from there.
    The trail does not go down toward Oak Creek. Instead, it hugs the west wall of the canyon. The trail is easy. For about the first 0.15 miles, it moves along a redrock ledge. In some spots stones have been mortared into place to pave the trail and to make steps. You walk along the base of a 100 foot tall red cliff, which is undercut and is very interesting. The cliff is not nearly so towering as many in the Sedona area, but it has its own charm and is more human sized and intimate. The creek is to your right (east) at all times, anywhere from 20 to 100 yards away.
    At 0.19 miles you reach a fork. The main trail is the left fork. The right one goes to the creek, to a scenic spot that is well worth a short detour. The trail is shaded all the way and the creek—if by nothing other than its sound—offers refreshment.
    Just beyond this fork take a look to your left and you will see what appears to be a small Indian ruin in a shallow cave.
    The vegetation along the trail is agreeable, a forest of sycamores,

cypress, juniper and shrubbery.

At 0.41 miles you reach another fork. You are almost at the end of the trail here. To your left you will see an abandoned stone building and some rock walls and a flat area. This is an old campground. The building was a public toilet. If you take the left fork, you will go uphill and join Highway 89A at the **Casner Canyon** trailhead. If you go right, you will end at a nice scenic place on the creek.

The Allens Bend Trail is a sleeper. Many hikers who prefer to hike in remote country away from crowds might feel it unworthy of a look when they find out where it is located. We prefer the back country but every trail has its charm and its contribution to make. This is a pretty trail that is accessible any time of year, unlike some of the wild backcountry hikes, the trailheads of which can't be reached when the roads are muddy. Allens Bend is also valuable as a hike that goes right along the creekbank.

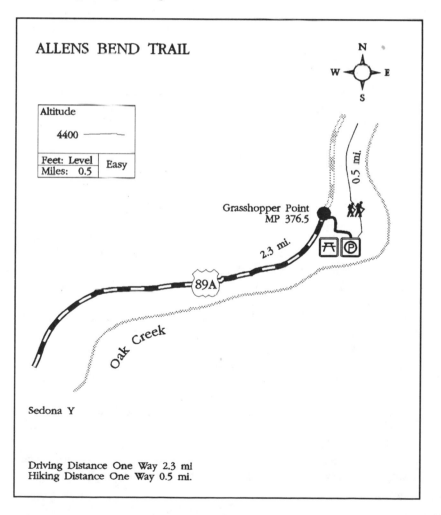

ALLENS BEND TRAIL

N
W — E
S

Altitude

4400 ————

| Feet: Level | Easy |
| Miles: 0.5 | |

Grasshopper Point
MP 376.5

0.5 mi.

2.3 mi.

89A

Oak Creek

Sedona Y

Driving Distance One Way 2.3 mi
Hiking Distance One Way 0.5 mi.

ANGEL FALLS

General Information
Location Map D4
Wilson Mountain USGS Map
Coconino Forest Service Map

Driving Distance One Way: 1.5 miles (Time 10 minutes)
Access Road: All cars, Last half mile is unpaved
Hiking Distance One Way: 2.5 miles (Time 90 minutes)
How Strenuous: Moderate
Features: Waterfall

NUTSHELL: You start this hike on a maintained trail then bushwhack along a streambed to reach a box canyon where two waterfalls are located.

DIRECTIONS:
From the Sedona Y Go:

North on Highway on 89A (toward Flagstaff) for 0.30 miles to Jordan Road, which is in the middle of uptown Sedona. Turn left and take Jordan Road to its end, where the paving stops. Keep going on the unpaved road. Your goal is the Shooting Range. At 1.1 miles, you will intersect a private road. Turn left here. You will reach the Shooting Range fence at 1.5 miles. Park outside unless you have a key. You don't want to get locked in.

TRAILHEAD: Start this hike at the Brins Mesa Trailhead.

DESCRIPTION: Start measuring trail mileage from the outside gate. It is 0.26 miles across the Shooting Range lot to the Brins Mesa Trailhead, where you will find a rusty sign reading **Brins Mesa #119**. The first mile of the trail from the sign follows a closed jeep road, and it is wide and easy. It takes you to the foot of Brins Mesa.

Stay at the bottom of the mesa and follow an old road to your right. It disappears in about 0.2 miles. From there a footpath is marked by cairns. You are walking along the base of Brins Mesa. The trail goes onto a redrock ledge, and here the cairns become tricky. Some lead you directly toward Brins Mesa while others take you downhill, into a side canyon. These downhill cairns into the canyon mark the trail that you are to take.

The trail goes into a small wash that runs parallel to Mormon Canyon. You must come out of the wash and move across country for about 0.1 mile, and then enter Mormon Canyon, which is much bigger.

From that point, you work your way upstream. There is an irony here: if there is water in the streambed, you may not be able to hike it. If there is no water, you can hike it, but there will be no water coming over Angel Falls.

Walking the stream is hard, but a payoff comes when you get to the end of the canyon. It stops in a spectacular box against the flank of Wilson Mountain, where Angel Falls is located. This place feels truly remote and is fun to explore. You can work your way up into the box, where there are some fascinating redrock ledges and sculptures.

Wilson Mountain is the tallest mountain in the Sedona area and its land mass is huge. There are two good hikes to the top of Wilson: **Wilson Mountain North** and **Wilson Mountain South**, but this is one of the rare hikes that takes you to the base of the mountain. **The Old Jim Thompson Road** is another, although it is at a higher level than the Angel Falls hike.

Generally we have tried to focus our attention in this book on established trails. However where there is a special hike that can only be reached by bushwhacking, we include it—such as Angel Falls.

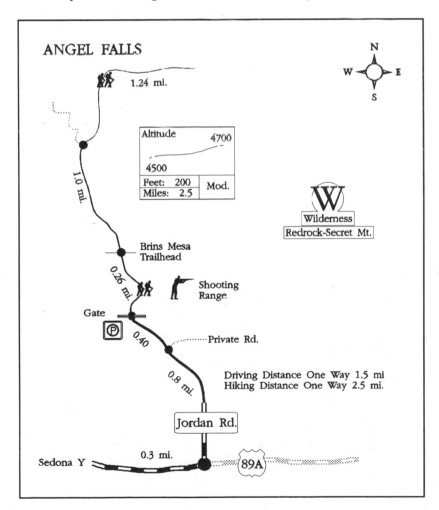

ANGEL FALLS

1.24 mi.

N
W · E
S

Altitude 4700
4500
Feet: 200 | Mod.
Miles: 2.5

1.0 mi.

Wilderness
Redrock-Secret Mt.

Brins Mesa
Trailhead

0.26 mi.

Shooting
Range

Gate

0.40

Private Rd.

0.8 mi.

Driving Distance One Way 1.5 mi
Hiking Distance One Way 2.5 mi.

Jordan Rd.

0.3 mi.

Sedona Y

89A

APACHE FIRE TRAIL

General Information
Location Map F3
Sedona USGS Map
Coconino Forest Service Map

Drive Distance One Way: 8.8 miles (Time 15 minutes)
Access Road: All vehicles, All paved
Hiking Distance, Complete Loop: 1.95 miles (Time 1.0 hours)
How Strenuous: Moderate
Features: Oak Creek, Red Rock State Park, Views

NUTSHELL: This moderate trail is located in Red Rock State Park 8.8 miles southwest of Sedona. It takes you to the top of the hill on which the exotically named House of Apache Fire is located.

DIRECTIONS:
From the Sedona Y Go:
　　　　Southwest on Highway 89A (toward Cottonwood) for a distance of 5.5 miles (MP 368.6) to the Lower Red Rock Loop Road. Turn left on the Lower Red Rock Loop Road and follow it to the 8.5 miles point, where you will see the entry to Red Rock State Park. Turn right into the park. You will come to a toll booth where an admission is charged. From that point, drive to the Visitor Center and park there, at 8.8 miles.

TRAILHEAD: This is a marked and maintained trail, part of the network of seven trails planned for the park. Go through the Visitor Center. Though the center is not marked as the trailhead for this hike, it is the starting point.

DESCRIPTION: Enjoy the Visitor Center and then walk through it, turning right on the paved trail. At 0.08 miles you will come to the first trail junction. Here the **Smoke Trail** forks to the right, where Sentinel Crossing is located. Go straight here. The sign at this junction shows your destination as *"Kingfisher Crossing, House of Apache Fire."*
　　　　Soon after this you will reach another junction. Turn right here, to Kingfisher Crossing, which is a major bridge across the creek. You will see the House of Apache Fire on top of a knoll. It is a pueblo style house built of native rock.
　　　　When you cross the bridge you will reach another trail junction, where the **Kisva** and **Eagles' Nest** trails go right. You will go left there and shortly thereafter will be at the base of the knoll on which the house is located. You will see a driveway going uphill to your right to get to the house. To your

left is a short flight of redrock steps and a sign for the Apache Fire Trail and the **Frye Wash Trail.** This is the place where the Apache Fire Trail starts.

Walk up the steps and you will find yourself on a nice gentle trail heading south, away from the park and into undeveloped country. This part of the trail is a welcome getaway from the developed area. The trail makes a big loop. Toward the far end of the loop the Frye Wash Trail takes off. From here you begin to turn north and climb the knoll.

At the top of the knoll you will be at eye level with the House of Apache Fire and you will have a good view of this interesting structure. A bench has been thoughtfully placed at about the one mile point. It is a good place to sit and enjoy the views. Just beyond the bench the **Coyote Ridge Trail** forks to the left.

From this point the trail comes down the knoll and intersects the Kisva Trail. Turn right here and you will return to the bridge at Kingfisher Crossing. From the bridge you go back to the Visitor Center

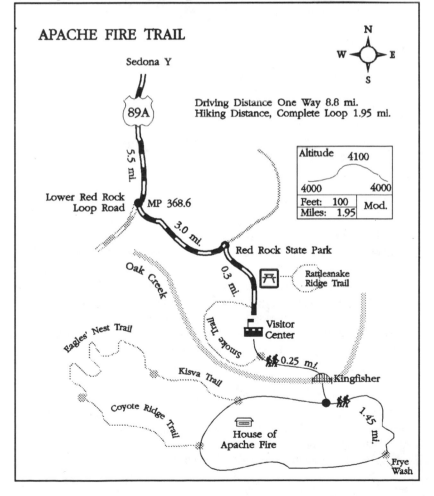

APACHE FIRE TRAIL

Sedona Y

89A

Driving Distance One Way 8.8 mi.
Hiking Distance, Complete Loop 1.95 mi.

N
W — E
S

5.5 mi.

Lower Red Rock Loop Road

MP 368.6

3.0 mi.

Altitude 4100
4000   4000
Feet: 100   Mod.
Miles: 1.95

Red Rock State Park

Oak Creek

0.3 mi.

Rattlesnake Ridge Trail

Eagles' Nest Trail

Smoke Trail

Visitor Center

0.25 mi.

Kisva Trail

Kingfisher

Coyote Ridge Trail

1.45 mi.

House of Apache Fire

Frye Wash

APACHE MAID TRAIL

Great View of Area
Peace & quiet

General Information
Location Map G6
Casner Butte and Apache Maid USGS Maps
Coconino Forest Service Map

Driving Distance One Way: 17.2 miles (Time 30 minutes)
Access Road: All cars, Last 2.5 miles gravel, in good condition
Hiking Distance One Way: 3.75 miles (Time 2 hours)
How Strenuous: Hard
Features: Views of Wet Beaver Creek Country, Rock Art

NUTSHELL: You hike the Bell Crossing Trail for two miles, then branch off to climb Casner Butte, 17 miles south of Sedona.

DIRECTIONS:
From the Sedona Y Go:
South on Highway 179 (toward Phoenix) for 14.7 Miles (MP 298.9), to the I-17 intersection. Go straight here rather than getting on I-17. You will see a sign for Beaver Creek Ranger Station. At 15.2 miles, there is a junction, where FR 618 goes left. Take FR 618.
At 16.9 miles, just before the ranger station, you will see a sign for the Bell Crossing Trailhead. Turn left here. The well marked parking lot is at 17.2 miles.

TRAILHEAD: Signed and marked at the parking lot.

DESCRIPTION: From the trailhead, take the Bell Crossing Trail. It goes upcanyon along Wet Beaver Creek, sometimes near it, sometimes away from it, but always following its path. Even when you are not near the creek, you can hear water running, a pleasant sound in desert country. The waterway is lined with typical riparian vegetation: tall sycamores and cottonwoods.
As you look up the canyon, you see a flank of the Mogollon Rim, a giant uplift running across Arizona and New Mexico. The top of the rim marks the southern boundary of the Colorado Plateau. Its base is the northern boundary of the Sonoran Desert, so it is a highly significant land feature.
The trail is an old jeep road, broad and easy to walk. As you walk along the trail, note the canyon walls: they contain the same redrock as in Sedona in the lower layers but the top is covered with a thick cap of lava. If it weren't for that top layer of hard rock, this country would be just as eroded and colorful as Sedona.
At about 0.6 miles, look for a large boulder on the left side of the trail.

On the side facing away from you is some rock art.

At the 2.0 mile point you will hit a fork where the Apache Maid Trail, #15, branches to the left and climbs Casner Butte. This is a steep climb, rising about 1000 feet in 1.75 miles. You will be rewarded by good views at the top, but the trail itself is uninteresting. We suggest stopping at the top.

The trail goes on to the head of Wet Beaver Creek, and is the point of departure for the rugged types who hike Wet Beaver Creek from top to bottom, a multi-day trip, definitely not an undertaking for casual hikers.

The Apache Maid Trail was built as a cattle trail, not as a scenic trail. Sedona ranchers would graze their animals in the lower warm country in winter and then take them to the high county on top of the rim for summer. Apache Maid is the name of a mountain on top of the rim where one of the largest ranches of its day was located. There is a fire lookout tower on top of Apache Maid Mountain. You can drive all the way to the tower. Take the Stoneman Lake Road to get there.

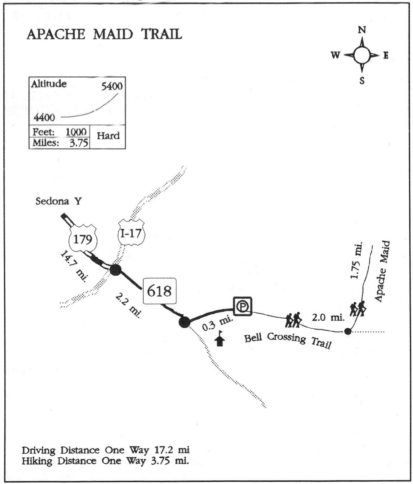

APACHE MAID TRAIL

Driving Distance One Way 17.2 mi
Hiking Distance One Way 3.75 mi.

BATTLEMENT MESA

General Information
Location Map E5
Sedona USGS Map
Coconino Forest Service Map

Driving Distance One Way: 2.0 miles (Time 10 minutes)
Access Road: All cars, Paved all the way
Hiking Distance One Way: 1.5 Miles (Time 60 minutes)
How Strenuous: Moderate
Features: Devil's Dining Room (sinkhole), Views

NUTSHELL: This trail is located in Sedona's "backyard" at the south end of Marg's Draw. It requires a moderate climb among interesting rocks for a great view.

DIRECTIONS:
From the Sedona Y Go:

South on Highway 179 (toward Phoenix) for 1.4 miles (MP 312.1) to Morgan Road in the Broken Arrow Subdivision. Turn left on Morgan Road and follow it to its end, at 2.0 miles, where you park at the cattle guard or just beyond it.

TRAILHEAD: This is an unmarked, unmaintained trail. Walk the road, FR 179F, to Devil's Dining Room, where this trail starts.

DESCRIPTION: Walk along the dirt road. This road is popular with the jeep tours, and you may have to share it. At 0.34 miles, turn off to the right on a sunken road. At 0.42 miles, you will reach the **Devil's Dining Room,** a sinkhole surrounded by boulders and a fence, and worth a look. Behind the sinkhole is a hill. You will see a path going up this hill. Take this path. It is your trail.

At 0.65 miles, you will come out onto a redrock ledge. Walk along it toward the saddle you can see on the skyline. In a little over one hundred feet you will see a trail marked by cairns to the left. It is the trail you want. First, however, you might enjoy walking to the end of the ledge, to see the interesting rock formations. Ignore cairns at end of ledge.

Then, it's up to the top. Go back to the trail and follow it to the saddle, where you will get great views to the north toward Sedona and to the south toward Poco Diablo. The **Twin Buttes** Trail takes off to the left from here, but you want to go up to the right, toward the "castle" rock formation on top of Battlement Mesa.

      Once there, you can explore, working your way around the mesa if you choose. It's a fascinating place.

      We like the name Battlement Mesa. It is a little more high-falutin' than some of the more mundane Sedona names such as Rabbit Ears or H. S. (for horse s—) Canyon, but it describes perfectly the appearance of this formation. A battlement is the kind of toothed wall that you would see on a castle. The knob on the top of Battlement Mesa looks like a castle and the ledges below it are scalloped in some places so that they look toothed. Seen from the right angle, this formation is aptly named.

      Battlement Mesa is another one of those places that has a deceptive appearance. From the ground you get the impression that it is flat and bare on top and that you would be able to walk around it as if you were on a football field. Not so. The top is rugged and by no means flat. It is broken by fissures and declivities so that you have to pick your way around. In spite of this, it is possible to circle the top if you want to make the effort.

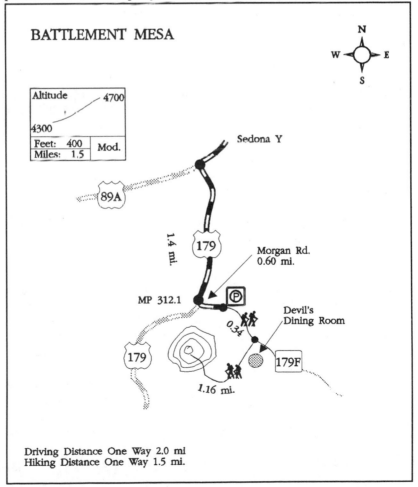

BATTLEMENT MESA

Driving Distance One Way 2.0 mi
Hiking Distance One Way 1.5 mi.

BEAR MOUNTAIN

General Information
Location Map C2
Wilson Mountain USGS Map
Coconino Forest Service Map

Driving Distance One Way: 8.9 miles (Time 20 minutes)
Access Road: All cars, Last 1.2 miles dirt, in good condition
Hiking Distance One Way: 2.2 miles (Time 90 minutes)
How Strenuous: Hard, Very steep
Features: View

NUTSHELL: Climbing this prominent mountain 8.9 miles northwest of Sedona is a challenge, but the views from the top are superb.

DIRECTIONS:
From the Sedona Y Go:
Southwest on Highway 89A (toward Cottonwood) for 3.2 miles (MP 371) to Dry Creek Road. Go right on Dry Creek Road to the 6.1 mile point, where Dry Creek Road joins the Long Canyon Road, both paved. Turn left here, on FR 152C, and go to the 7.7 mile point, where it joins the Boynton Canyon Road.
Turn left here on the Boynton Pass Road, FR 152C. The paving soon ends, to be replaced by a good dirt road. Stop at the 8.9 mile point, just before a cattle guard. The parking area is on the right.

TRAILHEAD: The Bear Mt. Trail shares its parking space with the **Doe Mt. Trail**, and you will see signs for both trails there. Crawl through the "window frame" in the fence to begin the Bear Mt. Trail, #54.

DESCRIPTION: The first 0.25 miles of the hike are across what seems to be flat land to the base of the mountain. In fact, the land is badly eroded and there are many gulches. You have to cross three of them. The trail is marked by cairns. Be sure to follow them, because this is cattle country, and wherever the cattle wander in this dry soil they leave what appears to be a trail but is really an aimless meander.
Bear Mountain will surprise you. As you climb, you keep thinking that you have reached the top. Actually, you will encounter five steppes or terraces. You are climbing steeply almost all the way. The good news is that the beautiful views begin with the first steppe. The higher you go, the more of a panorama you get and the better the views are.
At 2.2 miles, you reach the base of steppe number five, the true top.

It's a good stopping place. We quit here, but the trail goes on, making what appears to be a hard climb over slickrock.

The bulk of the mountain is on steppe four. The surface here is eroded along crossbedding lines and a tiny amount of soil has formed in the cracks. Sparse vegetation grows in this soil, making the grasses and other plants form lines and rows that match the seams in the stone. In the right light, this causes fascinating patterns.

The top could well be called *Bare* Mountain rather than Bear Mountain, for there is precious little growing on it.

Friends tell us that from Capitol Butte you are supposed to be able to see a bear in the contours of the top of Bear Mountain. We have tried this from several viewpoints but were never able to see the bear. That's the way it is with these landmark figures: sometimes you can see them readily and sometimes you can't see them at all no matter how hard you try. According to our sources, the bear is recumbent and it is his round ears that really make the formation.

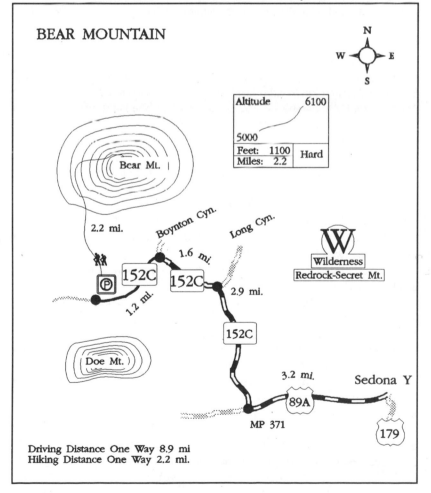

BEAR MOUNTAIN

N
W — E
S

Altitude 6100

5000

| Feet: | 1100 | Hard |
| Miles: | 2.2 | |

Bear Mt.

2.2 mi.

Boynton Cyn.

Long Cyn.

1.6 mi.

152C

152C

2.9 mi.

Wilderness
Redrock-Secret Mt.

1.2 mi.

Doe Mt.

152C

3.2 mi.

Sedona Y

89A

MP 371

179

Driving Distance One Way 8.9 mi
Hiking Distance One Way 2.2 mi.

BEAR SIGN TRAIL

General Information
Location Map   C4
Loy Butte and Wilson Mountain USGS Maps
Coconino Forest Service Map

Driving Distance One Way: 9.6 miles (Time 45 minutes)
Access Road: Last 4.4 miles very rough, High clearance best
Hiking Distance One Way: 3.25 miles (Time 90 minutes)
How Strenuous: Moderate
Features: Secluded canyon, Beautiful redrocks

NUTSHELL: Located 9.6 miles north of Sedona, this is a wilderness hike that follows a streambed to the base of the Mogollon Rim.

DIRECTIONS:
From the Sedona Y Go:
　　　　Southwest on Highway 89A (toward Cottonwood) for 3.2 miles (MP 371) to the Dry Creek Road. Turn right on Dry Creek Road and follow it to the 5.2 mile point, where FR 152 branches off to the right. Turn right and follow FR 152 to its end. At 9.6 miles, just 100 yards before the Vultee Arch parking area, pull off to the left and park.

TRAILHEAD: At parking area. There is a rusty sign: Dry Creek #52.

DESCRIPTION: You will walk across a little arroyo and around the toe of a hill for about 0.1 miles, where you will encounter Dry Creek. At the entry point, the canyon cut by Dry Creek is rather shallow and wide. The trail follows up the creek, which usually *is* dry, northerly. If any appreciable amount of water is running in the creek, you might want to postpone this hike until the creek is dry, for the trail crosses the creek at least a dozen times.
　　　　As you walk, the trail climbs, but this is gradual and you are barely conscious of it.
　　　　At 0.63 miles, you reach a point where the creek forks at a reef. The left-hand channel is the Bear Sign Trail, and the right fork is the **Dry Creek Trail**. There is a rusty sign in the left channel marked "Bear Sign #59."
　　　　From this point, the canyon deepens and you are treated to the sight of giant redrock buttes on both sides of the creek. As you proceed, you will notice a change in the flora, as the rise in altitude changes the life zones.
　　　　The trail ends where it intersects a channel running east and west. We are informed that this channel can be hiked. To the east, it would connect with Dry Creek Pack Trail. Maps show that you could do a loop, going up the Bear

Sign Trail and coming back via the Dry Creek Pack Trail, but we have not tried this.

Both the Bear Sign Trail and its neighboring Dry Creek Trail take you far away from habitation. They are nice if you want to get away into pristine country. Both trails head toward the Mogollon Rim and bump right against the base of it. The beauty of such trails is that even though they take you into wild and primitive country they are not dangerous. Stay in the canyons that define these trails and you won't get lost.

What is bear sign? Bears leave a number of marks. Their droppings are distinctive. They scratch trees in a characteristic way. They uproot anthills. Also they will eat small animals such as squirrels very neatly, separating the hide and skeleton from the flesh and leaving a little fur coat behind. We haven't seen any bear sign in Bear Sign, but it is bear country. Experts estimate that there are about four thousand bears in Arizona and they thrive in brushy country at Sedona's elevation.

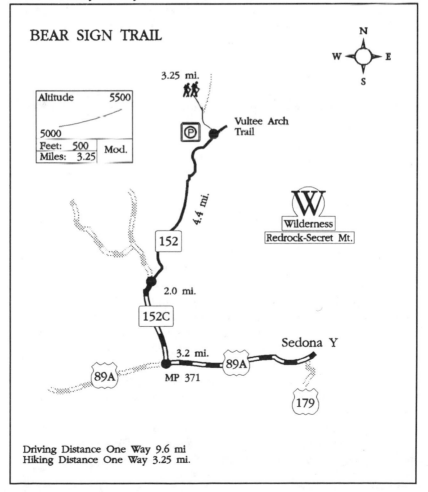

BEAVERHEAD

General Information
Location Map G5
Casner Butte and Lake Montezuma USGS Maps
Coconino Forest Service Map

Driving Distance One Way: 11.2 miles (Time 20 minutes)
Access Road: All paved
Hiking Distance One Way: 1.1 miles (Time 45 minutes)
How Strenuous: Moderate
Features: Historic road, Views

NUTSHELL: Located 11.2 miles south of Sedona, you hike 1000 feet to the top of the Mogollon Rim along an ancient Hopi trail that was converted into a wagon road in the 1870s.

DIRECTIONS:
From the Sedona Y Go:
　　　　South on Highway 179 (toward Phoenix) for a distance of 11.2 miles (MP 302.2) where you will see a gravel driveway to your left. Turn in on it and park by the gate in the barbed wire fence.

TRAILHEAD: You will follow the old road from the gate.

DESCRIPTION: From the unlocked gate where you parked, walk up the dirt road a distance of 0.1 miles. There you will see a road to your right that has been blocked by a dirt berm. Walk over the berm and you will pick up the old road. You follow it uphill.
　　　　At the start of the hike, take a moment to look at your objective. High above, you will see a ridge with a long section of jagged cliffs. This is not an isolated ridge but a part of the Mogollon Rim. You are about to walk a short stretch of The Palatkwapi Trail, used by the Hopi Indians for more than 1200 years. The trail starts at the Hopi mesas and ends at Camp Verde (with a branch to Jerome). The challenge to the pathfinders as they came off the high country was to find a gentle way down from the top of the Mogollon Rim to the Verde Valley. The route went from the Hopi mesas to Sunset Crossing (Winslow), Chavez Pass, Stoneman Lake, and Rattlesnake Canyon to the top of the Rim. As you walk along this trail, you can admire the choice that the ancients made. Except for being rocky, the way is excellent.
　　　　Spanish explorers followed the trail in the late 1500s. It was explored by army scouts in the 1860s and then, after the Civil War, when the army undertook to subdue hostile Indians, the old trail was improved as a wagon road

linking Fort Apache and Camp Verde. Once established by the military, private operators became interested in the road and a stage line ran over it between 1876-1882. Until the Schnebly Hill Road was built in Sedona in 1902, the Beaverhead Road was the only road Sedona residents had to get to Flagstaff in a wagon. Think about these things as you enjoy this hike.

The road is easy to follow and the area has a pleasant feel. You soon climb high enough to get good views of the scenic surrounding country. At 0.75 miles you will reach the beginning of an incredibly rocky passage. Many a wagon wheel must have broken here.

At 0.85 miles you will reach the first top. In this area the old road looks almost like a trench, as it is deeply lined by the stones that were rolled to the sides. At 1.1 miles you will be at the true top. Here there are some exceptional views. Walk to your left a bit to stand on the cliff tops for unimpeded sightseeing. The road veers away from the cliffs and continues its long journey northward (it is 145 miles long) from here over drab country.

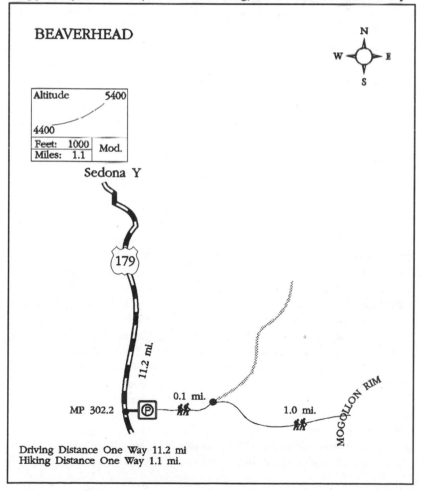

BEAVERHEAD

| Altitude | 5400 |

4400

| Feet: | 1000 | Mod. |
| Miles: | 1.1 | |

Sedona Y

179

11.2 mi.

MP 302.2

0.1 mi.

1.0 mi.

MOGOLLON RIM

Driving Distance One Way 11.2 mi
Hiking Distance One Way 1.1 mi.

BELL CROSSING TRAIL

General Information
Location Map G6
Apache Maid and Casner Butte USGS Maps
Coconino Forest Service Map

Driving Distance One Way: 17.2 miles (Time 30 minutes)
Access Road: All cars, Last 2.5 miles gravel, in good condition
Hiking Distance One Way: 4.0 miles (Time 2 hours)
How Strenuous: Moderate
Features: Permanent Stream, Rock Art

NUTSHELL: This trail follows the course of Wet Beaver Creek, 17.2 miles southwest of Sedona. The trail is broad and easy, with many attractions.

DIRECTIONS:
From the Sedona Y Go:
    South on Highway 179 (toward Phoenix) for 14.7 miles, to the I-17 Interchange. Instead of going onto I-17, go underneath it onto the dirt road. At 15.2 miles, you will come to a junction. The right fork goes to Montezuma Castle. Take the left fork (FR 618). It is a good dirt road. At 16.9 miles, you are almost to the Beaver Creek Ranger Station. You will see a sign showing a left turn for the Bell Crossing Trail. Take it. At 17.2 you will reach the parking area for the trailhead.

TRAILHEAD: Well marked with signs at the parking area.

DESCRIPTION: From the trailhead, the trail goes upcanyon along Wet Beaver Creek, sometimes near it, sometimes away from it, but always following the stream.
    The trail is broad and easy to walk. It was built by a cattle rancher named Earl Bell in 1932, as a means for taking his cattle to the top of The Mogollon Rim in the spring.
    At about 0.6 miles, look for a large boulder on the left side of the trail. On the side that faces away from you are a number of interesting petroglyphs.
    At the 2.0 mile point you will hit a fork where the **Apache Maid Trail, #15** branches to the left and climbs Casner Butte.
    Just beyond this fork you will find a signboard containing a map and discussion of the geology, plant and animal life of the area. The life is richer than you might think. Just beyond the billboard is a trail going off to the right, down to the water. This is the **Weir Trail.** It is only 0.5 miles long.
    Bell Crossing is 2.0 miles up the canyon from the signboard. There

the trail narrows and crosses the creek. Along the creekside from the crossing are delightful places for a picnic. We recommend that you go upstream about 100 yards to check out a large pool known as The Crack.

From the crossing, the trail goes 2.5 miles on up to the top of The Rim. The full hike is scenic, but is much longer and harder. We recommend stopping at the crossing for most day hikers.

Most of the cattle ranchers for whom trails were named were hardscrabble impecunious people who scratched out trails due to necessity and at a cost they could hardly afford. Earl Bell was different. He was a wealthy Easterner who fell in love with the Beaver Creek area when he was a guest at one of the dude ranches that flourished there from the 1920s through the 1940s. Such places as the Soda Spring Ranch and Rancho Roca Roja had a national reputation and became winter retreats for the wealthy, who would sign up for long stays. Bell bought some fine properties and gave ranching a go, but his heart was not really in it.

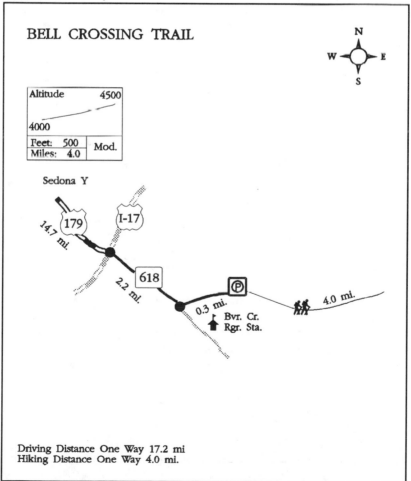

BELL CROSSING TRAIL

Altitude 4500
4000
Feet: 500
Miles: 4.0 Mod.

Sedona Y

179 I-17
14.7 mi.
618
2.2 mi.
0.3 mi.
Bvr. Cr.
Rgr. Sta.
4.0 mi.

Driving Distance One Way 17.2 mi
Hiking Distance One Way 4.0 mi.

BELL ROCK

General Information
Location Map F5
Sedona USGS Map
Coconino Forest Service Map

Driving Distance One Way: 5.6 miles (Time 15 minutes)
Access Road: All cars, All paved
Hiking Distance One Way: 1.0 mile (Time 45 minutes)
How Strenuous: Moderate
Features: Vortex Spot, Views

NUTSHELL: This landmark south of Sedona is one of the famed Vortex Spots. No defined trail. You explore as you wish.

DIRECTIONS:
From the Sedona Y Go:
South on Highway 179 (toward Phoenix) a distance of 5.6 miles. On the right side of the road, you will see the Bell Rock Vista. You can park at the Vista or go across the highway and park on the shoulder of the road.

TRAILHEAD: Not a marked trail, but hundreds of visitors have worn an easy-to-see path up to the rock. At the rock there are some cairns.

DESCRIPTION: As you near the rock, there are many trails. Don't be concerned about these. Just pick out one that strikes your fancy. All of them go to the rock. Once you are there, you may or may not see cairns marking trails going up onto the rock. If you see none, just pick a likely access and ascend. You are on your own.
Y ou probably will encounter medicine wheels or other outlines on the rock made by New Agers. We know of no particular spot that is regarded as *the* vortex spot on Bell Rock. Different people get different responses. Other vortex spots covered in this book are shown in the Index, pages 253-254.
The redrock around Sedona was laid down in layers and has weathered in such a way that it has created ledges that are almost like stairsteps. This is especially true on Bell Rock, with its conical slopes. What you will do on this hike is look for likely ways to go up. Even the timid hiker should be able to get quite close to the top in comfort. We find it too daunting to go to the very top, however.
As you wind your way around the rock, you are treated to great views in all directions.
The early settlers in the area were hard pressed to come up with names

for all of the rock formations around Sedona. There is controversy over the correct names for some of them. Nobody ever disagreed about Bell Rock, however. It *looks* like a bell. This is a very popular place because it is so well known and easy to reach, and is also on the road to Phoenix. So, you won't have a wilderness experience here, but it is a lot of fun, and you may even get a significant experience from the vortex power.

Bell Rock is often a busy place and it doesn't look very big. For those who like solitary places, its aspect is off-putting when you see people of all stripes, including whining infants and disrespectful teenagers assaying its slopes. A funny thing happens when you get to the rock, however. It suddenly seems much bigger than it looked from afar. You can pick out a way that no one else is using and before you know it, you are having an enjoyable peaceful experience in spite of the Coney Island atmosphere. Give it a try in spite of the crowds. It is a special place.

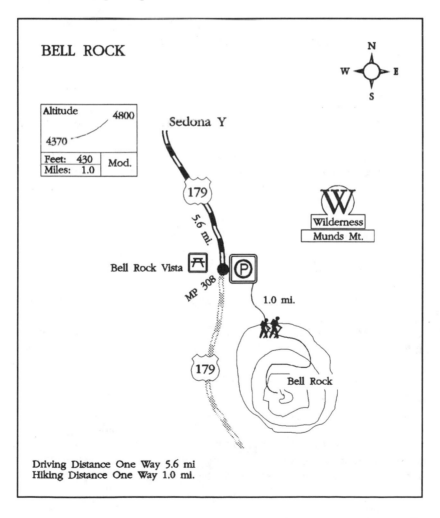

BELL ROCK

N
W — E
S

| Altitude | 4800 |
| 4370 | |

| Feet: | 430 | Mod. |
| Miles: | 1.0 | |

Sedona Y

(179)

5.6 mi.

W
Wilderness
Munds Mt.

Bell Rock Vista

(P)

MP 308

1.0 mi.

(179)

Bell Rock

Driving Distance One Way 5.6 mi
Hiking Distance One Way 1.0 mi.

BLACK MOUNTAIN

General Information
Location Map C1
Clarkdale, Loy Butte,
Page Springs and Sycamore Basin USGS Maps
Coconino Forest Service Map

Driving Distance One Way: 28.3 miles (Time 45 minutes)
Access Road: High clearance vehicles, Last 2.1 miles very rough
Hiking Distance One Way: 2.25 miles (Time 90 minutes)
How Strenuous: Moderate
Features: Views

NUTSHELL: Located 28.3 miles southwest of Sedona, Black Mt. borders Sycamore Canyon. This hike follows a road to the top to a lookout point.

DIRECTIONS:
From the Sedona Y Go:
Southwest on Highway 89A (toward Cottonwood) a distance of 16.0 miles (MP 358) to FR 761, the unpaved Bill Gray Road. Turn right and take FR 761 to the 25.5 miles point, its junction with FR 258A, Buckboard Road. Go right here, staying on FR 761. At 26.2 miles, you will see a road to your left marked FR 9761A, with a sign saying that it is a Forest Protection Road. Turn left onto this road. Up to this point, the road has been good, but now it gets quite rough. A high clearance vehicle with sturdy tires is recommended, and only when the road is dry. At 28.3 miles, you reach a Y fork, with FR 9761A going right and FR 9761C going left. Park and walk FR 9761C, the road going uphill left. We would not drive any vehicle we ever owned up this road.

TRAILHEAD: Walk the road, FR 9761C.

DESCRIPTION: The road and the surroundings are rather bleak. There isn't much of interest near at hand. However, you are treated to some great views.
You will see some signs of yesteryear's flagstone quarrying here and there along the road. This is great country for javelina, and you may see some of them. We were treated to the sight of a whole family of javelina on the road ahead of us peacefully grazing. Then they caught our scent and disappeared. It is amazing how they can melt into the brush in an instant.
You will reach the top at 1.25 miles, and may be surprised to find that the top is larger than you'd have thought. The top is a juniper/pinon pine life zone. There are no cliffs along the rim to furnish natural viewpoints, as the

sides are rounded.

At about 2.0 miles, the road forks where there is a steel fence post. The left fork takes you to the south, onto the bulk of the mountain, where the road peters out in about a quarter mile. The fork to the right takes you to the north. We recommend taking it. You can bushwhack to the edge of the mountain in a quarter mile for colorful views into Sycamore Canyon.

This is not a premier hiking trail, but makes an interesting mountain bike ride. The road is plenty good for that. The grades are not bad. The problem with driving it is the danger of getting high centered, which would not be a problem for a mountain bike.

Black Mountain looks black when the sun is high but in the evening when the light is low you can see that it is just about as red as it is black. The red strata occur in the lower parts of the mountain. On some places the red is exposed by erosion and very visible, such as the north face that you see from **The Dogie Trail.**

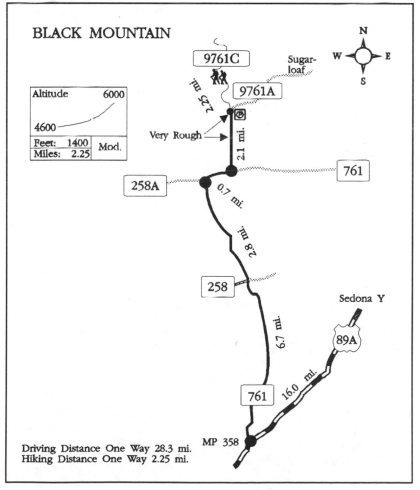

BLACK MT. MYSTERY HOUSE

General Information
Location Map C1
Clarkdale, Loy Butte,
Page Springs and Sycamore Basin USGS Maps
Coconino Forest Service Map

Driving Distance One Way: 31.0 miles (Time 60 minutes)
Access Road: High clearance vehicles, Last 4.8 miles awful
Hiking Distance One Way: 0.4 miles (Time 20 minutes)
How Strenuous: Moderate
Features: Strange abandoned house in remote area, Views

NUTSHELL: After a rough drive, you hike an old road to a strange abandoned house high on Black Mountain, where you have million dollar views.

DIRECTIONS:
From the Sedona Y Go:
　　　　Southwest on Highway 89A (toward Cottonwood) a distance of 16.0 miles (MP 358) to FR 761, the unpaved Bill Gray Road. Turn right and take FR 761 to the 25.5 miles point, its junction with FR 258A, Buckboard Road. Go right here, staying on FR 761. At 26.2 miles, you will see a road to your left marked FR 9761A, with a sign saying that it is a Forest Protection Road. Turn left onto this road. Up to this point, the road has been good, but now it gets quite rough. A high clearance vehicle with sturdy tires is recommended, and only when the road is dry. At 28.3 miles, you reach a Y fork, with FR 9761A going right and FR 9761C going left. Drive FR 9761A, to the right. This is a very rough but spectacular road. At the 31.0 mile point you will reach the remains of a barbed wire fence. You can drive farther, but it's a killer. Park at the fence.

TRAILHEAD: Walk the old road.

DESCRIPTION: We became aware of the mystery house one day when we were hiking the **Casner Mountain South Trail.** We looked over at Black Mountain and saw the sun glinting off of something. We checked it with our field glasses and were astonished to see the spooky remains of an old house. After a lot of map work and trial and error, we figured out how to get there.
　　　　When you get to the site, you will find the ruins of a fairly modern house. It is situated uniquely, with a million dollar view, but also a million miles from anywhere. It was a split level, the front being about 60 feet long, with view windows all along it.

We have puzzled over the mystery of the house. The boards used in the walls came from World War II ammunition boxes, so our best guess is that it was built between 1946 and 1948, when such boxes were plentiful as war surplus items.

From the flagstone rubble that is seen all around the premises, we would guess that whoever built the house operated a flagstone quarry here. Under the influence of some Frank Lloyd Wright designs, it was popular in the late 40s and early 50s to use brick sized pieces of flagstone as a building material. The 1955 addition to the Coconino County Courthouse in Flagstaff is an example of this. The fashion died out at the end of the 50s, so maybe the quarry was abandoned then. It seems obvious that at times there was a sizable quarry operation here. You can see where almost a whole cliff face was cut away if you walk the road to its end.

You have to wonder as you stand on this site how these people hauled things in and out. There is nothing like this ruin that we have found in the area.

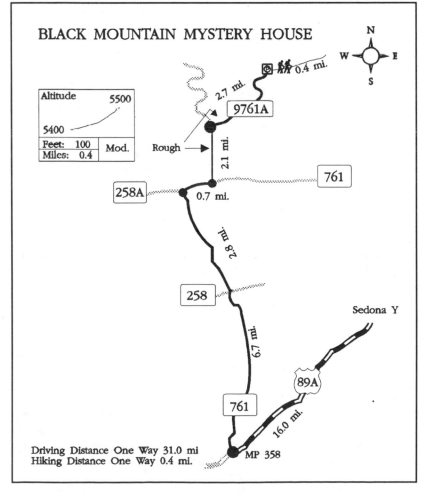

BLODGETT BASIN

General Information
Location Map G6
Walker Mtn. USGS Map
Coconino Forest Service Map

Driving Distance One Way: 28.7 miles (Time 1 hour)
Access Road: All cars, Last 14.0 miles good dirt road
Hiking Distance One Way: 2.0 miles (Time 1.5 hours)
How Strenuous: Hard
Features: Views

NUTSHELL: This trail runs from a point high on the Mogollon Rim to the bottom of the wonderful chasm of West Clear Creek, a 2000 foot drop in 2.0 miles.

DIRECTIONS:
From the Sedona Y Go:
        South on Highway 179 (toward Phoenix) for 14.7 miles, to the I-17 Interchange. Instead of going onto I-17, go underneath it onto the dirt road. At 15.2 miles, you will come to a junction. The right fork goes to Montezuma Castle. Take the left fork (FR 618), toward Beaver Creek Ranger Station. It is a good dirt road. Several minor roads branch off FR 618, but it is always obvious that it is the main one. Follow FR 618 to the 24.5 mile point, where you will see a dirt road branching left, marked "Cedar Flat." Take this left road, and you will soon see a sign identifying it as FR 214. FR 214 takes you to the top of the Mogollon Rim, about a 2000 foot climb. There are some great views along the way. At the 28.7 mile point, high up on the road, you will see the sign for the Blodgett Basin Trail to your right through a fence with tall gate posts. Pull in and park by a number of circular rusty water troughs.

TRAILHEAD: You will see cairns marking the trail as it goes downhill from the parking area.

DESCRIPTION: There is very little shade on this trail and you will be dangerously exposed to the sun. It can get very hot. We recommend that you do not even try this hike in full summer. If you do, please be prepared with lots of water, hats, sunscreen, etc.
        From the place where you park, you can see the huge chasm of West Clear Creek before you. Only in a state containing such famous canyons as Grand Canyon, Oak Creek Canyon and Sycamore Canyon would such a marvelous canyon as West Clear Creek go unsung. It is huge, scenic and wild.

You will wind around the sides of several hills as you work your way down to the bottom. You will have good views, particularly of Wingfield Mesa and later the trees lining the bottom of West Clear Creek Canyon. Though the gorge of West Clear Creek is clearly before you, you never come to a lip from where you can look directly down into the main canyon; instead, you will come into it by means of a sidecanyon.

At the end of the trail, you will intersect the **West Clear Creek Trail #17** (also known as the Bull Pen Trail), on a shelf some distance from the creek. It's about 0.20 miles down to the water; turn right and you will come to the parking area at the Bull Pen trailhead, from where it's a short hop to the creek.

We definitely recommend using two cars on this hike. Park the first car in the West Clear Creek Campground at the West Clear Creek #17 trailhead. You reach this by following FR 618 south 2.0 miles from its intersection with FR 214, then turning left (east) on FR 215 and going 3.0 miles to the campground. Take the second car to the top as described herein.

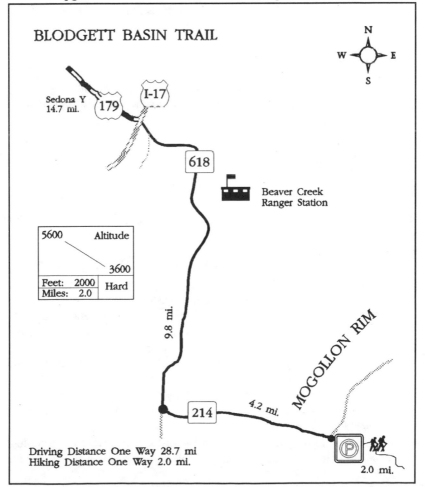

BLODGETT BASIN TRAIL

Sedona Y 14.7 mi. 179 I-17

618

Beaver Creek Ranger Station

5600 Altitude 3600
Feet: 2000 Hard
Miles: 2.0

9.8 mi.

214 4.2 mi. MOGOLLON RIM

Driving Distance One Way 28.7 mi
Hiking Distance One Way 2.0 mi.

2.0 mi.

BOYNTON CANYON

Vortex

General Information
Location Map C3
Wilson Mountain USGS Map
Coconino Forest Service Map

Personal
Favorite

Driving Distance One Way: 8.0 miles (Time 20 minutes)
Access Road: All cars, All paved
Hiking Distance One Way: 3.25 miles (Time 90 minutes)
How Strenuous: Moderate
Features: Indian Ruins, Vortex

NUTSHELL: This wonderful canyon is located just 8.0 miles northwest of uptown Sedona, and is easily reached by paved roads. Its beauty is unsurpassed. **A personal favorite.**

DIRECTIONS:
From the Sedona Y Go:
Southwest on Highway 89A (toward Cottonwood) a distance of 3.2 miles (MP 371), to Dry Creek Road, where you take a right turn onto Dry Creek Road (FR 152C). Follow it to the 6.1 mile point, where it joins Long Canyon Road. Take a left here, staying on FR 152C. At the 7.7 mile point, you reach another junction. Go right. At 8.0 miles, just before the gatehouse to the Enchantment Resort, you will see a parking area to the right. Park there. There is also a small parking area on the left side of the road.

TRAILHEAD: It is marked at the parking area by a sign reading, "Boynton Canyon #47."

DESCRIPTION: This trail is gentle and wide. For the first mile it overlooks the Enchantment Resort. The trail winds along the south face of the canyon, hugging the towering ruin-dotted red cliffs so as to skirt the resort property. At the 0.85 mile point you will see a path going off to your right. This leads uphill to Indian ruins in two caves, and is well worth a detour. It takes a bit of scrambling and climbing to get up to the ruins, but even if you don't climb to them, it is worth going over to the face of the cliff on which they are located for a look. This is a detour of about 0.25 miles each way.

Just beyond this point the trail turns away from the cliffs and follows along the canyon floor. It is much wider and easier to walk from this point on.

At 1.0 miles you will cross a shallow wash, beyond which the vegetation changes. As you go up canyon, the altitude increases and it is cooler.

At about 3.0 miles, the trail pinches down suddenly as the canyon narrows. This is a good stopping place. However, you can bushwhack another 0.25 mile and see the head of Boynton, which is a box canyon against the side of Secret Mountain. The streambed forks here. Take the right fork and you will soon see a primitive path, which is almost a tunnel through the lush growth at stream level. You will emerge into the box, which is ringed with towering buff cliffs.

Boynton Canyon is considered to be one of the Sedona Vortex spots. We have been to all of them, and this is the only one that really gives us any special feeling. The red cliffs here can really be spectacular. We love them at about four o'clock in the afternoon on a winter's day. There is something about the angle and clarity of the light resonating on the beautiful red rocks that is really special at such times.

This hike has become very popular and you are almost certain to have company.

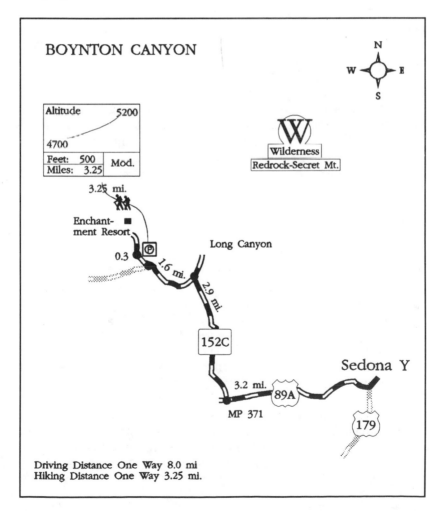

BOYNTON SPIRES

General Information
Location Map C3
Wilson Mountain USGS Map
Coconino Forest Service Map

Vortex

Driving Distance One Way: 8.0 miles (Time 20 minutes)
Access Road*:* All cars, All paved
Hiking Distance One Way*:* 0.25 miles (Time 30 minutes)
How Strenuous*:* Moderate
Features*:* Vortex, Interesting rock formations, Views

NUTSHELL: Located next door to the popular Boynton Canyon hike, this shorty takes you to a vortex spot and a scenic viewpoint.

DIRECTIONS:
From the Sedona Y Go:
          Southwest on Highway 89A (toward Cottonwood) a distance of 3.2 miles (MP 371), to Dry Creek Road, where you take a right turn onto Dry Creek Road (FR 152C) Follow it to the 6.1 mile point, where it joins Long Canyon Road. Take a left here, staying on FR 152C. At the 7.7 mile point, you reach another junction. Go right. At 8.0 miles, just before the gatehouse to the Enchantment Resort, you will see a parking area to the right. Park there. There is also a small parking area on the left side of the road.

TRAILHEAD: It is marked at the parking area by a rusty sign reading, "Boynton Canyon #47."

DESCRIPTION: From the trail sign at the parking lot, take a look to your right, where you will see two spires on the toe of a ridge. The saddle between these spires on the back side of the ridge is your target.
          Begin walking down the main trail. In about 220 feet (30 paces before a small pole bridge) you will see side trails branching to your right. The challenge of this hike is to pick the right one. The bad news is that the trail is not marked, not even with cairns. The good news is that if you keep your eye on the target and follow the trails that look like they go there, you will succeed.
          The trail climbs uphill and winds around the toe of the ridge. Boynton Canyon is regarded as a Sedona Vortex Center and some psychics think the vortex point is located below the back of the toe. We found a little crystal shrine there. Another theory holds that the spires are points on the Vortex, one female the other male.

Once you are around the toe you have your choice of paths up to the saddle. All are obvious. The saddle is a nice vantage point from which to see down onto the Enchantment resort on the left and **Mescal Mountain** and the approach to **Long Canyon** on the right.

From there you will see a trail over to the taller spire. It requires a brief, relatively safe bit of climbing to get to the spire's base. Fit hikers should have little trouble with it. To that point you will have hiked 0.25 miles.

Some maps show a cliff dwelling farther along the butte at its base. There are some primitive trails along the base, some of them aimless game trails. We went to the half mile point, where there is a shallow alcove with a low line of stones covered by a fallen boulder. There are graffiti on the cliff walls here, one of which is *EHP 1901*. This was probably done by Elmer Purtymun, a Sedona pioneer. See the **Purtymun Trail** for a bit of information about the Purtymun family.

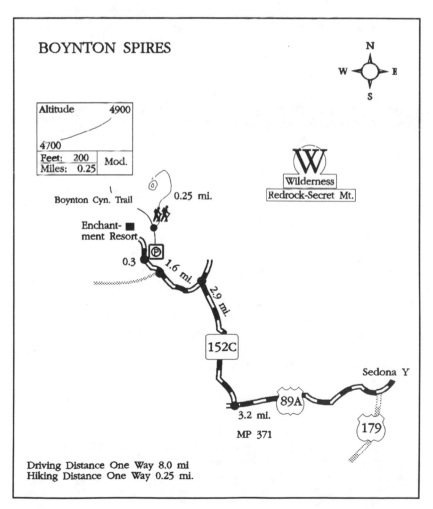

BOYNTON SPIRES

N
W — E
S

Altitude	4900
4700	

Feet:	200	Mod.
Miles:	0.25	

Boynton Cyn. Trail

0.25 mi.

Wilderness
Redrock-Secret Mt.

Enchant-ment Resort

0.3

1.6 mi.

2.9 mi.

152C

Sedona Y

3.2 mi.

89A

MP 371

179

Driving Distance One Way 8.0 mi
Hiking Distance One Way 0.25 mi.

BRIANT CANYON

General Information
Location Map E5
Munds Mt. and Sedona USGS Maps
Coconino Forest Service Map

Driving Distance One Way: 3.6 Miles (Time 15 minutes)
Access Road: All cars, Paved all the way
Hiking Distance One Way: 2.4 Miles (Time 75 minutes)
How Strenuous: Moderate
Features: Beautiful rock formations, Cypress forest

NUTSHELL: Starting at the Chapel of the Holy Cross, this trail hugs Twin Buttes, then goes beyond it into a scenic canyon.

DIRECTIONS:
From the Sedona Y Go:
South on Highway 179 (toward Phoenix) for 2.9 miles (MP 310.6) to Chapel Drive. Turn left on Chapel Drive and follow it to the Chapel of the Holy Cross. Park in the lower parking lot.

TRAILHEAD: This is an unmarked, unmaintained trail. Just above the first Chapel of the Holy Cross parking lot, where the road finishes a big curve and starts to curve in the other direction, you will see a trail going to your right.

DESCRIPTION: For the first half mile, the trail seems urban, but after that the sight of habitation is lost and it feels nice and remote. It stays in the shadow of Twin Buttes and offers marvelous views of its impressive rock formations.
At 0.80 miles, you will reach a fence with an unlocked gate. Just beyond that, you reach **Chicken Point**, located above you on top of rounded ledges. At 1.0 miles you will reach a Wilderness boundary marker. There are great views into **Marg's Draw** from here.
The trail is well marked with cairns and lines of stone. At 1.5 miles you will enter Briant Canyon, where you pass through a lovely cypress forest. You cross the canyon and climb up onto a ledge about 200 feet above the canyon floor, then hike the ledge.
The cairns end at 2.4 miles and the trail just quits for no apparent reason. It seems that you could bushwhack to the end of the canyon, which is probably no more than a half mile from the end of the trail.
Just above the point where the trail quits you can see Lee Gap, which is a significant notch in Lee Mountain. Perhaps the trail was designed to provide access to the gap but we could find no side trail going up to the gap.

Briant Canyon is one of those hidden canyons that you can't see unless you come across its opening unexpectedly. Or, of course, unless you have a nifty hike book to guide you.

While taking this hike in the spring of 1991 we were treated to a most unusual sight. At the fence below Chicken Point we could hear animals and people approaching us. We expected that this would be a party of horse riders. Instead it turned out to be a llama trek. There were two of these beautiful animals being led by guests who were on a day hike being conducted by a local guide. We stopped and visited with these people for a while and had a chance to pet the llamas, one of which enjoyed being petted while the other was aloof. Their huge soulful eyes are captivating. Their hooves also are a wonder, being so broad and soft that they leave almost no footprints. The party had just finished a picnic in Briant Canyon, with all the gear packed in by the llamas. For a moment we thought we must have taken a wrong turn and wound up in Peru.

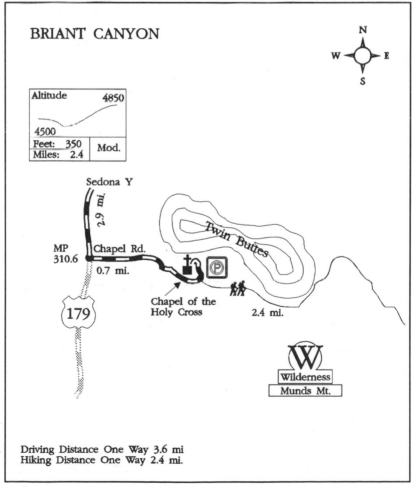

BRIANT CANYON

N
W — E
S

Altitude   4850
4500
Feet: 350   Mod.
Miles: 2.4

Sedona Y
2.9 mi.
MP
310.6   Chapel Rd.
0.7 mi.

Twin Buttes

Chapel of the
Holy Cross   2.4 mi.

W
Wilderness
Munds Mt.

Driving Distance One Way 3.6 mi
Hiking Distance One Way 2.4 mi.

BRINS MESA EAST

General Information
Location Map D4
Wilson Mountain USGS Map
Coconino Forest Service Map

Driving Distance One Way: 1.5 miles (Time 10 minutes)
Access Road: All cars, Last 0.40 miles gravel, in medium condition
Hiking Distance One Way: 2.5 miles (Time 75 minutes)
How Strenuous: Moderate
Features: Easy to reach, Good views

NUTSHELL: You hike a maintained trail to the top of Brins Mesa, then you go across country to a stunning rock formation on the lip of the mesa next to Wilson Mountain.

DIRECTIONS:
From the Y in Sedona, Go:
        North on Highway 89A (toward Flagstaff) a distance of 0.30 miles, to Jordan Road, a main street in uptown Sedona. Follow Jordan Road to its end, beyond the point where the paving disappears. At 1.1 miles, you reach a junction with a private drive, turn left here and follow the road to the Shooting Range, at 1.5 miles. Park outside the gate.

TRAILHEAD: Walk through the parking area of the range about 0.26 miles, where you will see a Rusty Sign reading *Brins Mesa #119* at the entrance to an old road.

DESCRIPTION: The trail follows a closed jeep road for just over a mile. It is wide and crosses over rolling hills on a moderate incline. It takes you to the foot of Brins Mesa. The next half mile climbs the mesa. It is fairly steep and moderately strenuous, a 500 foot climb in half a mile. When you begin the climb, look behind you. As you rise, you will get better and better views.
        When you top out on the mesa, you will be treated to great views. The trail continues across the mesa to the west, where it intersects a trail coming up from the **Soldier Pass Trail** and then goes all the way to the **Brins Mesa West** trailhead on the Vultee Arch Road. However, we are suggesting a different hike. This is to turn right at the mesa top and go north along the rim of the mesa. There is an ill-defined trail there, but it is easy to find your way by just following the rim. You will go a mile to the end of the mesa.
        About half way along, there is a great vantage point where a bare redrock cliff juts out like the prow of a ship. Beautiful sights from here. But

the best is yet to come. At the very end of the mesa, there is an eroded redrock turret that is easily climbed. The sculptures and carvings in the redrock are a true delight to the eye. There is a deep crevice between the end of the mesa and gigantic Wilson Mountain. This is one of the best sitting and gazing points in all Sedona, one of our all-time favorite spots in the redrock country.

From this point, you will have the best possible place to watch **Angel Falls** and its unnamed neighbor waterfall when they are running. There is a problem with this waterfall viewing, and that is that if it is wet enough for the falls to be running, it probably will be quite muddy on the mesa.

When the mesa is muddy, hiking there is miserable. There is no way to avoid the mud.

Brins Mesa is one of those places that is totally visible but that you pay no attention to until you have it called to your consciousness. After you have hiked it, look at it from Sedona and you will realize what a significant land feature it is.

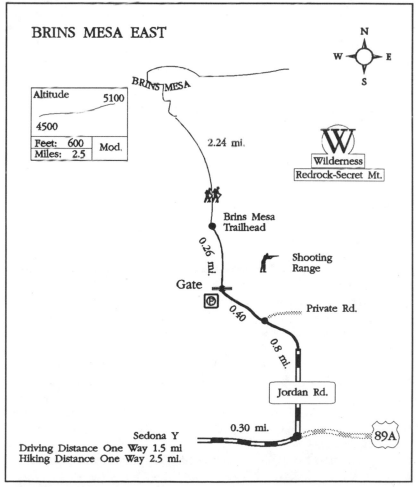

BRINS MESA EAST

N
W ◄—◇—► E
S

Altitude 5100

4500

Feet: 600 — Mod.
Miles: 2.5

2.24 mi.

W
Wilderness
Redrock-Secret Mt.

Brins Mesa
Trailhead

0.26 mi.

Shooting
Range

Gate

0.40

Private Rd.

0.8 mi.

Jordan Rd.

0.30 mi.

89A

Sedona Y
Driving Distance One Way 1.5 mi
Hiking Distance One Way 2.5 mi.

BRINS MESA WEST

General Information
Location Map D4
Wilson Mountain USGS Map
Coconino Forest Service Map

Driving Distance One Way: 7.7 miles (Time 30 minutes)
Access Road: Rough road last 2.5 miles, High clearance best
Hiking Distance One Way: 2.5 miles (Time 75 minutes)
How Strenuous: Moderate
Features: Views

NUTSHELL: Brins Mesa overlooks uptown Sedona, giving fine views of the south face of Wilson Mountain and the Dry Creek drainage to the west.

DIRECTIONS:
From the Sedona Y Go:
Southwest on Highway 89A (toward Cottonwood) for 3.2 miles (MP 371) to Dry Creek Road. Turn right on Dry Creek Road (FR 152C) and proceed to the 5.2 mile point. Turn right on FR 152, the Vultee Arch Road, and follow it to the 7.7 mile point. Pull off to the right and park.

TRAILHEAD: There is a rusty sign marking the trailhead at the parking area reading, "Brins Mesa #119."

DESCRIPTION: FR 152 is very rough, one of the worst ones in the book. Too bad, as it gives access to several excellent hikes. You need a high clearance vehicle to get very far, and it is very slow going. The problem is that the topsoil has blown or washed away from many portions of the road leaving the underlying rock exposed. In some places this means sharp individual rocks and in other places whole ledges.

The trail seems to be a combination of an old jeep road and stock path. It crosses a streambed ten times. Usually this is dry, and is no problem. If it is carrying much water, wait for another day. At the 1.0 mile point you climb out of the streambed. You then begin to climb to the top of the mesa. This is a fairly gradual climb, because this side (the west side) of Brins Mesa slopes, forming an inclined plane, which makes for easy access. At 2.0 miles you are near the top, out on the mesa, where you begin to have some fine views. You can look to your right into Soldier Pass, at **Coffee Pot Rock**. Straight ahead you look at Sedona. To your left you see Wilson Mt. Behind you are views of the Dry Creek area.

The mesa top is quite flat and broad. There are some junipers growing there but in many places the mesa is rather bare. It was good grazing land for cattle, though it isn't big enough to support many of them. The mesa itself is not particularly interesting but it provides a fine viewpoint.

You walk all the way across the mesa and peer down a fairly steep drop into the area of Mormon Canyon and Jordan Road, which is the **Brins Mesa East Trail** access. It is possible to work these two hikes as a two-car shuttle, parking a car at each trailhead. The Brins Mesa West hike has a more gradual climb, is less scenic at the beginning and has more difficult access than the Brins Mesa East hike.

Brins Mesa is a large, interesting place. It forms a low barrier between Sedona and the Dry Creek backcountry. The legend is that in the old ranching days a brindle steer managed to avoid roundup and went wild on the mesa. Cowboys who tried to capture him became so frustrated by his escapes that they finally shot him. Their nickname for the critter was Brins or Brinds because of his brindle coloration, hence the name Brins Mesa.

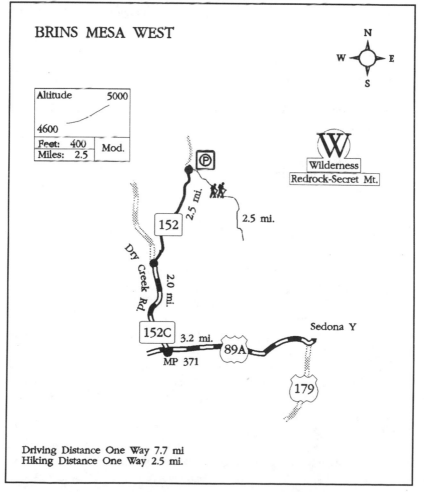

BRINS MESA WEST

Driving Distance One Way 7.7 mi
Hiking Distance One Way 2.5 mi.

BROWN HOUSE CANYON

General Information
Location Map C4
Wilson Mt. USGS Map
Coconino Forest Service Map

Driving Distance One Way: 6.9 miles (Time 15 minutes)
Access Road: All cars, All paved
Hiking Distance One Way: 0.3 miles (Time 20 minutes)
How Strenuous: Moderate
Features: Scenic canyon, Slide Rock State Park

NUTSHELL: While the hordes enjoy the creekside pleasures at Slide Rock State Park, you can enjoy this little-known scenic canyon hike there.

DIRECTIONS:
From The Y in Sedona Go:
　　North on Highway 89A (toward Flagstaff) a distance of 6.9 miles (MP 381.1) to the entrance to Slide Rock State Park. The park is well marked and signed and you will have no trouble finding it. Park in the main parking lot as near the brown house as you can.

TRAILHEAD: This trail is not signed or maintained. You will see the trail leading west from the picnic tables at the Ponderosa Picnic Area, immediately west of the brown house.

DESCRIPTION: You will have to pay an entrance fee to get into this state park ($3.00 per car in 1992). The brown house is used by the Park Department as its headquarters, and is where you buy entrance tickets. This hike goes up the canyon behind the house. Walk up to the Ponderosa Picnic Area (signed) and you will see the trail going west of the picnic tables.

　　Those who are familiar with the landscape around Sedona are amazed to find out how different things are in the upper canyon. The altitude at Slide Rock is about 5100 feet and you are going into a shaded moist canyon. As a result, you will find a dense alpine forest of pine, oak and maple. Near the entrance to the canyon blackberry bushes grow profusely.

　　The trail is one of those now-you-see-it, now-you-don't affairs, but you can't go wrong because the canyon is narrow and you just keep following the main channel to the canyon's end. There is a small streambed in the canyon and the trail crosses it several times.

　　As you begin the hike, your attention is on the trees, but as you go higher, you begin to see interesting redrock formations on either side of you.

You get rather mysterious peekaboo glimpses of these through the thick foliage. At about the quarter mile point you come into sight of immense white and gray cliffs.

The canyon ends in a box and you cannot get right to the base of the cliffs without some serious bushwhacking as the place is so overgrown. The trail plays out on a ridge some distance from the cliffs, a remote silent place surrounded by towering cliffs.

This is a good hike for a summer day, cool and delicious.

The area where Slide Rock State Park is located was once an apple orchard owned and operated by the Pendley family. It was the Pendleys who built the long irrigation flume that allowed their orchards to succeed where others had failed. Many apple trees are still on the grounds. One of the main old orchards was cut down in 1991 and new trees were planted as the old ones had lost their vigor. There are many signs placed around Slide Rock Park showing points of interest.

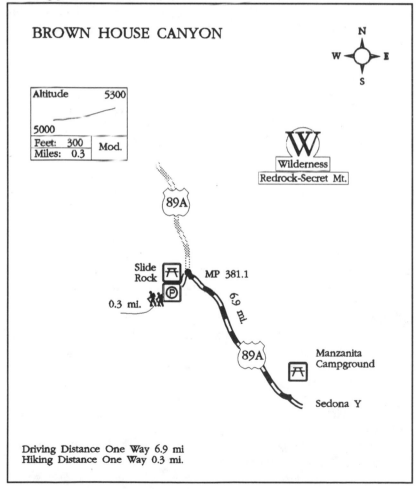

BROWN HOUSE CANYON

Altitude 5300
5000
Feet: 300
Miles: 0.3 Mod.

Wilderness
Redrock-Secret Mt.

89A

Slide Rock   MP 381.1

0.3 mi.

6.9 mi.

89A   Manzanita Campground

Sedona Y

Driving Distance One Way 6.9 mi
Hiking Distance One Way 0.3 mi.

CAPITOL BUTTE

General Information
Location Map D4
Wilson Mt. USGS Map
Coconino Forest Service Map

Driving Distance One Way: 5.2 miles (Time 15 minutes)
Access Road: All cars, All paved
Hiking Distance One Way: 0.5 miles (Time 30 minutes)
How Strenuous: Moderate
Features: Views

NUTSHELL: Capitol Butte is one of the main Sedona landmarks, and the town partly wraps around it. This hike takes you to the top of a ridge radiating from the west face of the butte for fine views out over scenic country.

DIRECTIONS:
From the Sedona Y Go:
    Southwest on Highway 89A (toward Cottonwood) for a distance of 3.2 miles (MP 371) to the Dry Creek Road, FR 152C. Turn right onto Dry Creek Road and follow it to the 5.2 mile point, where FR 152 branches off to the right. The road is paved to this point. Pull onto FR 152 just far enough to find a parking place and park.

TRAILHEAD: This trail is not marked, but the trailhead is easily found. From where you park, you will see a large metal sign frame, about 8 feet high. Walk up the road about 75 paces from it and look to your right, where you will see a ditch and a blocked dirt road. This is the trailhead.

DESCRIPTION: Walk up the old road a few yards, where you will meet another trail. Go right. At 0.15 miles, the trail forks. The left fork is an old jeep road, and takes you on the **Chinup** hike. Take the right fork instead. It will lead you down into a little wash and then back up the other side.
    At 0.18 miles, you will have partly climbed a ridge. Here the main trail, which is a horse trail leading to stables on Dry Creek Road, goes straight ahead, at the same level. You will find a fainter trail going uphill, toward the top of the ridge. This is the trail you want.
    After a short, stiff climb, you will find yourself on the ridge top at 0.4 miles. Though the top is covered with vegetation, it is not dense and it is easy to walk through it. Go to your right (west), to the clear edge of the ridge, where you can see down onto Dry Creek Road. This is a nice view, though you are looking down at a lot of homes in subdivisions.

After this, work your way east toward the cliffs that top the butte. High above you is the formation called Lizard Head. Seen from the right angle, it fully lives up to its name. Look to your left (north) in the middle distance and you will see an urn-shaped balanced rock on the skyline.

We bushwhacked around this ridge, did a bit of climbing up the redrock, and felt that we had had a nice outing. While we were there we noticed a hiker coming down from a saddle at the top. He might have even been able to get to the base of Lizard Head from the saddle. As it was late, we were unable to see whether this adventurer had a trail or was just picking his way. You might want to do some exploring here if steep climbing is your fancy.

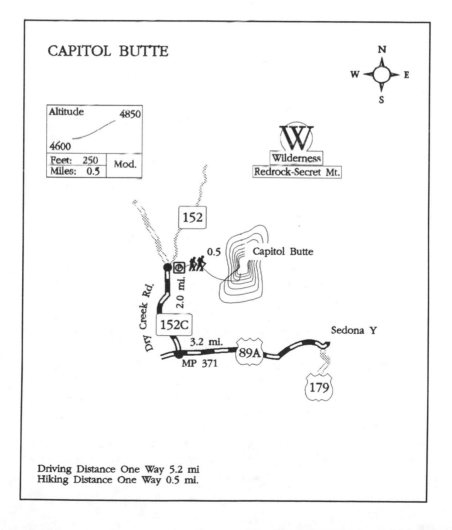

CAPITOL BUTTE

N
W — E
S

| Altitude | 4850 |
| 4600 | |

| Feet: | 250 | Mod. |
| Miles: | 0.5 | |

W
Wilderness
Redrock-Secret Mt.

152

0.5   Capitol Butte

Dry Creek Rd.

2.0 mi.

152C

Sedona Y

3.2 mi.   89A

MP 371

179

Driving Distance One Way 5.2 mi
Hiking Distance One Way 0.5 mi.

CARROLL CANYON

General Information
Location Map E4
Sedona USGS Map
Coconino Forest Service Map

Driving Distance One Way: 7.3 miles (Time 20 minutes)
Access Road: All cars, Last 0.20 miles gravel, in good condition
Hiking Distance One Way: 1.25 miles (Time 40 minutes)
How Strenuous: Easy
Features: Arch

NUTSHELL: This canyon, located 7.3 miles southwest of Sedona, runs just south of Airport Hill. An easy walk, it features a "pocket-sized" arch.

DIRECTIONS:
From the Sedona Y Go:
> Southwest on Highway 89A (toward Cottonwood) a distance of 5.3 miles (MP 368.9) to the Upper Red Rock Loop Road. Turn left and follow the Loop to the 7.1 mile point, where you turn left, heading toward Red Rock Crossing on a dirt road. At 7.30 miles, you will come to a bridge. Park just beyond the bridge.

TRAILHEAD: No marked trail. You walk up the floor of the canyon.

DESCRIPTION: The bridge that you reach at the 7.30 mile point spans Carroll Canyon, so park anywhere near it. There is space for a couple of cars just beyond the bridge.
> Get out and go into the wash and walk upstream. There are many places where the stream has cut down to a redrock shelf, where it is almost like walking on pavement. In other places, you must do a bit of boulder hopping. In about 0.25 miles, you will be out of sight of habitation, although you will hear lots of airplane activity because the big hill to your right is Airport Hill.
> As you go, the canyon gets deeper and more interesting. At about 0.6 miles, you reach an area where the canyon falls steeply and has carved out a series of terraces. You can keep climbing upstream over these ledges.
> Many pools have formed in declivities in the rock and some appear to be deep enough to hold water year around.
> At 0.9 miles, you reach a place where the words "Arch Spring" have been carved into a rock near a pool. The lettering looks old fashioned and may have been carved there many years ago when the spring was active. It seems inactive now, or perhaps it is active only during the time of snow melt. The

arch is at ground level—just about big enough for your cocker spaniel to squeeze through.

Although the canyon goes all the way to Sedona (it crosses under Highway 89-A at Coffee Pot Rock Road), the scenic part of the canyon ends at 1.25 miles. Beyond there, the channel flattens and due to the nearness of "civilization" becomes littered with trash.

Carroll Canyon is named after the Carroll family, which home-steaded in Sedona in its earliest days. The Carrolls occupied a tract of land on what is now the Red Rock Loop Road. Exhausted by their hardscrabble existence, they sold the land to Henry Schuerman, a hard working German immigrant of many talents. Schuerman was able to develop the property successfully and his descendants lived there for many years. Local landmarks bear the names of both families, Carroll Canyon and Schuerman Mountain. On the latter mountain you will find the **Schuerman Trail.**

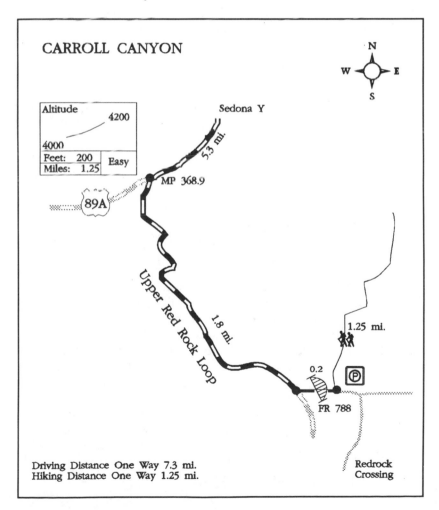

CARROLL CANYON

Driving Distance One Way 7.3 mi.
Hiking Distance One Way 1.25 mi.

CASNER CANYON NORTH

General Information
Location Map D5
Munds Park USGS Map
Coconino Forest Service Map

Driving Distance One Way: 2.6 miles (Time 10 minutes)
Access Road: All cars, All paved
Hiking Distance One Way: 2.0 miles (Time 75 minutes)
How Strenuous: Hard
Features: Views

NUTSHELL: Located just north of Sedona, this trail takes you across Oak Creek, then up Casner Canyon to a point on the Schnebly Hill Road just north of Schnebly Hill Vista.

DIRECTIONS:
From the Sedona Y Go:
    North on Highway 89A (toward Flagstaff) a distance of 2.6 miles (MP 376.8) where you park at the mouth of a closed road.

TRAILHEAD: Walk down the old road a few feet and you will see a rusty sign reading, "Casner Canyon #11" where the trail goes downhill to your left.

DESCRIPTION: Follow the path down to Oak Creek. You have to wade across the creek here. We like to bring a towel along to dry our feet when we get to the other side. This is not a hike you would want to do while wearing wet tennies. A good method is to pack a pair of Tevas or other sandals, as walking the creek is tricky. Use the sandals for crossing the creek, then dry your feet and switch back to your hiking shoes on the other shore. You don't want to fall in. Count on wading, because even though there may be stepping stones, our experience is that they are unreliable.
    Once you are across the water and have dry shoes on, you will see Casner Canyon. You head right up the canyon on its right (south) side. Soon the trail lifts out of the canyon and climbs the north wall of the canyon, meaning that you are on a southern exposure. There is no shade and you are fully exposed to sun. Don't do this hike on a hot day.
    From the point where you rise above the crowns of the trees growing in the bottom of the canyon, the trail just goes to the top in a very businesslike way. It cuts a straight diagonal line from the bottom of the canyon to the top of Schnebly Hill. There is no scenery along the trail. In fact, it is quite drab. You do climb to the point where you get sweeping views. Some of these are

very nice.

You reach the top at a place that is close to the Schnebly Hill Vista, going through a gate in a barbed wire fence; so one way to do this hike is to use the two-car switch, parking one at Schnebly Hill Vista and the other at the Casner Canyon Trailhead. The easy way to do the hike is to start at the top, from Schnebly Hill. It is easy to recognize the start of the trail there by looking for the gate in the fence.

When you stand at the Schnebly Hill Vista you can see the Casner Canyon Trail. Sometimes, when the light is just right, it looks like a road and you wonder what on earth it can be, because no car could drive straight up the mountain as the trail goes. The trail was built by the Casner ranching operation as a livestock trail in the late 1890s.

The Casner family left its name in several areas: **Casner Mountain**, south of Sedona, the **Casner Canyon South** Trail in the Wet Beaver Creek Country, Casner Canyon Draw near Woody Mountain and others.

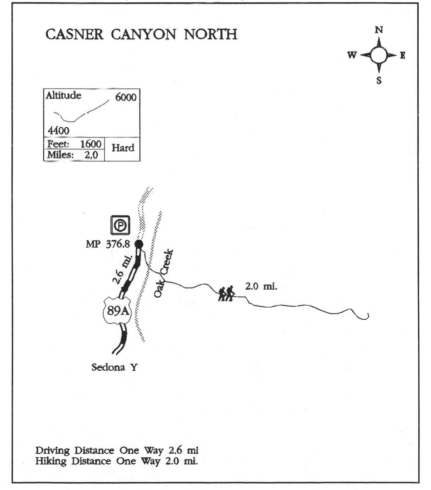

CASNER CANYON NORTH

Driving Distance One Way 2.6 mi
Hiking Distance One Way 2.0 mi.

CASNER CANYON SOUTH

General Information
Location Map G6
Casner Butte USGS Map
Coconino Forest Service Map

Driving Distance One Way: 17.2 miles (Time 30 minutes)
Access Road: All cars, Last 2.5 miles gravel, in good condition
Hiking Distance One Way: 2.0 miles (Time 1.25 hours)
How Strenuous: Moderate
Features: Permanent Stream, Rock Art, Views

NUTSHELL: This trail follows the Bell Crossing Trail along the banks of Wet Beaver Creek and then branches off to climb to the top of a mesa.

DIRECTIONS:
From the Sedona Y Go:
South on Highway 179 (toward Phoenix) for 14.7 miles, to the I-17 Interchange. Instead of going onto I-17, go underneath it onto the dirt road. At 15.2 miles, you will come to a junction. The right fork goes to Montezuma Castle. Take the left fork (FR 618). It is a good dirt road. At 16.9 miles, you are almost to the Beaver Creek Ranger Station. You will see a sign showing a left turn for the Bell Crossing Trail and others. Take it. At 17.2 you will reach the parking area for the trailhead.

TRAILHEAD: Several hiking trails here share a common trailhead that is well marked with signs at the parking area.

DESCRIPTION: From the trailhead, the **Bell Crossing Trail** goes up canyon along Wet Beaver Creek, sometimes near it, sometimes away from it, but always following the stream.

The trail is an old road, broad and easy to walk. It was built by a cattle rancher named Bell in 1932, as a means for taking his cattle to the top of The Mogollon Rim in the spring.

At about 0.6 miles, look for a large boulder on the left side of the trail. On the side that faces away from you are a number of interesting petroglyphs.

The Forest Service's parking lot sign indicates that the Casner Canyon Trail is 1.5 miles from the trailhead. When you make the hike, you will see a small sign for the trail to your left just before the Bell Trail dips down into a gully.

The trail goes up the south wall of Casner Canyon in a straight line, not zigzagging as many trails do. It is not terribly strenuous, though it does climb 1000 feet in 0.70 miles. Along the way you are treated to some good views and some shows of colorful redrock.

The top of the mesa is covered by a hundred foot thick layer of lava, which is typical of all the mesas in this area. In most places there are sheer cliffs at these mesa rims. This trail takes advantage of a gap in the caprock and emerges at the top without requiring any rock climbing. On the top the trail just ends at a cairn at a point 2.0 miles from the beginning.

We suggest that you turn left and walk to the edge of the mesa overlooking Beaver Creek (about 0.20 miles) for some excellent views of the creek and the Verde Valley. Hikers along the Bell Crossing Trail will wonder how you got there.

The Casner family was very active in the livestock business and left its name in several locations. In this book you will find the **Casner Mountain South** and **Casner Canyon North** hikes in addition to this hike.

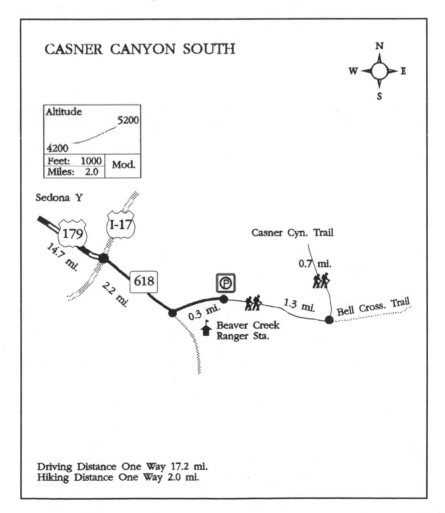

CASNER MOUNTAIN SOUTH

General Information
Location Map C1
Loy Butte and Clarkdale USGS Maps
Coconino Forest Service Map

Driving Distance One Way: 19.6 miles (Time 30 minutes)
Access Road: All cars, Last 10.0 miles good dirt road
Hiking Distance One Way: 2.0 miles (Time 1.5 hours)
How Strenuous: Hard
Features: Views

NUTSHELL: This hike takes you to the top of a mountain overlooking Sycamore Canyon and the Sedona back country.

DIRECTIONS:
From The Y in Sedona Go:
Southwest on Highway 89A (toward Cottonwood) a distance of 9.6 miles (MP 364.5) to the Red Canyon Road. Turn right on Red Canyon Road, also known as FR 525, and follow it to the 12.4 mile point where FR 525C branches to the left. Turn left on FR 525C and stay on it to the 15.6 mile point, the next major junction. Here FR 761, the Bill Gray Road, goes to the left. Stay on FR 525C, the right fork, and follow it to the 19.6 mile point, where you will see a trail sign marked "Casner Mtn. #8." There is a very small parking spot, just enough for one car, right at the trailhead.

TRAILHEAD: The trailhead is marked with a sign. The trail follows the power line up the south face of Casner Mountain, and you can see clearly from the start of the hike where the trail goes.

DESCRIPTION: Casner Mountain is bare of shade trees except for a few junipers and the trail takes you up its south face. Because of that, you are in full sunlight with no shade, so take a hat and plenty of water and don't try this hike on a hot day. The trail follows along a jeep road created for the construction of the power line. You will climb about 0.4 miles to join the power line, then hike across a gradually rising shelf. From there you will begin the steepest ascent. Look over to your right (east) and you will see the rounded red butte known as **Robber's Roost.**
The payoff for this hike is the viewing that you will enjoy. Casner is a tall mountain and is situated so that you can see into some beautiful country. To the south you see the Black Hills and can even pick out Jerome. To the east you will see many familiar Sedona landmarks and parts of the town. As you

climb higher you will begin to see the red towers of Sycamore Pass to your left (west).

From the end of the shelf, the trail goes straight up the mountain to about the halfway point, where the pitch becomes quite steep, and from there the trail serpentines. At the 1.6 mile point you come to a sharp switchback at the west edge of the mountain where you break over a shoulder so that you can suddenly see into the whole of Sycamore Canyon. It is a vast and soul-stirring view, worth the trip all by itself.

From this point you will make the final push and stop at the top, at the highest point. Though Casner Mountain looks like a detached free-standing mountain when you start the hike, it is actually attached to the Mogollon Rim by a ridge. The power line runs across this ridge and you can continue hiking the power line road for four miles to the rim. This hike from Casner's summit to the rim we have described in our *Flagstaff Hikes* book as **Casner Mountain North.**

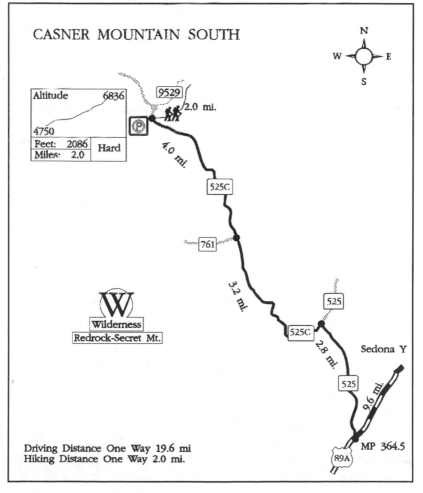

CATHEDRAL RIDGE

General Information
Location Map F4
Sedona USGS Map
Coconino Forest Service Map

Driving Distance One Way: 7.0 miles (Time 15 minutes)
Access Road: All cars, All paved
Hiking Distance One Way: 1.5 miles (Time 60 minutes)
How Strenuous: Moderate
Features: Views

NUTSHELL: Located 7.0 miles south of Sedona, this interesting ridge connects Cathedral Rock and Little Park Heights. You hike a closed road to the base of the ridge and then make a moderately strenuous climb from there.

DIRECTIONS:
From the Sedona Y Go
        South on Highway 179 a distance of 7.0 miles (MP 309.4) to a point where a dirt road to the left is visible. Turn left onto the dirt road and park there.

TRAILHEAD: This is not a marked trail. Walk across Highway 179, where you will find an old closed road. Then you walk the road.

DESCRIPTION: Like several other hikes in the book, the trail is a road that has been closed to vehicular travel. You will see a marker at the start of this road indicating that it has been closed. Here and there you will see places where the roadbed has been torn up to discourage vehicles from using it. Because it was once a road, it is wide and makes for easy walking.
        At the first part of the hike you will walk up a little crest and then go down into a bottom where there is a gully. This is usually dry. We were lucky enough to make the hike in late March when water was running in it and it was lovely.
        The gully is not deep and you should have no trouble getting across it. The road is a bit hard to follow as you come down the hill to the streambed, as there is a berm of dirt across the road, and a false road takes off to the left, where it ends in an old materials pit. You should have no trouble getting back on track, though, because you can plainly see the true road on the other side of the streambed.
        After crossing the gully, you climb gently until you come into a basin at the foot of Cathedral Ridge. Behind you are fine views of the Chapel of the Holy Cross. The road ends here. The ending isn't obvious. There is no visible

reason for the road to quit where it does, but you will become aware that it has ended. Keep walking forward, toward the ridge, and you will soon come to a path at a T intersection. Take the left fork, which goes uphill. You should begin to see cairns marking the trail from this point.

The trail climbs up the ridge. It is gradual at first and then becomes steeper. It is less than a half mile to the top. Before you get to the crest, you will come out onto a redrock ledge that is over one hundred feet thick. It forms some beautiful cliffs. It is fun to walk along this ledge and peer down. There are many interesting eroded rock sculptures and formations.

Once you have had your fill of the ledge, you can make the final push to the top. This requires another short steep climb. At the top you have your choice of going either north toward **Cathedral Rock** or south toward **Little Park Heights**, or both. The mileage shown here is just to the top. If you do any exploring, then you can add another half mile or more to the mileage we have shown in the heading for this hike.

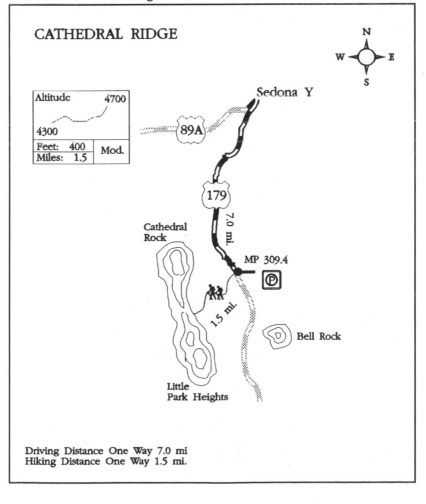

CATHEDRAL RIDGE

Driving Distance One Way 7.0 mi
Hiking Distance One Way 1.5 mi.

CATHEDRAL ROCK, BACK O' BEYOND

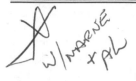

General Information
Location Map F4
Sedona USGS Map
Coconino Forest Service Map

Driving Distance One Way: 4.1 miles (Time 15 minutes)
Access Road: All cars, Last 0.7 miles good dirt road
Hiking Distance One Way: 1.0 miles (Time 30 minutes)
How Strenuous: Easy
Features: Views, Vortex spot

NUTSHELL: Cathedral Rock, a prominent Sedona landmark, is accessible from several points. This is the easiest and one of the most satisfying routes, featuring a marvelous natural walkway partly around the butte.

DIRECTIONS:
From the Sedona Y Go
        South on Highway 179 a distance of 3.4 miles (MP 310.2) to a point where you see a dirt road to the right into an area signed Back O' Beyond. Turn right onto the dirt road and follow it to the 4.1 mile point, where you will see a marked and fenced parking area to your left.

TRAILHEAD: This is not a marked trail. It starts at the fence at the parking lot.

DESCRIPTION: At the parking area you are quite close to Cathedral Rock, and it dominates the skyline to your right. Enjoy the views of it before starting on the hike. You will see one of its outstanding features on the left end, a spire called The Mace, which is a large column that is larger at the top than the bottom.
        The butte consists of two major parts, the upper sheer-walled cliffs and a lower platform with sloping sides. These slopes make it possible to climb to the top of the platform with relative ease.
        Go through the gap in the fence and you will see several trails. Cattle used to graze this area and there are numberless false trails caused by them. Pass by the first trail that forks right and take the second right fork, about 40 paces from the fence. It goes downhill into a wash and up the other side.
        Once across you will find another network of trails. Stay on the main one, which heads uphill toward the butte. At 0.2 miles you will come to the top of a red slickrock ledge. Keep going up toward the central mass and in a short distance you will find a wide lip that makes a natural walkway to your

left. From here you simply hike the lip around to the south, hugging the butte all the way. This natural path is an unusual and delightful feature.

The views of the butte are eye-pleasing at every turn and you will also have some great views in the distance. This is a very restful and quieting kind of hike. Stop at the 1.0 mile point, where the trail turns away from the butte and goes downhill into the junipers, a place where you encounter the remains of an old barbed wire fence. The trail goes on but is not very interesting beyond the fence.

We have not found a particular point that seems to be *the* Vortex spot on Cathedral Rock: no medicine wheels or other markers; but the place does have a nice restorative feeling of silent energy to both of us.

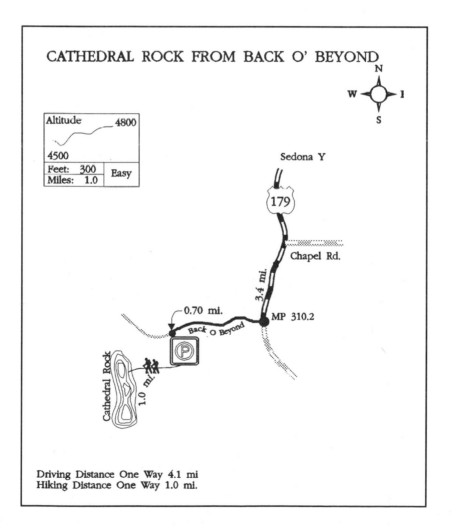

CATHEDRAL ROCK FROM BACK O' BEYOND

Altitude 4800

4500

Feet:	300	Easy
Miles:	1.0	

Sedona Y

179

Chapel Rd.

3.4 mi.

0.70 mi.

Back O Beyond

MP 310.2

Cathedral Rock

1.0 mi.

Driving Distance One Way 4.1 mi
Hiking Distance One Way 1.0 mi.

CATHEDRAL ROCK FROM V. V. SCHOOL

General Information
Location Map F4
Sedona USGS Map
Coconino Forest Service Map

Driving Distance One Way: 11.0 miles (Time 20 minutes)
Access Road: All cars, Last 0.5 miles good gravel road
Hiking Distance One Way: 1.2 miles (Time 1 hour)
How Strenuous: Moderate
Features: Rock formations, Views

NUTSHELL: Cathedral Rock is a prominent butte located about 4 miles south of Sedona. This hike is a bushwhacking, scrambling adventure to its south face.

DIRECTIONS:

From the Sedona Y Go:

South on Highway 179 (toward Phoenix) for a distance of 7.5 miles (MP 306.1), to the Verde Valley School Road. Turn right onto Verde Valley School Road. The first 3.0 miles of this road are paved. Follow it to the 11.0 mile point where you will see an unmarked dirt road to your right just past the Verde Valley School. Pull off onto it and park.

TRAILHEAD: Not marked as a hiking trail. See description below.

DESCRIPTION: The turnoff for this hike is about 0.5 miles from where the paving ends on the Verde Valley School Road, just beyond the entrance to the Verde Valley School. There are several roads branching to the right in this area, which obviously go to private homes. Don't take any of these roads. The road you are looking for is not marked. It is a good wide road to the right that ends in about 100 yards in a clearing. The road is blocked there with a row of boulders. This is where you should park.

From the parking area you will see several trails crisscrossing the area. Head toward Cathedral Rock and at the back of the parking area you will pick up the main travelled road, which runs parallel to the Verde Valley School Road. Hike it to its end.

From the end of the road you will have to bushwhack. There were a few cairns present when we made this hike, but they did not seem to have been erected systematically and they are not completely reliable. We also followed footprints part of the time.

The trail goes up a fin that radiates from the butte. It is easy to climb this fin, which takes you to a ledge top. In fact, this is a good place to stop for the faint of heart. You can walk along this extensive red sandstone ledge and enjoy superb views.

You can also go higher. To go higher requires a bit of climbing. There are clefts and ravines in the slopes of the butte that furnish natural ways to climb. We were able to pick them out readily and get up to the base of the cliffs, quite a bit higher than the first ledge top.

There are great views from this higher point. From the bottom as you start this hike, it seems that you could not get up to the base of the cliffs, but you can do it without a great deal of risk, and it is worth the effort.

As with some of the other vortex spots, we don't know of any one particular place on Cathedral Rock that is regarded as *the* power point or vortex spot. Keep yourself attuned as you explore this magnificent butte and see how it affects you.

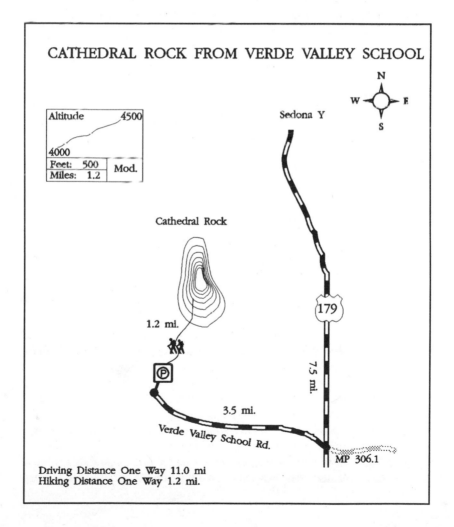

CATHEDRAL ROCK FROM VERDE VALLEY SCHOOL

N
W E
S

Sedona Y

Altitude   4500
4000
Feet: 500   Mod.
Miles: 1.2

Cathedral Rock

179

1.2 mi.

7.5 mi.

3.5 mi.

Verde Valley School Rd.

MP 306.1

Driving Distance One Way 11.0 mi
Hiking Distance One Way 1.2 mi.

CHICKEN POINT

General Information
Location Map E5
Sedona and Munds Mt. USGS Maps
Coconino Forest Service Map

Driving Distance One Way: 2.0 miles (Time 10 minutes)
Access Road: All cars, All paved
Hiking Distance One Way: 1.2 miles (Time 40 minutes)
How Strenuous: Moderate
Features: Rock formations, Views

NUTSHELL: Only a couple of miles southeast of Uptown Sedona, Chicken Point is a scenic gap that gives great views of Marg's Draw to the north and the Bell Rock country to the south. Short and easy, with good side tours, it is a great introductory hike to the area.

DIRECTIONS:
From the Sedona Y Go:
South on Highway 179 (toward Phoenix) for a distance of 1.4 miles (MP 312.1), to Morgan Road. Turn left onto Morgan Road. Follow it to the 2.0 mile point where you will see a cattle guard and the paving ends. Drive just beyond the cattle guard and park.

TRAILHEAD: Walk along the jeep road, FR 179F.

DESCRIPTION: Walk down the jeep road. You will see a sign at the cattle guard reading "Trail Walk-Through." We suggest that you disregard the walkthrough and just stay on the road. The road is widely used by the jeep tours that have proliferated in Sedona, so the road is well maintained, although sharing it with motor vehicles does detract from the natural qualities of the scene.
As you walk the road, you will reach a spot at 0.34 miles where a sunken road goes off to the right (south). This is the trail to the **Devil's Dining Room**, a large sinkhole. It is a short jaunt and worth seeing.
At 0.4 miles, the road splits but it doesn't matter which fork you take, as the roads converge on the other side of a hill. The high road gives better views. At 0.67 miles you reach a T fork. Go straight here. The right fork goes up to a nice viewpoint, again worth a short detour. The jeep tour drivers go up to the point for the view and to thrill the tourists, as they climb up a steep ledge. At 0.71 miles you come to a Y fork. The left branch goes down into a gully and up to **Submarine Rock**, again a worthwhile side tour and a short easy

one. Take the right fork here to go to Chicken Point. You will hit another T intersection at 0.94 miles. Go left.

At this part of the trail you are climbing and will get good views of the area to the north and east, a beautiful place known as Marg's Draw. It seems rather wild and remote and yet it is just a stone's throw from heavily populated areas of Sedona.

Chicken Point is a gap between Twin Buttes and the West Ridge of Lee Mountain. It is a great place for views both north and south and you stand right on beautiful red slickrock formations and are surrounded by interesting cliffs. Look for a famous formation called the Madonna and Nuns in the flutes of the rock face to your right. Depending on the light, it may be very obvious or you may have to use your imagination. It always seems to be windy at Chicken Point. Unfortunately this is not a place of solitude as it is very popular and when the jeep tours are running, load after load of them come to this justifiably popular spot.

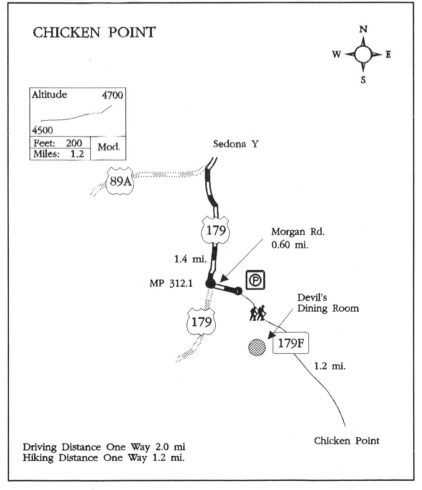

CHICKEN POINT

N
W — E
S

Altitude	4700
4500	

Feet:	200	Mod.
Miles:	1.2	

89A

Sedona Y

179

Morgan Rd.
0.60 mi.

1.4 mi.

MP 312.1   Ⓟ

Devil's
Dining Room

179

179F

1.2 mi.

Chicken Point

Driving Distance One Way 2.0 mi
Hiking Distance One Way 1.2 mi.

CHIMNEY ROCK

General Information
Location Map D4
Sedona USGS Map
Coconino Forest Service Map

Driving Distance One Way: 3.6 miles (Time 10 minutes)
Access Road: All cars, All paved
Hiking Distance One Way: 0.65 miles (Time 30 minutes)
How Strenuous: Moderate
Features: Rock formations, Views

NUTSHELL: This landmark located 3.6 miles southwest of uptown Sedona can be climbed with moderate effort for great views.

DIRECTIONS:
From the Sedona Y Go:
     Southwest on Highway 89A (toward Cottonwood) for a distance of 2.5 miles (MP 371.7), to Andante Drive. Turn right onto Andante Drive. Follow it to the 3.6 mile point where it intersects Skyview. Drive just across Skyview onto a parking area on the dirt near the water tank.

TRAILHEAD: No signs posted. Follow the fence surrounding the water tank to the end of the fence. You will pick up the trail there.

DESCRIPTION:
     As you begin the hike, there are not many clues to the presence of the trail. You will see signs that people have parked just outside the fence surrounding the water tank. Walk along the fence to your left from where you parked and you will spot the trail heading down into a gully. Chimney Rock is in plain sight here, so it is obvious to you which way you have to walk.
     After going down into the wash, go upstream about 12 paces and you will find the trail going up the other side. In a couple of hundred feet, the path will intersect a major trail. Take the fork to the right, going uphill.
     At 0.5 miles you will reach the top of a saddle between Chimney Rock and a ridge running over toward Capitol Butte. Take some time to explore around this ridgetop if you like. It is a good place. There are some great views.
     After you have explored the ridge, get back on the trail. It will now be clear to you that this trail is a horse trail. It goes down the other side of the ridge to stables located along Dry Creek Road. Follow this trail for a short distance, looking for a faint trail to your left, which heads toward Chimney Rock.

The trail up to the Chimney is not well developed, but this doesn't matter much, as your objective is in sight always so that all you need to do is to keep working toward it. It is a bit of a scramble. From a distance Chimney Rock looks like a monolith, but when you get up close to it you can see that the formation is composed of three pillars. These probably were a single column thousands of years ago, but weathering has divided it. You can walk right up to the base of these pillars. They are fun to look at and you will have a great platform from which to view the surrounding countryside. You can see in all directions except to the north where Capitol Butte blocks your view.

It is possible to walk all the way around the Chimney. The ground is not level but making the loop is well worth the toil. We found it helpful to build a cairn to mark our starting point when we began the loop so that we would know where to descend. From the main trail up to the Chimney, around the Chimney and back down to the main trail is only 0.3 miles.

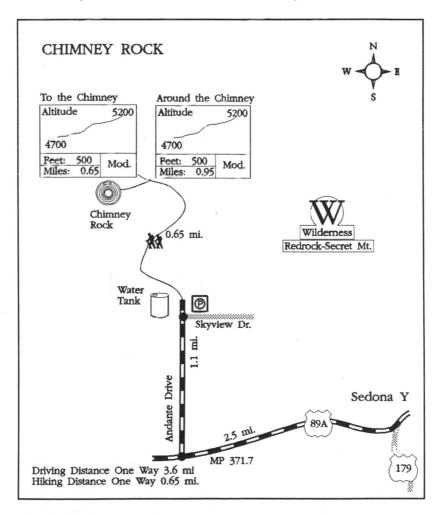

CHIMNEY ROCK

N
W — E
S

To the Chimney

Altitude	5200
4700	
Feet: 500	Mod.
Miles: 0.65	

Around the Chimney

Altitude	5200
4700	
Feet: 500	Mod.
Miles: 0.95	

Chimney Rock

0.65 mi.

Water Tank

Skyview Dr.

W
Wilderness
Redrock-Secret Mt.

1.1 mi.

Andante Drive

Sedona Y

89A

2.5 mi.

MP 371.7

179

Driving Distance One Way 3.6 mi
Hiking Distance One Way 0.65 mi.

CHINUP

General Information
Location Map D4
Wilson Mt. USGS Map
Coconino Forest Service Map

Driving Distance One Way: 5.2 miles (Time 15 minutes)
Access Road: All cars, All paved
Hiking Distance One Way: 0.5 miles (Time 30 minutes)
How Strenuous: Moderate
Features: Views

NUTSHELL: This hike takes you to the top of a ridge projecting from the west face of Capitol Butte for fine views out over scenic country.

DIRECTIONS:
From the Sedona Y Go:
Southwest on Highway 89A (toward Cottonwood) for a distance of 3.2 miles (MP 371) to the Dry Creek Road, FR 152C. Turn right onto Dry Creek Road and follow it to the 5.2 mile point, where FR 152 branches off to the right. The road is paved to this point. Pull onto FR 152 just far enough to find a parking place and park.

TRAILHEAD: This trail is not marked, but the trailhead is easily found. You will see a large metal sign frame, about 8 feet high just up the road from where you park. Walk up the road about 75 paces from the sign frame and look to your right, where you will see a ditch and a blocked dirt road. This is the trailhead.

DESCRIPTION: Walk up the blocked road a few yards, where you will meet another trail. Go to your right. At 0.15 miles, the trail forks. Go to your left. At 0.08 miles you will reach another fork. The left fork (north), going uphill, is an old jeep road, and takes you on the Chinup hike. The right fork takes you on the **Capitol Butte** hike.

Walk up the old jeep road. At 0.13 miles it makes a hairpin turn to your left (northwest). Keep following the road. It will wind completely around the face of the ridge, climbing gradually as it does so. This gives the hiker the chance to see a panoramic view.

At 0.238 miles you will be around the side of the ridge at a point where there is a fork, with one branch going downhill. You want to turn right here and go uphill. In a few yards from this point you will come out onto a high shoulder of the ridge.

The road becomes less distinct on top and there are confusing cattle trails all over the ground. Look to your left (east), where you will see a knob about one hundred feet high. The top of this knob is your objective.

Keep picking your way through the scrub until you have climbed to the top of this knob. At the high point you will have great views. To the north you will see into the Dry Creek back country, to the west and south are equally fine views though not as wild, as you can see many habitations. To the north look for an urn-shaped balanced rock on one of the cliffs of Capitol Butte. In the other direction, you will have a fine view of Lizard Head, a rock formation on the skyline.

You can then bushwhack to the head of the ridge, where it joins Capitol Butte and enjoy looking at the cliffs. This could even be the jumping off point for more exploration for those who have the time and energy.

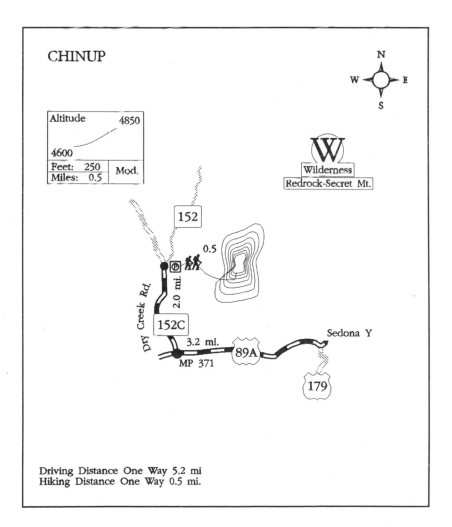

CHINUP

Altitude 4850
4600
Feet: 250   Mod.
Miles: 0.5

Wilderness
Redrock-Secret Mt.

152
0.5
Dry Creek Rd.
2.0 mi.
152C
3.2 mi.
MP 371
89A
Sedona Y
179

Driving Distance One Way 5.2 mi
Hiking Distance One Way 0.5 mi.

CIBOLA MITTENS

General Information
Location Map D4
Munds Park and Wilson Mt. USGS Maps
Coconino Forest Service Map

Driving Distance One Way: 1.5 miles (Time 10 minutes)
Access Road: All cars, Last 0.4 miles good gravel road
Hiking Distance One Way: 1.5 miles (Time 1 hour)
How Strenuous: Moderate
Features: Rock formations, Views

NUTSHELL: This unmaintained trail takes you to a landmark butte in the Soldier Pass area just 1.5 miles north of the Sedona Y.

DIRECTIONS:
From the Sedona Y Go:
    North on Highway 89A (toward Flagstaff) for a distance of 0.3 miles to Jordan Road. Turn left onto Jordan Road. Follow it to the end. You will run out of paving and see signs indicating that the road ends, but do not be bothered by that, as the paving simply changes into a good gravel road. Your target is the Shooting Range. At 1.1 miles you will reach an intersection. The road to your right is a private drive. Go left here to the Shooting Range gate. Park outside the gate. It is kept locked unless it is being used and you don't want to get locked in. (The Shooting Range was closed after this was written.)

TRAILHEAD: Walk across the parking area of the range, about 0.26 miles, where you will pick up the **Brins Mesa East** trailhead. Follow it.

DESCRIPTION: Start measuring trail mileage from the outside gate of the Shooting Range, where you will park. It is 0.26 miles to the Brins Mesa trailhead, where you will find a rusty sign reading "Brins Mesa #119." Follow the Brins Mesa Trail to the 0.70 mile point, where a wide trail takes off to the left, marked by a cairn.
    Follow this left trail. At 0.75 miles take the fork to the right.
    You will come out on top of the north end of **Shooting Range Ridge**. Take a minute while you are there to enjoy the view. You might even want to explore it a bit. Look for cairns leading north. The trail you want first goes down into a gully and then it goes up onto a redrock ledge.
    Ahead of you, fully in view, is your objective, the gap between Cibola Mittens and Brins Ridge. The trail is fairly steep but it is short. Cairns mark the way.

At the top you will stand on a saddle from which you have outstanding views. To your right is the Mormon Canyon country, bounded to the north by Brins Mesa. To the east is Wilson Mountain. Behind you are good views of uptown Sedona and the country beyond. To your left, west, is the Soldier Pass area. The saddle you are standing on divides Mormon Canyon and Soldier Pass.

You are at the base of one thumb of the mitten at this place. Keep going toward the hand of the mitten. You will find trails there. They seem to be deer trails but they work fine for humans.

There is a truly scenic gap between the first thumb and the hand. Just above head level at this gap you will find a rusted piton that was driven into the rock by a climber years ago. You can keep working your way around the hand of the mitten on a narrow but safe ledge to the other thumb, where the trail ends.

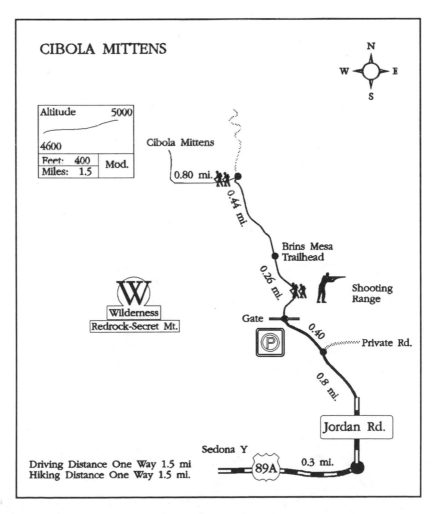

CIBOLA MITTENS

N
W — E
S

Altitude 5000

4600

Feet: 400 — Mod.
Miles: 1.5

Cibola Mittens

0.80 mi.

0.44 mi.

Brins Mesa
Trailhead

0.26 mi.

Shooting
Range

W

Wilderness
Redrock-Secret Mt.

Gate

0.40

Private Rd.

0.8 mi.

Jordan Rd.

Sedona Y

Driving Distance One Way 1.5 mi
Hiking Distance One Way 1.5 mi.

89A

0.3 mi.

COCKSCOMB, THE

General Information
Location Map C3
Wilson Mountain USGS Map
Coconino Forest Service Map

Driving Distance One Way: 6.7 miles (Time 20 minutes)
Access Road: All cars, All paved
Hiking Distance One Way: 2.5 miles (Time 1.5 hours)
How Strenuous: Moderate
Features: Views

NUTSHELL: The trailhead is easy to reach, 6.7 miles on paved roads. You hike 2.5 miles along pleasant abandoned roads, then climb 400 feet to the top of a landmark butte southwest of Sedona.

DIRECTIONS:
From the Sedona Y Go:
Southwest on Highway 89A (toward Cottonwood) a distance of 3.2 miles (MP 371) to Dry Creek Road (FR 152C) where you take a right turn onto Dry Creek Road. Follow it to the 6.1 mile point, where it joins Long Canyon Road. Take a left here, staying on FR 152C. At the 6.7 mile point, you will see a dirt road, FR 9586B, to your left (south). Pull off on it and park.

TRAILHEAD: Walk the closed road you park on.

DESCRIPTION: FR 9586B is a jeep road that goes to the south over gently rolling hills. Four-wheelers have driven all over the first part of this road, creating a confusing welter of tracks. The best clues to stay on the right path are: it is the main road everywhere; you always head southwesterly on it, never veering sharply east or west; look for bicycle tracks, as they mark the right route. You will hike the road a distance of 0.8 miles, to a point where you will meet a power line. Make a short jog to your left (southeast) here and then continue taking the road southwesterly.

You are not in remote country as you move along this old road, but the juniper forest screens you so that you feel as if you are really out in the country. From the power line onward you will be close to **Doe Mountain** and will move along beside it. At the 1.66 mile point you will see an unexpected sight, a line of green-leafed deciduous trees and even bamboo at a boggy place where the road crosses a drainage. The fence you will see here surrounds The Tree Farm. You will pass through a gate and begin to climb uphill, moving away from the fence.

Ahead of you now, looming large, is the Cockscomb. At the 2.0 miles point you will come to another corner of The Tree Farm fence at a point where the trail makes a hairpin turn to the east at the base of the Cockscomb. Look for a footpath to your right (south) here, going uphill. It is marked by cairns. The trail moves diagonally from the bottom right of The Cockscomb to its top left. About half way up you will meet the main trail, which is easy to follow. Stay on it, as it goes to the only place where you can climb up the top ledge.

At the base of the ledge keep moving to your left (east). You will go just around the corner of the north face and climb three notches in the ledge. These are slightly risky but even with our aversion to risk we did not hesitate to make the climb. It's that safe. You will come out on top of the Cockscomb. The top is small and quite barren so you have good views all around. Walk about and enjoy looking. The cliffs of the Cockscomb itself are attractive. On the southern face you will look down on the three spires that give the formation its name.

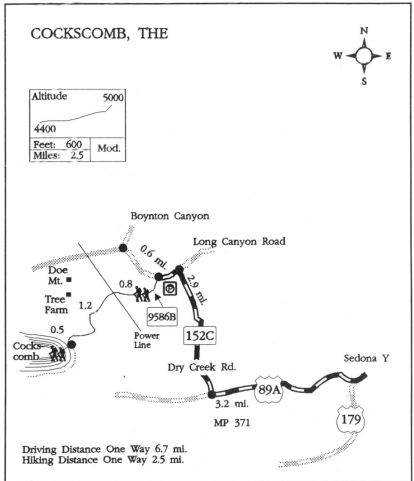

COCKSCOMB, THE

Altitude   5000
4400
Feet: 600   Mod.
Miles: 2.5

N
W — E
S

Boynton Canyon

Long Canyon Road

0.6 mi.

Doe
Mt.

0.8

2.9 mi.

Tree
Farm   1.2

9586B

0.5

152C

Cocks-
comb

Power
Line

Dry Creek Rd.

Sedona Y

89A

3.2 mi.

MP 371

179

Driving Distance One Way 6.7 mi.
Hiking Distance One Way 2.5 mi.

COFFEE POT TRAIL

General Information
Location Map D4
Sedona and Wilson Mt. USGS Maps
Coconino Forest Service Map

Driving Distance One Way: 2.6 miles (Time 10 minutes)
Access Road: All cars, All paved
Hiking Distance One Way: 1.0 miles (Time 45 minutes)
How Strenuous: Easy
Features: Rock formations, Views

NUTSHELL: Coffee Pot Rock is one of the most familiar Sedona landmarks. This trail allows you easy access to its base. You walk to a point under the "spout" where you enjoy great views.

DIRECTIONS:
From the Sedona Y Go:
 Southwest on Highway 89A (toward Cottonwood) for a distance of 1.7 miles (MP 372.5), to Mt. Shadows Street. Turn right onto Mt. Shadows Street. Follow it to the 2.6 mile point, where it intersects Fabulous Texan Way. (The streets in this area are named after movies that were filmed in Sedona). There you will find a large water storage tank and a microwave transmitter inside a chain link fence. Drive across the road up onto the dirt apron around the fenced area, where there is parking space for a couple of cars.

TRAILHEAD: At the parking area. No signs posted. Follow the instructions below.

DESCRIPTION: To begin the hike, go through a crawl-through in the fence, a sort of window frame. On the other side you will find several trails, which can be confusing. We found no cairns or other markers. You can see Coffee Pot Rock ahead of you. Your first objective is to circle to the back of **Sugarloaf**, the hill at the parking place. At every trail fork take the branch that leads toward the back of the Sugarloaf, usually the left fork. The correct path circles the base of Sugarloaf and takes you around to the north side.
 You will pass under a power line. Beyond that there is a wide cleared place. This is about 0.33 miles from the beginning. In the clearing you will see a road going up Sugarloaf. The entrance to the road has been blocked by a row of flat red stones. Instead of going up Sugarloaf, look for a jeep road to your right. It heads up a low ridge that connects to the base of the cliffs where Coffee Pot Rock is located.

Once you get safely on this old road, the rest of the hike is easy. Whenever you come to a side path (and there are several of them), just remember where Coffee Pot Rock is and keep moving toward it.

The trail will take you to the base of the cliffs and then move along a ledge toward Coffee Pot. You will enjoy looking at the cliffs here, as they are very colorful and highly sculptured. As the trail nears Coffee Pot it becomes rougher and you have to watch carefully to see where it goes. Eventually the ledge you walk on will reduce down to the point where you can't walk it any further. Here you can look up and see the spout of Coffee Pot towering hundreds of feet above your head. It will seem that you are right under it, though you will be a little west of it.

At this farthest point, about 1.0 mile from the parking spot, you will have some great views. The views to the north are marred by the substantial home building that has occurred there, but otherwise the views are fine.

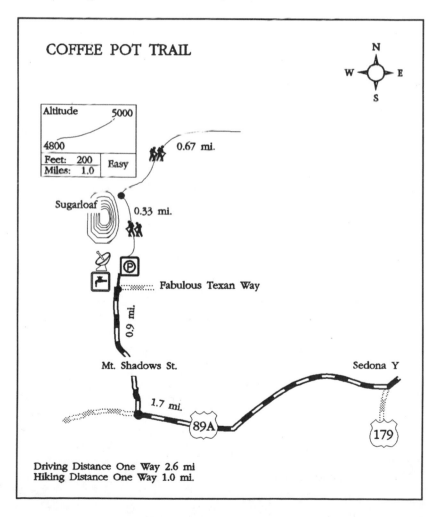

COFFEE POT TRAIL

COOKSTOVE TRAIL

General Information
Location Map B5
Mountainaire USGS Map
Coconino Forest Service Map

Driving Distance One Way: 12.7 miles (Time 20 minutes)
Access Road: All cars, All paved
Hiking Distance One Way: 0.75 miles (Time 45 minutes)
How Strenuous: Hard
Features: Views

NUTSHELL: This is a marked and posted trail located just across Highway 89A from the Pine Flat Campground 12.7 miles north of Sedona. It climbs the east wall of Oak Creek Canyon.

DIRECTIONS:
From the Sedona Y Go:
    North on Highway 89A (toward Flagstaff) for a distance of 12.7 miles (MP 386.9) to the Pine Flat Campground. On your left at the upper end of the campground on the shoulder of the highway, you will see a structure about 5 feet high and 4 feet square made of round stones that houses a spring. You will see water flowing out of a pipe that protrudes from the structure. Park anywhere near here. There are wide aprons on both shoulders in this area.

TRAILHEAD: On the east side of the road just across Highway 89A from the spring. It is marked by a rusty sign reading, "Cookstove Trail #143."

DESCRIPTION: The water in the spring at Pine Flat is potable. You will see people fill bottles and jugs for drinking water. We do this ourselves. There is a caution about this water, however: even though it is pure, it contains microbes that *your* system may not handle well, whereas local residents can drink it with impunity.
    The Cookstove Trail is typical of all trails in upper Oak Creek Canyon that climb the east wall of the canyon: namely, it goes virtually straight up with little finesse. Similar trails are **Harding Spring, Purtymun, Thomas Point** and **Thompson's Ladder.** They are all strenuous hikes.
    The trail starts right by the highway and immediately begins to climb. At first the trail parallels Cookstove Draw. At 0.1 miles you get a great view down into the draw, where there is a small waterfall during snow melt and after hard rains. Then the trail veers away from Cookstove Draw as it rises.
    The forest through which this trail passes is typical for upper Oak

Creek Canyon, with pine at the beginning, changing into mixed pines and firs as you climb and the altitude increases.

The trail does a little zigging and zagging. When you top out, you are in a spot where you get good views of the west wall of Oak Creek Canyon, but the views are not as good as the views you get at the top of the Harding Spring trail.

The altitude at the rim is about 6600 feet, almost as high as Flagstaff, and the climate is similar to Flagstaff's climate. These hikes can often be pleasant in summer when hiking in Sedona would be too hot.

On the rim the country is flat and not scenic. The old-timers who built these trails would travel to Flagstaff once they got to the top. They didn't build trails for the scenery. We like to walk along the rim looking for viewpoints, which are plentiful.

One wonders how Cookstove Draw got its name. Did one of the old timers wrestle a cook stove down this steep canyon wall?

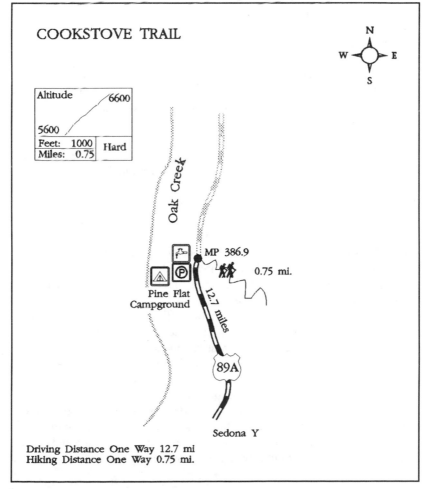

COOKSTOVE TRAIL

Altitude 6600
5600
Feet: 1000   Hard
Miles: 0.75

Oak Creek

MP 386.9
0.75 mi.

Pine Flat
Campground

12.7 miles

89A

Sedona Y

Driving Distance One Way 12.7 mi
Hiking Distance One Way 0.75 mi.

COURTHOUSE BUTTE BRIDLE TRAIL

General Information
Location Map F5
Mountainaire and Munds Mt. USGS Maps
Coconino Forest Service Map

Driving Distance One Way: 6.1 miles (Time 20 minutes)
Access Road: All cars, All paved
Hiking Distance, Complete Loop: 6.0 miles (Time 3.0 hours)
How Strenuous: Easy
Features: Views

NUTSHELL: This easy trail features Courthouse Butte, a landmark located 6.1 miles south of Sedona.

DIRECTIONS:
From the Sedona Y Go:
South on Highway 179 (toward Phoenix) for a distance of 6.1 miles (MP 307.5) to a place where you will see crawlthrough frames in the barbed wire fence on the left side of the roadway. Pull over and park on the left shoulder near a crawlthrough.

TRAILHEAD: You will not find any signs marking this trail. Crawl through a frame in the fence and follow the unmistakable trail to the left.

DESCRIPTION: This trail looks like a jeep road at the start, then turns into a horse trail. It is often used by horse riders, so it is easy to follow.

You will soon come to Bell Spring, which is located just below the famous **Bell Rock**. The spring can be located by the presence of the water-loving tall cottonwoods that grow around it. After that, you will come to a slickrock drainage coming from the spring and then the trail will take you along the south face of Courthouse Butte.

Unlike many of the rock formations in Sedona that are attached to ridges, mountains or the rim, Courthouse Butte is freestanding and isolated.

Courthouse Butte is very attractive and seems to be "built" on a more human scale than some of the gigantic formations around Sedona. It has undergone weathering that has created some very interesting erosion carvings and features. It seems to have a friendly feel.

The trail will take you beyond Courthouse Butte to a ridge behind a small subdivision. At 3.0 miles the trail forks at a fence corner and turns left toward Lee Mountain. The trail takes you close to Lee Mountain and climbs higher, up a talus slope, as it approaches the mountain. At the trail's highest point you have fine views to the south into the Jack's Canyon and Village of Oak Creek areas. The trail does not go very high against the side of Lee Mountain, just climbing the talus slope and then descending. From this point you follow a wash back to the beginning.

What is now called Courthouse Butte was originally called Cathedral Rock and *vice versa*. One of the early government map makers confused the two names and switched them. It doesn't seem to matter much, as either name seems appropriate, but some old-timers were pretty irate about the change.

The country through which this trail passes is cut by several arroyos that carry water that comes off Lee Mountain. These arroyos are fun to explore and can make hikes or hikelets in their own right.

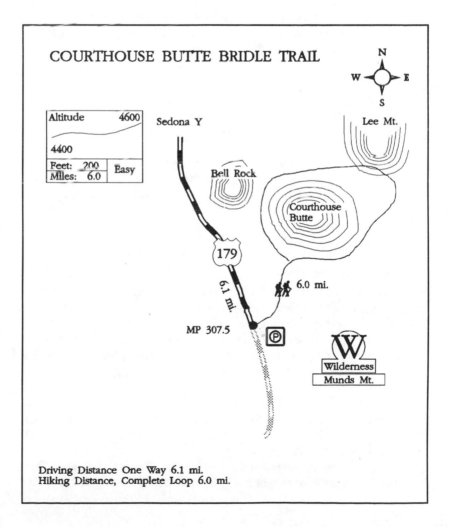

COURTHOUSE BUTTE BRIDLE TRAIL

Altitude 4600
4400
Feet: 200 Easy
Miles: 6.0

Sedona Y

Bell Rock

Lee Mt.

Courthouse Butte

179

6.1 mi.

6.0 mi.

MP 307.5

Wilderness
Munds Mt.

Driving Distance One Way 6.1 mi.
Hiking Distance, Complete Loop 6.0 mi.

COW PIES

Vortex

General Information
Location Map D5
Munds Mt. and Munds Park USGS Maps
Coconino Forest Service Map

Personal Favorite

Driving Distance One Way: 3.8 miles (Time 20 minutes)
Access Road: All cars, Last 2.5 miles good gravel road
Hiking Distance One Way: 1.5 miles (Time 40 minutes)
How Strenuous: Easy
Features: Views, Fascinating rock formations and sculptures, Vortex

NUTSHELL: An ugly name for a beautiful area. The Cow Pies are redrock formations just off the Schnebly Hill Road, 3.8 miles east of uptown Sedona. If you like redrocks, you will love the Cow Pies. **A personal favorite.**

DIRECTIONS:
From the Sedona Y Go:
        South on Highway 179 (toward Phoenix) for a distance of 0.3 miles (MP 312.8) to the Schnebly Hill Road. It is just across the bridge past Tlaquepaque. Turn left onto the Schnebly Hill Road. It is paved for the first mile and then turns into a gravel road that is all right for any car unless the road is muddy. At the 3.8 mile point, pull over and park. There is an area off the road to your right for parking and there are more spaces on the shoulder.

TRAILHEAD: There are no signs. You will see a trail going over the left side of the road (to the west). Follow it.

DESCRIPTION: What's in a name? Many Sedona landmarks have grand names, such as the Crimson Cliffs. This hike takes place on a formation known by the ugly name, Cow Pies. The name does describe the appearance of the rock forms, but utterly fails to convey a sense of how beautiful and interesting they are. The "pies" look like hardened blobs of soft warm red mud, dropped into Bear Wallow Canyon the way you'd drop cookie dough onto a baking sheet. They are a unique Sedona experience, easy to reach and hike on. We prefer to call these formations "muffins."
        At 0.2 miles you will come to the first muffin, a redrock shelf that had a very thin crust of volcanic basalt on top. This crust has broken up into small black stones which New Agers have arranged into a giant medicine wheel. This place is one of the fabled Sedona Vortex spots.
        At 0.43 miles you reach the next muffin. The trail you have been following continues in a straight line (for a hike called **Mitten Ridge**). You

want to quit the trail here and turn to the left. Now you will get a better idea of the muffins. They are mounds of slickrock with many ridges and levels. Walk west, to your left, on the level area to the end of this muffin, where at 0.52 miles you will find a land bridge linking it to the largest muffins, which sit by themselves in the bottom of the gorge.

You will top out on the Master Muffin at about 0.59 miles. There is usually a cairn marking this spot. Take note of it, since it will help you find your way down on the return trip. From this point there is no trail. You just walk around and explore this unusual place to your heart's content. In fact, it is so easy to walk around on these formations that you won't realize how substantial they are until you get to their edges and look down

The farthest extension of these rocks takes you out about 1.5 miles from the parking place, which brings you to the tip, which is rather like the prow of a ship jutting out into Bear Wallow Canyon, a wonderful place to stand and admire the beauties of the scene.

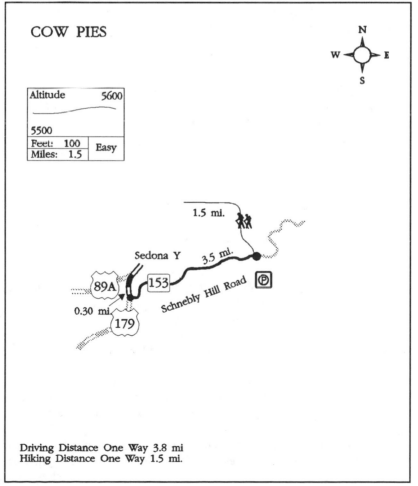

COW PIES

N
W — ◇ — E
S

Altitude	5600

5500

| Feet: 100 | Easy |
| Miles: 1.5 | |

1.5 mi.

Sedona Y   3.5 mi.

89A   153   Schnebly Hill Road   ℗

0.30 mi.   179

Driving Distance One Way 3.8 mi
Hiking Distance One Way 1.5 mi.

COYOTE RIDGE TRAIL

General Information
Location Map F3
Sedona USGS Map
Coconino Forest Service Map

Driving Distance One Way: 8.8 miles (Time 15 minutes)
Access Road: All vehicles, All paved
Hiking Distance One Way: 1.0 miles (Time 40 minutes)
How Strenuous: Moderate
Features: Creekside walk, views

NUTSHELL: This hike takes you from the Visitor Center at Red Rock State Park, 8.8 miles southwest of Sedona, along the banks of Oak Creek, then to the top of a ridge where you have delightful views.

DIRECTIONS:
From the Sedona Y Go:
Southwest on Highway 89A (toward Cottonwood) for a distance of 5.5 miles (MP 368.6) to the Lower Red Rock Loop Road. Turn left on the Lower Red Rock Loop Road and follow it to the 8.5 miles point, where you will see the entry to Red Rock State Park. Turn right into the park. You will come to a toll booth where an admission is charged. From that point, drive to the Visitor Center and park there, at 8.8 miles.

TRAILHEAD: This is a marked and maintained trail, part of the network of seven trails planned for Red Rock State Park. Go down through the Visitor Center. Though the center is not marked as the trailhead for this hike, it is the starting point for it.

DESCRIPTION: Enjoy the Visitor Center and then walk through it, turning right on the paved trail. At 0.08 miles you will come to the first trail junction. Stay on the main path, going to Kingfisher Crossing.
At about one quarter of a mile you will come to Kingfisher Crossing. Go across the bridge there and turn right (toward **Eagles' Nest Trail**) at the trail junction just beyond the bridge. Soon after this you will reach the sign for the **Kisva Trail**. Walk along the Kisva Trail to a point where the Apache Fire Trail goes uphill to your left. Hike up the Apache Fire Trail to a point near the top of the hill, where you will see the Coyote Ridge trail branching to the right. It is signed.
You will then walk along a ridge heading west about a quarter of a mile. There you will meet the Eagles' Nest Trail coming in from your left. Turn

right and keep going along the ridge. In a few paces you will see a trail going downhill to your left. This connects to the Kisva Trail at the trail toilet in about 0.25 miles, and is an optional way to make the return on this hike, setting up a shortcut across the Sentinel Crossing. Ignore it for now and go to the end of the Coyote Ridge Trail, which is in sight. The trail ends at a loop on top of a knob, which is a fine viewpoint.

NOTE: This was written in February 1992, at a time when the Coyote Ridge Trail was not yet open. Check at the Visitor Center for trail information before you try this hike, to be sure the trail is open.

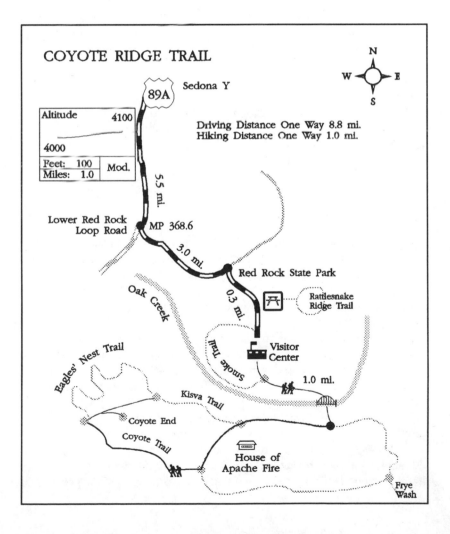

DAMFINO CANYON

General Information
Location Map D5
Munds Mt. and Munds Park USGS Maps
Coconino Forest Service Map

Driving Distance One Way: 1.55 miles (Time 20 minutes)
Access Road: All cars, Last 0.25 miles good gravel road
Hiking Distance One Way: 1.0 miles (Time 45 minutes)
How Strenuous: Moderate
Features: Views, Arches

NUTSHELL: Located off the Schnebly Hill Road, just a mile and a half from uptown Sedona, this hike takes you straight up a side canyon in wild and unspoiled country.

DIRECTIONS:
From the Sedona Y Go:
South on Highway 179 (toward Phoenix) for a distance of 0.30 miles (MP 312.8) to the Schnebly Hill Road, which is just across the bridge, past Tlaquepaque. Turn left onto the Schnebly Hill Road (the first mile of which is paved) and follow it to the 1.55 mile point.

TRAILHEAD: There are no signs marking this hike. There really is no trail. You work your way up the canyon floor.

DESCRIPTION: The Schnebly Hill Road is very popular and gets a lot of use. Sometimes it is in poor condition, but usually an ordinary passenger car can make it all right. If it is muddy you may need four-wheel drive.

At 1.55 miles, at a hairpin turn, you will see Damfino Canyon to your right. There is a clearing at its entrance that is wide enough for four cars. This is the place to park.

There is an apparent trail on the left bank of the canyon, but do not take it. It vanishes soon, going nowhere. Instead, walk straight up the bottom of the canyon. As you climb, some side canyons will appear. Don't go into these. Stay in the main canyon. At 0.40 miles you will reach a major fork. Go left there.

At 0.60 miles you will see an arch in a redrock cliff ahead of you to your left. At 0.75 miles you will see an even bigger arch also on the left. At 1.0 miles the going gets very rough and steep. This is a good place to stop although if you are hardy and in good shape you might try to struggle farther up the canyon. This is a good hike if you like rock hopping. You get right in amongst the beautiful cliffs which form the walls of this canyon. It has a great remote wilderness feeling.

The original Schnebly Hill Road was built by a coalition of Sedona residents and Coconino County in 1902. Before that time, the only wagon road from Sedona to Flagstaff was along the difficult **Beaverhead** road, which is 11.2 miles south of Sedona. Damfino Canyon got its name during the 1930s when government officials were surveying the Schnebly Hill Road in order to realign and improve it. The survey party had one of the pioneers who had participated in the original road construction along to impart local knowledge. When they came to this canyon, the head surveyor asked the old-timer for the name of the canyon. Although the veteran guide had provided the names of many a landmark for the engineer before that, this particular canyon stumped the old-timer and he replied, "Damn if I know," which came out sounding like "Damfino." The engineer thought he was reciting a name and wrote Damfino Canyon on the official map. There it has stayed to this day.

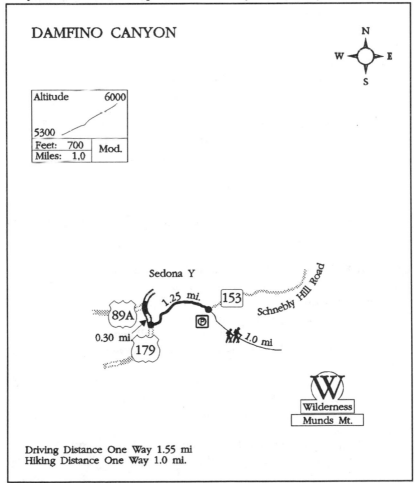

DAMFINO CANYON

Driving Distance One Way 1.55 mi
Hiking Distance One Way 1.0 mi.

DEVIL'S BRIDGE

General Information
Location Map D4
Loy Butte and Wilson Mt. USGS Maps
Coconino Forest Service Map

Driving Distance One Way: 6.5 miles (Time 30 minutes)
Access Road: All cars, Last 1.3 miles rough dirt road
Hiking Distance One Way: 1.0 miles (Time 30 minutes)
How Strenuous: Moderate
Features: Views, Arch

NUTSHELL: Located 6.5 miles northwest of Sedona, this is a short hike to a fascinating arch.

DIRECTIONS:
From the Sedona Y Go:
        Southwest on Highway 89A (toward Cottonwood) for a distance of 3.2 miles (MP 371) to the Dry Creek Road, FR 152C. Turn right onto Dry Creek Road and follow it to the 5.2 mile point, where FR 152 branches off to the right. The road is paved to this point. FR 152 is a dirt road that is often in miserable shape. Sometimes the first mile is graded but often it is not and the road is bad at such times. Ordinary passenger cars can make it but a higher clearance vehicle is recommended. At 6.5 miles you will reach a point where a dirt road takes off to the right. Turn onto it and park immediately.

TRAILHEAD: This is a marked and maintained trail. There is a rusty sign where you park reading "Devil's Bridge #120."

DESCRIPTION: You will walk up an old road for about 0.4 miles, to a point where a footpath forks off to your right. Follow this path. You will see that it leads up toward a red ledge on the east face of Capitol Butte. The path is steep but fairly short, being about 0.4 miles from the fork.
        Halfway up the trail from the fork you will begin to see the arch off to your left in the red ledge. It is hidden from your sight until you get to this point.
        The path itself is very interesting as it begins to climb up the cliff. The Forest Service has used some natural stairsteps made by erosion and has augmented these by cementing in some sandstone slabs to form stepping blocks.
        At the top you have great views into colorful backcountry.. You come out behind the arch. You can follow the trail to the end of the arch and loop

around to stand on the arch if you are daring. The trail places you in a spot where you are above the arch looking down on it.

To get under the arch, go back down to the bottom of the trail and look for cairns about 100 yards from the bottom, marking a small trail going off to your right. The trail goes down into a wash. You walk up the wash and find yourself under the arch.

This is a fine hike but attracts so many visitors that they may lessen your experience if you like solitude. Devil's Bridge is generally regarded as the largest of the natural arches around Sedona. It is an impressive sight.

If you face across the canyon you will be looking at the last leg of the **Lost Canyon Trail,** which is a personal favorite of ours.

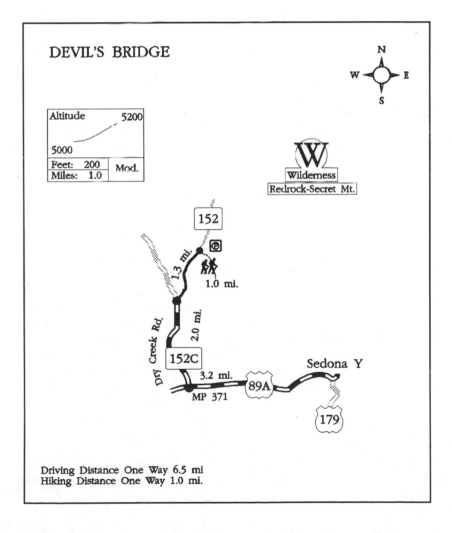

DEVIL'S DINING ROOM

General Information
Location Map E5
Sedona USGS Map
Coconino Forest Service Map

Driving Distance One Way: 2.0 miles
Access Road: All cars, All paved
Hiking Distance One Way: 0.42 miles
How Strenuous: Easy
Features: Sinkhole

NUTSHELL: The Devil's Dining Room is a sinkhole at the south end of Marg's Draw, only a few minutes from uptown Sedona. A short easy walk through scenic country brings you to this site, which is also the jumping off point for other good hikes.

DIRECTIONS:
From the Sedona Y Go:
South on Highway 179 (toward Phoenix) for a distance of 1.4 miles (MP 312.1) to Morgan Road. Turn left onto Morgan Road and follow it to the 2.0 mile point, where there is a cattle guard and the paving ends. Park just on the other side of the cattle guard.

TRAILHEAD: You will see no trail signs. Walk the road, which is FR 179F.

DESCRIPTION: At the cattle guard you will see a sign indicating a "Trail Walk-through." We have tried this and see no earthly reason for its existence. It is much better to walk right down the middle of the road.
This road is used by the jeep tours that abound in Sedona and you are likely to meet some of them on this hike in good weather. They act as if they own the road, and in a certain sense they do, as they have a maintenance agreement for it with the Forest Service.
At 0.26 miles turn right, going up on a red sandstone ledge. The jeeps go up there to thrill the dudes, so the trail is easy to follow. You stay on the lower part of the ledge and walk across it, where the dirt road resumes.
At 0.34 miles go to the right on a sunken road. This will lead you to the Devil's Dining Room at 0.4 miles. At the site, you will come out into a small clearing where you will see a line of boulders and a barbed wire fence. These mark the sinkhole.
This sinkhole isn't nearly as big as **Devil's Kitchen** but it is impressive. Sinkholes develop when underground cavities undermine a ledge

of rock to the point where it collapses into the void. Some geologists speculate that this sinkhole and Devil's Kitchen were both caused by the same underground river that removed the supporting subsoil from both places. After being "dormant" for decades, Devil's Kitchen became active again in November 1988, when a large chunk of ledge fell into the hole. We were at the site a month later and saw warning signs all around the rim. One of the jeep tour guides was there looking into the pit in awe and told us that he had gone to the bottom not long before the rockfall, being unaware of the danger. Since then there have been more cave-ins there. Devil's Dining Room appears to be stable, but so did Devil's Kitchen before November 1988. The natural undermining continues. Something for you to contemplate as you stand on the rim.

You will have some nice views to the north from here. This spot is the jumping off point for the **Battlement Mesa** and **Twin Buttes** hikes, both of which are recommended. You can get back on FR 179F and go to **Submarine Rock** and **Chicken Point**.

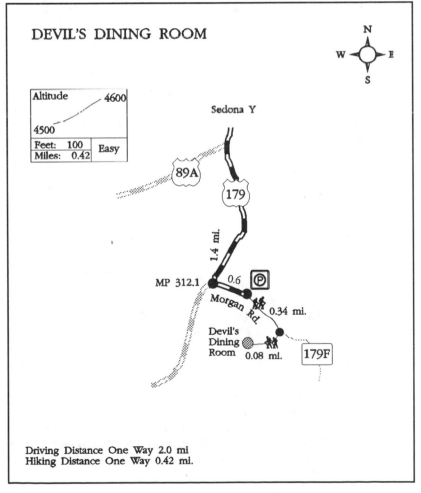

DEVIL'S DINING ROOM

Altitude 4600
4500
Feet: 100
Miles: 0.42 Easy

Sedona Y

89A
179
1.4 mi.
MP 312.1   0.6
Morgan Rd. 0.34 mi.
Devil's
Dining
Room   0.08 mi.   179F

Driving Distance One Way 2.0 mi
Hiking Distance One Way 0.42 mi.

DEVIL'S KITCHEN

General Information
Location Map D4
Sedona and Wilson Mt. USGS Maps
Coconino Forest Service Map

Driving Distance One Way: 1.55 miles (Time 10 minutes)
Access Road: All cars, All paved
Hiking Distance One Way: 0.35 miles (Time 15 minutes)
How Strenuous: Easy
Features: Sinkhole

NUTSHELL: The Devil's Kitchen is a sinkhole in the Soldier Pass area, only a few minutes from uptown Sedona. The hike is short, easy and scenic.

DIRECTIONS:
From the Sedona Y Go:
Southwest on Highway 89A (toward Cottonwood) for a distance of 1.2 miles (MP 372.8) to Soldier Pass Road. Turn right onto Soldier Pass Road and follow it to the 1.4 mile point, where it intersects Rim Shadows Drive, where you turn right. Follow Rim Shadows a short distance, to the 1.45 miles spot, where it intersects Canyon Shadows Drive. Turn left onto Canyon Shadows and follow it to the 1.5 miles point. There you will see a sign saying "Forest Service Access." Take the road to your left there. At 1.55 miles you will come to the parking area. This is well defined and spacious. Park there.

TRAILHEAD: You will see a rusty sign at the parking area reading "Soldier Pass Trail #66."

DESCRIPTION: The trail is an old jeep road and it is still in use by jeep tours. Walk down this road for 0.10 miles where you will see a road branching off to your right, marked FR 904B. Take this road. You will climb it uphill for a short distance and will reach Devil's Kitchen at 0.35 miles.
Devil's Kitchen is the biggest sinkhole in the Sedona area. The original cave-in occurred in the late 1800s, causing an implosion that was heard for miles. It raised a dust cloud that darkened the sky over a wide area.
Cave-ins here have not ceased. This is an active sinkhole. The hole was dormant for many years but then became active again in 1988 when a large chunk of the rim fell into the cavity. Since then there have been other collapses. There are warning signs around the perimeter of the crater warning you not to get close to the edge. They aren't kidding. Another collapse could happen at any time. This is an active sinkhole, rather like an active volcano. You can

see a thin white layer of mineral exposed on most of the sheared stone faces. This layer looks like a film of calcium that squirted into the layers of stone along fault lines, making a weak bond and creating natural weak points along which the collapsing occurs.

The hole is about one hundred feet deep. It was caused by an underground stream cutting away the strata underneath a redrock ledge. This created an underground cave. Deprived of its support, the cap eventually gave way along fault lines. Scientists believe that the same underground stream created the **Devil's Dining Room** several miles south of Devil's Kitchen.

There is a large tree, perhaps ninety feet tall, in the bottom of the crater. Since it is older than the crater it is assumed that it was growing on the top, fell in during the collapse and continued to grow. Plucky tree.

There is a culvert and derrick in the bottom of the pit. A rancher many years ago installed these during an attempt to tap the underground stream so that he could use the water. His efforts were unsuccessful.

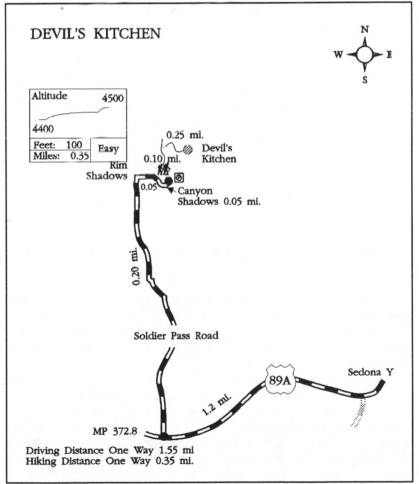

DEVIL'S KITCHEN

Altitude 4500
4400
Feet: 100 Easy
Miles: 0.35
Rim Shadows

0.25 mi.
0.10 mi. Devil's Kitchen
0.05 Canyon Shadows 0.05 mi.

0.20 mi.

Soldier Pass Road

89A Sedona Y

MP 372.8 1.2 mi.

Driving Distance One Way 1.55 mi
Hiking Distance One Way 0.35 mi.

DOE MOUNTAIN

General Information
Location Map D3
Wilson Mt. USGS Map
Coconino Forest Service Map

Driving Distance One Way: 8.9 miles (Time 20 minutes)
Access Road: All cars, Last 1.2 miles good dirt road
Hiking Distance One Way: 1.8 miles (Time 1 hour)
How Strenuous: Moderate
Features: Views

NUTSHELL: This small mesa, 8.9 miles west of uptown Sedona, is fairly easy to climb. Its weathered cliffs are a delight to explore and it provides great views. **A personal favorite**

DIRECTIONS:
From the Sedona Y Go:
Southwest on Highway 89A (toward Cottonwood) for a distance of 3.2 miles (MP 371) to Dry Creek Road. Turn right onto Dry Creek Road (also known as FR 152C) and follow it to the 6.1 mile point, where it intersects the Long Canyon Road, where you turn left. Stay on FR 152C to the 7.7 mile point, where it intersects the Boynton Canyon Road. Here you will turn left onto the Boynton Pass Road. It is paved for a short distance and then becomes unpaved. At the 8.9 mile point you will reach the parking area, which is off to your right just before a cattle guard. Park there. This is also the parking place for the **Bear Mountain** hike.

TRAILHEAD: You will see a rusty sign across the road reading "Doe Mountain #60."

DESCRIPTION: Doe Mountain is a small mesa standing by itself. It is one of the most southerly redrock formations in the west-of-Sedona area. Only the **Cockscomb** is farther south. The trail zigzags to the top of the mesa, climbing steadily. It is a good trail, but a fairly steep pull. Though it seems improbable, there are often cattle on top.
The top of Doe Mountain is not bare rock as you might think when you see it from a distance. Soil has formed through weathering and low junipers and shrubs grow there, plus forage for the cattle. The best part of this hike is working your way around the rim. The edge of the rim is mostly bare redrock. This means that there are no trees to obstruct your views, so Doe Mountain is a terrific viewpoint and it is situated so that there are interesting

things to look at. Views of Sedona are particularly good from here.

In addition to the views of far off objects, you will see some wonderful things nearby, where erosion has worked the cliff faces into some really fantastic rock sculptures. The Sedona Westerners report that there are Indian ruins on the top of the mesa but in three trips we have never seen any. The south side of Doe looks down on a tree farm, which is an unexpected and interesting sight. The farm lies between Doe Mountain and the Cockscomb.

On trips we took in 1988, 1989 and 1990 we saw three feral goats perched on a narrow ledge halfway up a cliff face. The first time we saw this we could not believe our eyes. Then we saw a ribbon around the neck of one goat and came to believe that these were pets who heard the call of the wild.

The peacefulness and wildness of this hike were spoiled for us twice when helicopter tours touched down here to show tourists the views. If this is progress, spare us. In June 1991 a major subdivision complete with golf course next to Doe Mountain was approved.

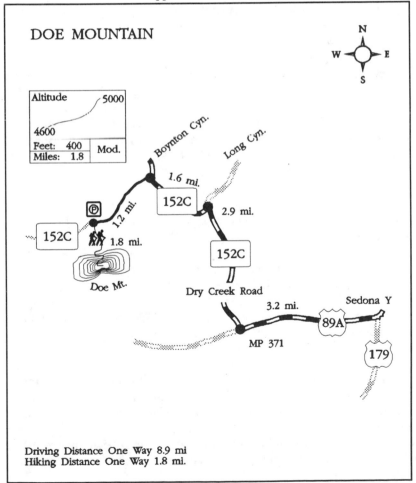

DOE MOUNTAIN

Altitude 5000
4600
Feet: 400 Mod.
Miles: 1.8

Driving Distance One Way 8.9 mi
Hiking Distance One Way 1.8 mi.

DOGIE TRAIL

General Information
Location Map C1
Loy Butte and Clarkdale USGS Maps
Coconino Forest Service Map

Driving Distance One Way: 20.6 miles (Time 45 minutes)
Access Road: All cars, Last 11.0 miles good dirt road
Hiking Distance One Way: 4.0 miles (Time 2.5 hours)
How Strenuous: Moderate
Features: Sycamore Canyon access, Views

NUTSHELL: This hike provides access into Sycamore Canyon at Sycamore Pass, located 20.6 miles northwest of Sedona.

DIRECTIONS:
From The Y in Sedona Go:
Southwest on Highway 89A (toward Cottonwood) a distance of 9.6 miles (MP 364.5) to the Red Canyon Road. Turn right on Red Canyon Road, also known as FR 525, and follow it to the 12.4 mile point where FR 525C branches to the left. Turn left on FR 525C and stay on it to the 15.6 mile point where it meets FR 761, the Bill Gray Road. Go right here, staying on FR 525C to the 19.7 mile point, where it meets FR 9529. Turn left here and go to the 20.6 mile point, where the road meets FR 9528. Park near this intersection. Don't try to drive on FR 9528.

TRAILHEAD: At the intersection near your parking spot you will see a road sign reading, *"Sycamore Pass, Dogie Trail"* with an arrow pointing to the right. Follow the arrow and walk down the road. You will reach a fork in the road, where you should take the right hand path. From there you will walk down a jeep road to the trailhead. Distance from the parking area to the trailhead is 0.5 miles.
At the trailhead you will see a sign: *"Sycamore Canyon 5 miles, Sycamore Basin Trail 5.5 miles, Road 525C 0.5 miles, Dogie Trail #116."*

DESCRIPTION: From the beginning, the trail slopes gradually toward Sycamore Canyon. You will walk down an old stock trail that is very rocky, but the grade is gentle. After hiking a few hundred yards, the landscape will open up to some great views ahead of you, where you will see redrock spires and buttes that are just as impressive as those nearer Sedona.
There are two cattle tanks on this trail. To get to the first one, you must detour to your left. The path goes right around the rim of the second one.

We recommend that you stop at about the 3.0 or 4.0 mile point rather than going all the way into Sycamore Canyon, for it is a pretty strenuous hike to go to the bottom. By staying on top you will have a fine hike and enjoy tremendous views. Remember that the return leg of this hike is all uphill.

Sycamore Canyon is a huge wild place. Even experienced hikers should not attempt a multi-day trip through it unless they are thoroughly prepared and know what they are doing. The brief sight of the canyon you get on a day hike like this is misleading and understates the rigors of the place. It is very beautiful and deserves to be better known and visited, as we hope to encourage in this book, but please do not overextend yourself.

Sycamore Canyon is so big and so long that we have put portions of it in two books. We have the Dogie Trail and the **Parsons Trail** in this book and nine hikes around the northern part of the canyon in our companion volume, "Flagstaff Hikes." Treated with knowledge and respect, Sycamore Canyon is a wonderful place.

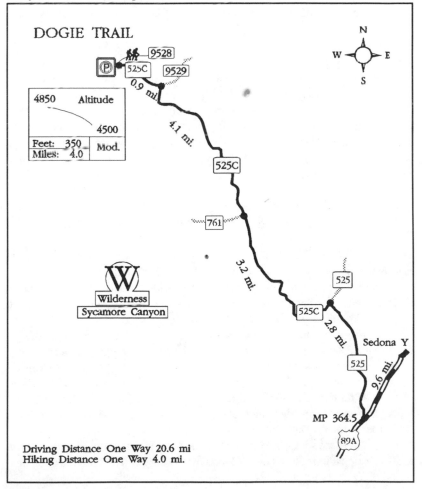

DRY CREEK TRAIL

General Information
Location Map C4
Loy Butte and Wilson Mt. USGS Maps
Coconino Forest Service Map

Driving Distance One Way: 9.6 miles (Time 45 minutes)
Access Road: High clearance car preferable, Last 4.4 miles rough dirt road
Hiking Distance One Way: 2.0 miles (Time 1 hour)
How Strenuous: Moderate
Features: Scenic canyon

NUTSHELL: Located 9.6 miles north of Sedona, this is a wilderness hike that follows the course of Dry Creek to its head at the base of the Mogollon Rim.

DIRECTIONS:
From The Y in Sedona Go:
    Southwest on Highway 89A (toward Cottonwood) a distance of 3.2 miles (MP 371) to the Dry Creek Road. Turn right on Dry Creek Road, also known as FR 152C, and follow it to the 5.2 mile point where FR 152 branches to the right. Take FR 152. You will see a sign for Vultee Arch on this road. Follow the road almost to its end, at 9.6 miles, a place where you can see the Vultee Arch parking area about 100 yards ahead of you. There is a small parking place to your left. Pull in and park there.

TRAILHEAD: The parking area is in a grove of trees. Walk west across a little gully. There you will see a rusty sign marked "Dry Creek #52."

DESCRIPTION: FR 152 can be a very rough road. Sometimes the first mile is graded but it is seldom graded after that. There are many places on the road where the soil has washed away from the surface leaving sharp projecting rocks that compete for the honor of tearing out your oil pan. In other places exposed ledges make for very rough encounters and must be crawled over.
    From the parking place walk across a little arroyo and around the toe of a hill for about 0.10 miles where you will encounter Dry Creek. At the entry point the canyon cut by Dry Creek is rather shallow and wide. The trail follows up the creek that usually is *dry*, living up to its name, in a northerly direction.
    If there is any appreciable amount of water in the creek, you might want to postpone this hike for another day when the creek is dry because the trail crosses the creekbed at least a dozen times.
    As you walk the trail gains altitude but this is a gradual climb and you are barely conscious of it. The walking is pretty easy and the trail is a good one.

At 0.63 miles you reach a point where the creek forks at a reef. The left hand channel is the **Bear Sign Trail** and the right fork is the Dry Creek Trail. There is a rusty sign in the left channel marked "Bear Sign #59." From this point the canyon deepens and you are treated to the sight of giant redrock buttes on both sides of the creek. As you proceed you will notice a change in the vegetation as the increase in altitude causes changes in the life zones.

The trail ends where it intersects a channel running east and west. We are informed that this channel can be hiked but it would be very steep and rugged, for advanced hikers only. To the east, it would go all the way to the top of the rim to East Pocket, where a Forest Service fire lookout tower is located.

To the west, the channel would connect with Bear Sign canyon. Maps indicate that you could do a loop, going up Dry Creek and coming back via Bear Sign, but we have not tried this.

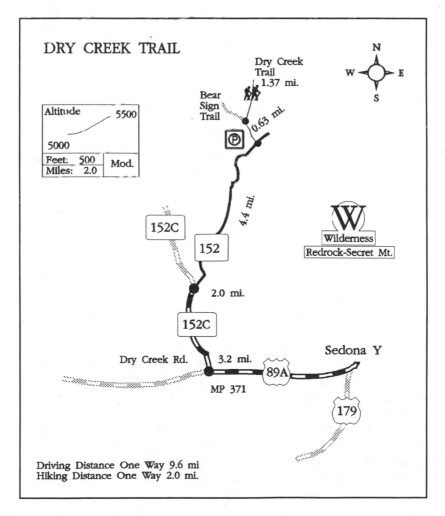

DRY CREEK TRAIL

Dry Creek Trail 1.37 mi.

Bear Sign Trail

0.63 mi.

N

W — E

S

Altitude 5500

5000

Feet: 500 Mod.
Miles: 2.0

152C

152

4.4 mi.

Wilderness
Redrock-Secret Mt.

2.0 mi.

152C

Dry Creek Rd. 3.2 mi. 89A Sedona Y

MP 371

179

Driving Distance One Way 9.6 mi
Hiking Distance One Way 2.0 mi.

EAGLES' NEST TRAIL

General Information
Location Map F3
Sedona USGS Map
Coconino Forest Service Map

Driving Distance One Way: 8.8 miles (Time 15 minutes)
Access Road: All vehicles, All paved
Hiking Distance One Way: 1.0 miles (Time 45 minutes)
How Strenuous: Moderate
Features: Oak Creek, Red Rock State Park, Views

NUTSHELL: This moderate trail is located in Red Rock State Park 8.8 miles southwest of Sedona. It takes you along the banks of a creek, then to the top of a redrock butte for exceptional views.

DIRECTIONS:
From the Sedona Y Go:
Southwest on Highway 89A (toward Cottonwood) for a distance of 5.5 miles (MP 368.6) to the Lower Red Rock Loop Road. Turn left on the Lower Red Rock Loop Road and follow it to the 8.5 miles point, where you will see the entry to Red Rock State Park. Turn right into the park. You will come to a toll booth where an admission is charged. From that point, drive to the Visitor Center and park there, at 8.8 miles.

TRAILHEAD: This is a marked and maintained trail, part of the network of seven trails planned for the park. Go through the Visitor Center. Though the center is not marked as the trailhead for this hike, it is the starting point for it.

DESCRIPTION: Enjoy the Visitor Center and then walk through it, turning right on the paved trail. At 0.08 miles you will come to the first trail junction. Here the **Smoke Trail** forks to the right, where Sentinel Crossing is located. Turn right here and go down to the creek. The Sentinel Crossing is a low wooden bridge that is hinged so that it swings downstream when the creek floods. When the water in the creek is running high, the bridge is not usable and you must go to the Kingfisher Crossing. You will see signs for it posted along the trail.

Once across the creek, you will hit the **Kisva Trail**. Turn right on Kisva and follow it to its end (about 0.5 miles from where you joined it). This portion of Kisva is lovely. The trail is bounded by the creek on your right and pretty redrock cliffs on your left. Large sycamores and other deciduous trees line the creek bank. The Armijo Ditch, an historic irrigation ditch, runs along the cliff base and its banks are covered with blackberries.

Where Kisva ends, the Eagles' Nest Trail goes off to your left, uphill. It takes you by twists and turns to the top of the red cliffs at the base of which you have been walking. At the top (1.0 miles from the Visitor Center) there is a viewpoint with a couple of benches. The views from this place are great. You see red buttes all around you forming a basin through which Oak Creek cuts a sinuous path.

The trail from the top drops down the other side of the butte, reaching ground level at the Kisva Trail where it joins the Kisva Trail by a trail toilet. You would then return to the Visitor Center the way you started, by going across the Kingfisher Crossing bridge.

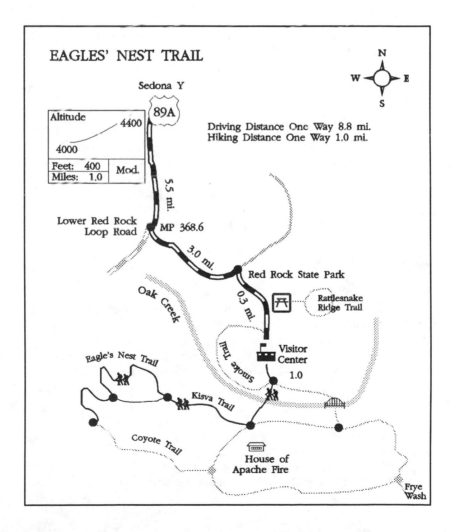

EAGLES' NEST TRAIL

N
W ← → E
S

Sedona Y

89A

Altitude
4400
4000

Feet: 400 Mod.
Miles: 1.0

Driving Distance One Way 8.8 mi.
Hiking Distance One Way 1.0 mi.

5.5 mi.

Lower Red Rock
Loop Road   MP 368.6

3.0 mi.

Oak Creek

0.3 mi.

Red Rock State Park

Rattlesnake
Ridge Trail

Smoke Trail

Visitor
Center

1.0

Eagle's Nest Trail

Kisva Trail

Coyote Trail

House of
Apache Fire

Frye
Wash

FAY CANYON

General Information
Location Map C3
Wilson Mt. USGS Map
Coconino Forest Service Map

Personal
Favorite

Driving Distance One Way: 8.2 miles (Time 20 minutes)
Access Road: All cars, Last half mile good dirt road
Hiking Distance One Way: 1.2 miles (Time 30 minutes)
How Strenuous: Moderate
Features: Views, Arch, Indian ruins

NUTSHELL: This is an easy hike 8.2 miles northwest of uptown Sedona, featuring a lovely canyon on the side of Bear Mountain with a natural arch and Indian ruins. **A personal favorite.**

DIRECTIONS:
From the Sedona Y Go:
Southwest on Highway 89A (toward Cottonwood) for a distance of 3.2 miles (MP 371) to Dry Creek Road. Turn right onto Dry Creek Road (also known as FR 152C) and follow it to the 6.1 mile point, where it intersects the Long Canyon Road, where you turn left. Stay on FR 152C to the 7.7 mile point, where it intersects the Boynton Canyon Road. Here you will turn left onto the Boynton Pass Road. It is paved for a short distance and then becomes unpaved. At the 8.2 mile point you will reach the driveway to the parking area, which is off to your right. Pull in and park there.

TRAILHEAD: You will see a rusty sign at the gate: "Fay Canyon #53."

DESCRIPTION: The trail is gentle and wide. You will find a forest of oaks, many of them quite sizable. Though the canyon is short, about one mile long, it is broad and very scenic. There are impressive red cliffs on both sides with buff colored cliffs rimming the back of the canyon.
At just over 0.50 miles, a side trail branches off to the right (east) and makes a sharp ascent up the east side of the canyon to Fay Arch. This trail is usually marked with cairns. The path to the arch is nothing like the main trail. It seems to have just been scratched out of the side of the canyon willy nilly. It is steep and there are places where the footing is tricky. Aunt Maude would have no trouble with the main trail along the canyon floor but the climb to the arch would be too much for her.
There is a small Indian ruin just before you reach the arch. This isn't much of a ruin, just knee high walls outlining one room in a low, shallow cave.

There are a few rock art figures on the cliff face above the ruin but we suspect that they are modern. Canyon wrens, tiny birds with a glorious call, live in this cliff face. If you are lucky you will hear one.

There is a narrow slot between the arch and the wall it has broken away from. You can stand underneath it and look up through it for an interesting view. The clamber up the side of the canyon would be worthwhile for the views even if there were no arch. Spectacular.

After visiting the arch, return to the main trail and continue up the canyon. Near its end it forks around a redrock fin that sticks out like the prow of a ship. You can quit right where you are for a 1.2 mile hike or you can climb up on the fin. You can go in either direction around the fin, but we recommend the left hand fork. It will take you up and out on a slickrock shelf where you will find a few caves that contain vestigial Indian ruins. The right hand fork takes you back a little deeper into the canyon but neither trail takes you all the way around the fin, for it is a peninsula, not an island.

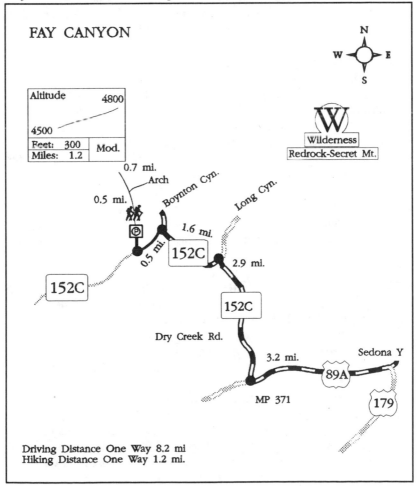

FAY CANYON

Altitude 4800
4500
Feet: 300   Mod.
Miles: 1.2

Wilderness
Redrock-Secret Mt.

0.7 mi.
Arch
0.5 mi.
Boynton Cyn.
Long Cyn.
1.6 mi.
0.5 mi.
152C
2.9 mi.
152C
152C
Dry Creek Rd.
3.2 mi.
Sedona Y
89A
MP 371
179

Driving Distance One Way 8.2 mi
Hiking Distance One Way 1.2 mi.

FRYE WASH TRAIL

General Information
Location Map F3
Sedona USGS Map
Coconino Forest Service Map

Driving Distance One Way: 8.8 miles (Time 15 minutes)
Access Road: All vehicles, All paved
Hiking Distance One Way: ?? miles (Time ??)
How Strenuous: ??
Features: Oak Creek, Red Rock State Park

NUTSHELL: This moderate trail is located in Red Rock State Park 8.8 miles southwest of Sedona. It takes you to undeveloped country behind the hill on which the exotically named House of Apache Fire is located.

DIRECTIONS:
From the Sedona Y Go:
         Southwest on Highway 89A (toward Cottonwood) for a distance of 5.5 miles (MP 368.6) to the Lower Red Rock Loop Road. Turn left on the Lower Red Rock Loop Road and follow it to the 8.5 miles point, where you will see the entry to Red Rock State Park. Turn right into the park. You will come to a toll booth where an admission is charged. From that point, drive to the Visitor Center and park there, at 8.8 miles.

TRAILHEAD: This is a marked and maintained trail, part of the network of seven trails planned for the park. Go through the Visitor Center. Though the center is not marked as the trailhead for this hike, it is the starting point for it.

DESCRIPTION: Enjoy the Visitor Center and then walk through it, turning right on the paved trail. At 0.08 miles you will come to the first trail junction. Here the **Smoke Trail** forks to the right, where Sentinel Crossing is located. Go straight here. The sign at this junction shows your destination as *"Kingfisher Crossing, House of Apache Fire."*
         At 0.24 miles you will reach another junction. Turn right here, to Kingfisher Crossing, which is a major bridge. You will see the House of Apache Fire on top of a knoll. It is a sort of modern pueblo style house built of native red rock.
         When you cross the bridge you will reach another trail junction, where the **Kisva** and **Eagles' Nest** trails go right. You will go left there and at 0.45 miles will be at the base of the knoll on which the house is located. You

will see a driveway going uphill to your right to get to the house. To your left is a short flight of redrock steps and a sign for the Apache Fire Trail and the **Frye Wash Trail**. This is the place where the Apache Fire Trail starts.

Walk up the steps and you will find yourself on a nice gentle trail heading south, away from the park and into undeveloped country. This part of the trail is a welcome getaway from the developed area. The trail makes a big loop. Toward the far end of the loop the Frye Wash Trail takes off.

When we hiked this trail in February 1992, it was incomplete. It ran back to a fence about 0.1 miles from its beginning. The trail is situated in beautiful country and when it is finished it should be a great trail. We don't see how it can miss and therefore we include it in this book even though we cannot fully describe it. By the time this book is printed and you are reading it, we hope that the trail is open. Check at the Visitor Center to see whether this trail is open before you try it.

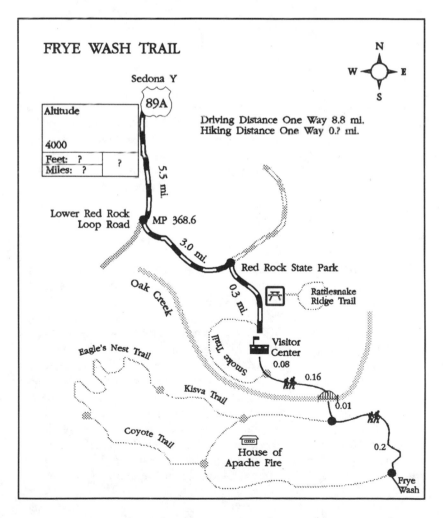

HS CANYON

General Information
Location Map C4
Loy Butte and Wilson Mt. USGS Maps
Coconino Forest Service Map

Personal Favorite

Driving Distance One Way: 8.6 miles (Time 30 minutes)
Access Road: High clearance vehicles, last 3.4 miles rough dirt
Hiking Distance One Way: 2.0 miles (Time 70 minutes)
How Strenuous: Moderate
Features: Views, Remote side canyon

NUTSHELL: This beautiful canyon, 8.6 miles northwest of uptown Sedona, provides a delightful hike but the access road is very rough. Leave the Cadillac at home and borrow a pickup. **A personal favorite.**

DIRECTIONS:
From the Sedona Y Go:
Southwest on Highway 89A (toward Cottonwood) for 3.2 miles (MP 371) to the Dry Creek Road. Turn right on Dry Creek Road and follow it to the 5.2 mile point, where FR 152 (the Vultee Arch Road) branches off to the right. Turn right and follow FR 152 to the 8.6 mile point. There you will find a short half hidden road to your left. A rusty sign at the roadside says, "Secret Canyon #121." Pull in on this road and park.

TRAILHEAD: Hike the Secret Canyon Trail, which starts at the parking area, for 0.6 miles to reach the HS Canyon trailhead.

DESCRIPTION: Look carefully for the side road that leads to the trailhead parking. There is a screen of trees and shrubs along the road in this area and the opening is just a gap in the screen. It is easy to drive right by it without noticing it.
The access road, FR 152, road is often very rough. The problem is not so much deep ruts that can cause high centering, as you may often encounter on heavily travelled dirt roads. The hazards here are exposed rocks and ledges over which you must drive. A high clearance vehicle is definitely the vehicle of choice on this road. We have made it several times in our Toyota Tercel but we cringe every time and have to crawl over some of the rough places.
Once you get to the trailhead, you follow the **Secret Canyon Trail**. It goes immediately over to Dry Creek and then proceeds along the Dry Creek drainage. If water is running in Dry Creek you may not be able to make this hike because the trail winds across the creekbed several times.

At 0.6 miles you will see a trail going off to the left marked with a rusty sign reading, "H S Canyon #50." Take this trail. H S Canyon is narrow. It goes mostly to the west toward the north face of Maroon Mountain. You can see a huge fin of Maroon Mountain in the distance. H S Canyon is a pretty little canyon and not very well known. We have never encountered any other hikers on this trail, but usually find them on the better known Secret Canyon Trail.

An easy walk, the trail is mostly shaded by a pleasant forest. It climbs but the climb is so gradual that it is not exhausting. There are great views. The canyon walls here are lower than those flanking some of the other hikes in this book. As a result they seem to be on a more human scale. Consequently the canyon has a nice friendly feeling.

The trail takes you to the base of Maroon Mountain where it ends in a box canyon surrounded by thousand foot high white cliffs. A truly impressive place. The end of the trail gives a false appearance of climbing out of the canyon but that is an illusion, for it plays out against the mountain.

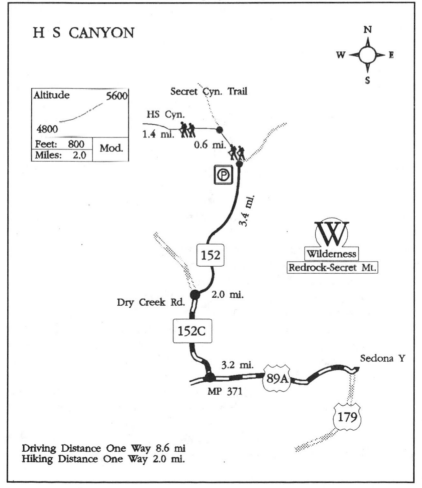

HARDING SPRING TRAIL

General Information
Location Map B5
Mountainaire and Munds Park USGS Maps
Coconino Forest Service Map

Driving Distance One Way: 11.4 miles (Time 20 minutes)
Access Road: All cars, All paved
Hiking Distance One Way: 0.80 miles (Time 45 minutes)
How Strenuous: Hard
Features: Views

NUTSHELL: This is a marked and posted trail located just across Highway 89A from the Cave Spring Campground 11.4 miles north of Sedona. It climbs the east wall of Oak Creek Canyon.

DIRECTIONS:
From the Sedona Y Go:
　　　　North on Highway 89A (toward Flagstaff) for a distance of 11.4 miles (MP 385.6) to the entrance to the Cave Spring Campground, which is on your left (west). Park anywhere around here on the shoulder of the road.

TRAILHEAD: On the east side of Highway 89A just across from the Cave Spring Campground entrance. It is marked by a rusty sign reading, "Harding Spring Trail #51."

DESCRIPTION: There is no official parking area for this hike. Cars park all along the shoulders of the road wherever there is a wide spot. If you are lucky you might find a parking spot in the Cave Spring Campground but don't count on it. Camping in the campground requires the payment of a fee.
　　　　Since you will be so near the Cave Spring Campground after you park, you might as well walk into the campground and take a look at Cave Spring. It is an interesting place.
　　　　Like the other trails going up the east wall of upper Oak Creek Canyon the Harding Spring trail goes virtually straight up with little finesse. You start in a pine and spruce forest and then get into a more open area as you climb above tree line. Then you get into a region of pine forest again at the top.
　　　　The trail zigzags in such a way that it isn't a killer, like the **Purtymun Trail** or **Thompson's Ladder**. It is more like the **Cookstove Trail** or the **Thomas Point Trail**.
　　　　The trail was built in the late 1800s to provide access to the canyon rim so that families living down in the canyon could get to the top and go to

Flagstaff. They could lead a horse on such a trail or walk it but it was not a wagon road, as you will see when you hike it. They would leave a wagon chained to a tree at the top and hitch the horse to it for the trip to town and return. When they brought their goods back, they would park the wagon and pack the goods down by horseback. Such a trip often took several days and was considered to be a major undertaking. Most of the east rim hikes are like that.

These east rim trails all predate the present Highway 89A, which is much newer than you might think. It was completed in the 1930s. Before that the only road good enough for a wagon was the Schnebly Hill Road and using it meant a long trip from the upper canyon south to Sedona then doubling back to the north to go to Flagstaff.

Once you have reached the top you can walk along the rim in either direction looking for views. We especially enjoy the view down into the Cave Spring Campground.

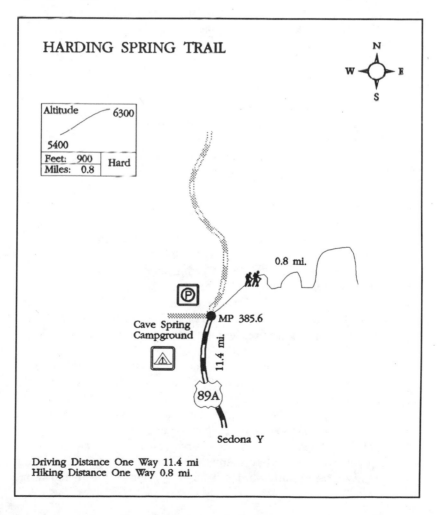

HERMIT RIDGE

General Information
Location Map D5
Munds Mt. and Munds Park USGS Map
Coconino Forest Service Map

Driving Distance One Way: 2.6 miles (Time 10 minutes)
Access Road: All cars, All paved
Hiking Distance One Way: 1.4 miles (Time 1.5 hours)
How Strenuous: Moderate
Features: Views

NUTSHELL: This hike is located 2.6 north of Sedona. There is no marked trail, but for those who enjoy bushwhacking and steep climbs, it is very rewarding.

DIRECTIONS:
From the Sedona Y Go:
North on Highway 89A (toward Flagstaff) a distance of 2.6 miles (MP 376.8) where you park at the mouth of a closed road.

TRAILHEAD: Walk down the closed road a few feet beyond a pole gate to a place where you will see a sign, "Casner Canyon #11."

DESCRIPTION: Follow the **Casner Canyon Trail** down to Oak Creek. When you get to the floor of the gorge, you will find it strewn with boulders. You will see a canyon on the other side. Head for it. When you get to the creek, you will have to wade or rock hop over it, depending on the depth of the water.

Once across, hike into Casner Canyon, its entrance marked by a high jutting ledge. Keep jumping boulders to get to the right hand (south) side, where you will soon pick up the Casner Canyon Trail. At 0.33 miles, the trail goes up a knob and then starts down at the base of an undercut cliff. At the top of this knob you will see a faint trail going steeply uphill by a barbed wire fence. Take it.

You will come out onto a shoulder of Hermit Ridge near a power line. The highest point of the ridge is just above your head here. You can make reaching the top easier by walking southwest along the shoulder for about 0.1 mile, then going up. There are no marked paths, but there are game trails. Look for a likely spot to make the short, steep climb to the top.

Hermit Ridge is quite narrow, covered with manzanita and other scrub through which there are many open lanes made by cattle. Your destination is to the south, toward Sedona, where you will see the towering cliffs of Mitten Ridge. Bushwhack, following open alleys through the growth.

We picked up a deer trail that follows along the west side of the ridge, overlooking the creek and the highway. Great views from here. On the east side of the ridge you have equally fine views. Near the 1.0 mile point you will be directly opposite the popular Grasshopper Point Picnic Ground. The creek makes a pretty picture here.

As you get closer to the buttes you will climb again and then reach an area where wide eroding ledges on the face of Mitten Ridge are almost like roadways. As you get closer to the cliffs, these turn into slickrock ledges. You have your choice of going up or down. We recommend going to a lower ledge. The obvious wide ledge for walking ends at 1.4 miles, at a lovely viewpoint. For the adventurous who are unafraid of high narrow ledges, follow an upper ledge lined by trees. It curves around into an impressive amphitheater before dwindling down into impossible-to-walk narrowness.

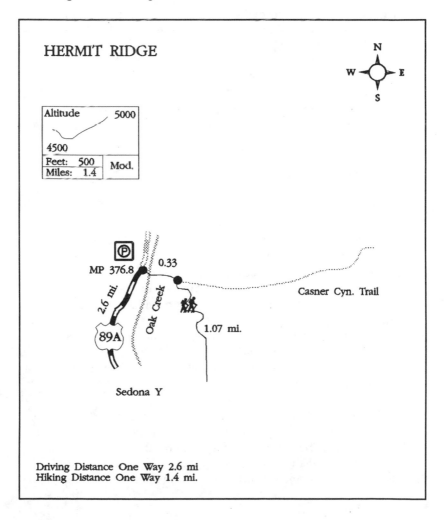

HERMIT RIDGE

Altitude   5000
4500
Feet: 500   Mod.
Miles: 1.4

MP 376.8   0.33

2.6 mi.

Oak Creek

89A

Casner Cyn. Trail

1.07 mi.

Sedona Y

Driving Distance One Way 2.6 mi
Hiking Distance One Way 1.4 mi.

HOT LOOP TRAIL

General Information
Location Map G5
Munds Mt. USGS Map
Coconino Forest Service Map

Driving Distance One Way: 8.7 Miles (Time 15 Minutes)
Access Road: All cars, Paved except last 0.10 miles
Hiking Distance One Way: 4.0 Miles (Time 75 Minutes)
How Strenuous: Hard
Features: Views

NUTSHELL: Located south of the Sedona Y 8.7 miles, this trail follows the Woods Canyon Trail and then branches off to the top of Wild Horse Mesa where you will have exciting views.

DIRECTIONS:
From the Y in Sedona, Go:
　　　South on Highway 179 (toward Phoenix) for 8.6 miles (MP 304.8) to an unmarked dirt road to your left. Turn left on the road, follow it for 0.10 miles and then park.

TRAILHEAD: Right at the highway you will see a gate and a rusty sign reading, "Woods Canyon #93."

DESCRIPTION: The gate is unlocked. Go through it. We recommend that you park just beyond the gate. You can drive farther but the road conditions are dicey, especially if the road is wet. We have driven in as far as a mile but do not recommend this unless you are sure your vehicle can handle it. If you park near the highway as we recommend this is a four mile hike each way.
　　　To follow the trail just walk along the main jeep road. At 2.0 miles from the highway you will come to a fence. Just beyond the fence you will find a rusty sign marked, "#93 Hot Loop." This is the place where the Hot Loop Trail branches off to the left, going uphill. It looks like a road. The **Woods Canyon Trail** path forks to the right here and turns into a footpath descending to the bottom of the canyon.
　　　From this place the Hot Loop Trail is a hard steep climb up the road. When you reach a point 3.0 miles from the highway the jeep road disappears and the road turns into a footpath over loose lava stones. It is hard to see the trail in these stones Be sure to look for the cairns that mark the trail.
　　　When you finally struggle to the top of Wild Horse Mesa at 3.7 miles from the highway, the trail gets better again with more soil and fewer rocks.

At a point 4.0 miles from the highway it will be obvious to you where the rim of the mesa is to your left. Walk over to it and see the view. It is a great vantage point from which to see Pine Valley, Jacks Canyon and Lee Mountain.

There is very little shade on this hike and the trail is rocky almost everywhere. It is not very scenic until you reach the top. This trail was built as a livestock trail not a scenic one.

When the first homesteaders came into the Sedona area after 1876 when the Apaches had been subdued by the federal troops located at Camp Verde, they found many wild horses in the grasslands. Some of the men made a pretty good living trapping these horses and selling them. Wild Horse Mesa was the location for a sizable horse herd and that is how it got its name. You will also hear it called Horse Mesa.

We hiked this trail last in February 1989. We understand that there are plans to extend the trail all the way to Jacks Point (which would be several miles) but cannot confirm this.

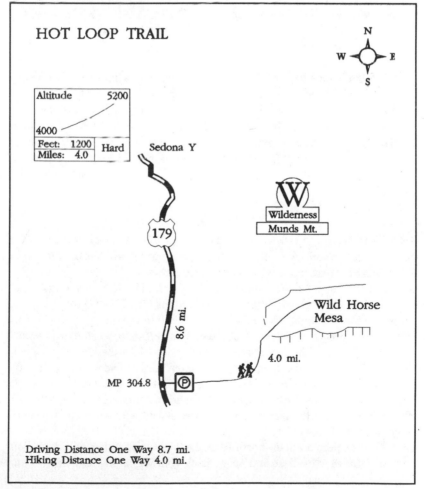

HOT LOOP TRAIL

Driving Distance One Way 8.7 mi.
Hiking Distance One Way 4.0 mi.

HOUSE MOUNTAIN

General Information
Location Map G3
Sedona and Lake Montezuma USGS Maps
Coconino Forest Service Map

Driving Distance One Way: 14.5 miles (Time 40 minutes)
Access Road: High clearance vehicles, last 3.9 miles dirt
Hiking Distance One Way: 2.25 miles (Time 70 minutes)
How Strenuous: Easy
Features: Views

NUTSHELL: This sprawling mountain located 14.5 miles south of Sedona is rather drab but is a platform for great views.

DIRECTIONS:
From the Sedona Y Go:
        South on Highway 179 (toward Phoenix) for a distance of 10.6 miles (MP 303) to unpaved road FR 120. Turn right on FR 120 and follow it to the 12.4 miles point, where FR 9120A intersects it. Turn right onto FR 9120A. The road up to this point has been good, but from here to the end it is rough, with deep ruts, rocks and other hazards. At the 14.5 mile point you will be on top of House Mountain. The road here becomes too rough to drive farther. Pull off the road and park in this area.

TRAILHEAD: No trail markings. Walk the road, FR 9120A.

DESCRIPTION: House Mountain is a shield volcano so it is more rounded than conical on top. A shield volcano doesn't erupt with a big upthrusting bang. It sort of rises like a pimple and then oozes lava. As a result it can create a sprawling low mountain, which is exactly what House Mountain is.
        The driving instructions take you to the top of House Mountain and along the top to a point where the road gets extremely rough. Using a truck with high clearance or a bike you could go two miles more on the road, almost to the north face of the mountain, the face that looks at Sedona.
        The top of the mountain is uninteresting. There has been some livestock activity here and some woodcutting. It was for these purposes that the road was built. As you walk along the road you are not close enough to the rim of the mountain to get any views. You must walk across the top to the north edge to get to a viewpoint.
        Once you are at the north edge, the location of the rim will be obvious to you. Just leave the road and bushwhack your way along to the rim. Once

there you will have tremendous views. You will find some places where lava has formed bare columns where no trees grow. These spots are excellent viewpoints.

There is another hike in the book that goes to the top of House Mountain. This is The **Turkey Creek Trail** that climbs the northwest face, with access from the Verde Valley School Road. Though the Turkey Creek Trail is a steep climb, it is much more scenic and enjoyable than the hike described in this article.

The top of House Mountain shows signs of considerable ranching activity. When we first began to hike around Sedona, we were surprised to find signs of cattle grazing (and sometimes the cattle themselves) on mountain tops, including some that must be hard for cattle to climb, such as **Doe Mountain**. House Mountain would be fairly easy to climb from the south approach used on this hike. So, if you hear a large animal crashing through the brush, it is much more likely to be a Guernsey than a Grizzly.

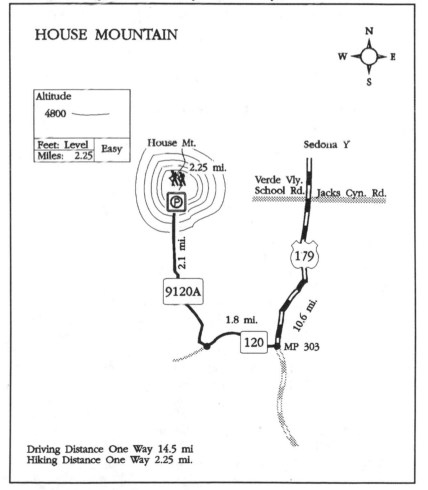

JACKS CANYON TRAIL

General Information
Location Map F5
Munds Mountain and Sedona USGS Maps
Coconino Forest Service Map

Driving Distance One Way: 9.6 miles (Time 15 minutes)
Access Road: All cars, Last 2.0 miles good dirt road
Hiking Distance One Way: 4.5 miles (Time 2.5 hours)
How Strenuous: Moderate
Features: Old cattle trail, Views

NUTSHELL: Located 9.6 miles south of the Sedona Y, this old cattle trail starts in an inhabited area. It then proceeds into some remote back country.

DIRECTIONS:
From the Sedona Y Go:
    South on Highway 179 (toward Phoenix) for a distance of 7.0 miles (MP 306.2) to Jacks Canyon Road. Turn left onto Jacks Canyon Road and follow it to the 7.9 mile point, where there is a stop sign. Turn right at the stop sign and follow the unmarked dirt road to the 9.6 miles point, where there is a cattle guard at the entrance to the Pine Valley subdivision. Park just on the other side of the cattle guard.

TRAILHEAD: Walk along the jeep road to the right of the house that sits by the cattle guard. You will see a rusty sign reading, "Jacks Canyon #55."

DESCRIPTION: You start this hike by following a road. The first mile of the hike is not very attractive because you are always in sight of the houses in a subdivision. For a time you will feel as if you are walking through people's backyards.
    Jacks Canyon runs between the substantial Lee Mountain on your left and the lower Wild Horse Mesa (also known as Horse Mesa) on your right and curves around Lee Mountain going to the north. Eventually it climbs up to the top of the Mogollon Rim at Jacks Point. The rim in that location is quite flat and open and makes a good grazing area for cattle. The purpose of this trail was to provide a means of taking cattle herds up to the top of the rim in the summer and bringing the critters back to the low country in the winter.
    The trail follows an eastward course for about 2.0 miles to Jacks Tank. Just beyond the tank the jeep road ends and your route turns into a foot path that branches off to the right, down into the canyon floor. The canyon curves at the tank and begins a northerly course from there. (The jeep road continues

about 0.50 miles from Jacks Tank parallel to the canyon but up on the shoulder of the hill. It terminates at a pasture. Not worth hiking).

The hiking trail is more interesting from Jacks Tank onward, especially if there is some water running in the canyon. You don't want a lot of water, just a bit, since you will be walking across the canyon bottom.

Over many centuries the intermittent flow of water has worn the soil in the channel down to redrock and in many places the water has carved interesting sculptures in the soft stone. The canyon is narrow and scenic.

We recommend stopping at the 4.5 mile point, which is where the trail leaves the canyon bottom and begins its steep ascent to the rim, which requires you to climb over 1200 feet in 2.0 miles. The trail tops out on Munds Ridge, near the **Munds Mt. North** and **South** Trailhead. From there you can turn right and walk on to Jacks Point, stopping at Committee Tank, a total of 7.0 miles from where you park.

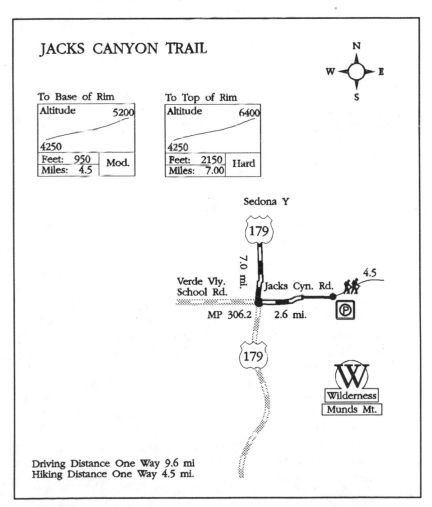

KISVA TRAIL

General Information
Location Map F3
Sedona USGS Map
Coconino Forest Service Map

Driving Distance One Way: 8.8 miles (Time 15 minutes)
Access Road: All vehicles, All paved
Hiking Distance One Way: 1.3 miles (Time 30 minutes)
How Strenuous: Easy
Features: Oak Creek, Red Rock State Park, Views

NUTSHELL: This easy trail is located in Red Rock State Park 8.8 miles southwest of Sedona. It takes you along the banks of Oak Creek on a level path.

DIRECTIONS:
From the Sedona Y Go:
Southwest on Highway 89A (toward Cottonwood) for a distance of 5.5 miles (MP 368.6) to the Lower Red Rock Loop Road. Turn left on the Lower Red Rock Loop Road and follow it to the 8.5 miles point, where you will see the entry to Red Rock State Park. Turn right into the park. You will come to a toll booth where an admission is charged. From that point, drive to the Visitor Center and park there, at 8.8 miles.

TRAILHEAD: This is a marked and maintained trail, part of the network of seven trails planned for the park. Go through the Visitor Center. Though the center is not marked as the trailhead for this hike, it is the starting point for it.

DESCRIPTION: Enjoy the Visitor Center and then walk through it, turning right on the paved trail. At 0.08 miles you will come to the first trail junction. Here the **Smoke Trail** forks to the right, where Sentinel Crossing is located. Keep going on the paved path to the Kingfisher Crossing, which you will reach at 0.24 miles. Go across the creek on the bridge, where you will emerge onto a sandy trail. Go straight for about ten yards, where you will find the trail junction for the **Apache Fire Trail** and the **Eagles' Nest Trail**.
Turn right. Soon you will see a sign marking the Kisva Trail. The trail follows an old ranch road that is still in use by officials of the Red Rock State Park, so it is wide and easy to walk. Kisva, the sign tells you, means "Shady Water" in Hopi. It is an appropriate name, as many trees grow along the creekbank and provide shade for the trail. The shade and the cool creek water make this a good hot weather trail.

Near the one mile point you come to a place where the trail goes along the base of a redrock ridge. There is an irrigation ditch to your left, at the cliff base, with the creek running along to your right. This abundance of water supports the growth of large sycamores, stunning with their beautiful white bark. They overarch the trail. There are many blackberries along the ditch bank. It is a gorgeous spot.

The trail ends at a point that is 1.3 miles from the Visitors Center. The road continues, but it is for use by park officials only. The Eagles' Nest Trail starts here, going uphill to your left.

This is a very pleasant and easy ramble that would be appreciated by people who are not strong enough to take a more strenuous hike yet want to experience a walk that will display the main attractions of Sedona: redrocks and Oak Creek.

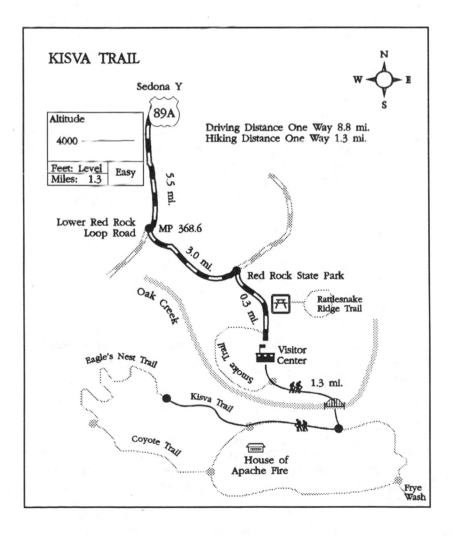

KUSHMAN'S CONE

General Information
Location Map E2
Page Springs, Sedona USGS Maps
Coconino Forest Service Map

Driving Distance One Way: 10.4 miles (Time 35 minutes)
Access Road: High clearance vehicle for last 0.5 miles
Hiking Distance One Way: 0.55 miles (Time 40 minutes)
How Strenuous: Moderate
Features: Views

NUTSHELL: This volcanic cone located 10.4 miles southwest of Sedona is a fairly hard climb but rewards the hiker with marvelous views.

DIRECTIONS:
From the Sedona Y Go:
Southwest on Highway 89A (toward Cottonwood) for a distance of 8.2 miles (MP 365.9) to a place where you will see a dirt road, FR 9573C, going off to your right through a gate in a barbed wire fence. Go through the gate and follow FR 9573C. At 8.3 miles, an unmarked road forks right. Ignore it. At 8.7 miles FR 9573 branches to the left. Ignore it. At 8.9 miles there is a fork. Take the right turn and begin to circle around the mountain headed north. At 9.3 miles you will be on the north side and you will see a big power line. FR 9573P branches to the left here. Go right, staying on FR 9573C. At 9.8 you reach a junction where FR 9573A goes to the left. Take FR 9573A. You will be at the power line. At 10.0 miles you will see FR 9544 going right. Take it. It follows the power line. Go down to the bottom of a long hill and park at 10.4 miles, where the road meets a wash. Don't try to cross the wash, as the road beyond is very bad and you will only gain 0.1 miles, as the road totally ends at 10.5 miles.

TRAILHEAD: There are no signs. You will see a faint jeep trail going into the wash and up the other side. This must have been a service road for the construction of the power line.

DESCRIPTION: Walk across the wash, and take the jeep road going up to the power line, then follow it to the Northeast. Soon after, the road disappears, but you can see a path along the power line. By now you are on the shoulder of the mountain. Kushman's Cone is a small extinct volcano, and broken lava is everywhere. The footing is very rocky and the going is quite slow. You will reach a point where it seems that there really is no trail, but you can see paths through the shrubbery all over the place. Don't worry, just keep picking your way along, following the power line until it starts to dip down, at which point you want to begin working uphill as you curve around to the east. At about 0.33 miles you will come to a worn path marked by cairns and you want to take this path to the top.

Many mountain tops are elusive. You think you have come to the mountain's crest only to find that it is merely a bench. That is not the case on Kushman's Cone, where you will find a definite pinpoint top. From the top you can enjoy thrilling views to the west. To the Northeast you can see parts of Sedona. Immediately below you to the east is a subdivision—not so thrilling—but the views beyond it are great.

On your way back down, don't follow the marked trail all the way, as it veers off to a subdivision. You will need to leave the trail and get back to the power line, using the line as your marker for the return to your car.

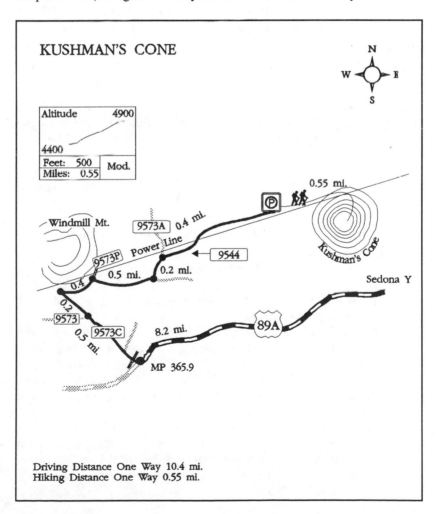

KUSHMAN'S CONE

N
W ← → E
S

Altitude   4900

4400
Feet: 500   Mod.
Miles: 0.55

0.55 mi.

Windmill Mt.

9573A   0.4 mi.

9573P   Power Line

9544

0.5 mi.   0.2 mi.

0.4

Kushman's Cone

Sedona Y

0.2

9573

9573C   8.2 mi.   89A

0.5 mi.

MP 365.9

Driving Distance One Way 10.4 mi.
Hiking Distance One Way 0.55 mi.

LITTLE HORSE TRAIL

General Information
Location Map E5
Munds Mt. and Sedona USGS Maps
Coconino Forest Service Map

Driving Distance One Way: 3.6 miles (Time 15 minutes)
Access Road: All cars, All paved
Hiking Distance One Way: 1.0 miles (Time 40 minutes)
How Strenuous: Easy
Features: Views

NUTSHELL: This easy trail starts at the famous Chapel of the Holy Cross south of Sedona 3.6 miles. It winds around Twin Buttes to the bottom of Chicken Point.

DIRECTIONS:
From the Sedona Y Go:
    South on Highway 179 (toward Phoenix) for a distance of 2.9 miles (MP 310.6) to Chapel Road. Turn left onto Chapel Road and follow it to the 3.6 mile point, where you find the lower parking lot for the Chapel of the Holy Cross. Park there.

TRAILHEAD: You will see no trail signs. Look for a footpath on the right side of the road.

DESCRIPTION: The trailhead is hard to see. As you come up to the Chapel of the Holy Cross you will drive around a big left curve. Just as the curve straightens and you begin a right curve the trail meets the driveway on your right. There is a wide paved apron at this place. The bank on the right hand side of the driveway tapers down to the road level at that spot. With all these clues you should find the trail easily.

    If you have not seen the Chapel of the Holy Cross by all means take a little time and see it while you are so close to it. Building it was an inspiration and the idea was carried out brilliantly. Even if you don't like churches you will be moved by this magnificent creation. Then, unlike the masses who gawk for fifteen minutes and pile back onto their tour busses, you can take a refreshing hike.

    You will see some cairns where the trail starts. The trail follows a drainage at the beginning and is somewhat hard to see. Once you get a little way beyond the beginning the trail becomes more defined and easy to follow.

    For the first half mile you are in sight of the Chapel and of homes in a subdivision. You walk along behind these homes. The trail follows south along the base of Twin Buttes. After this you drop out of sight of habitation and get a nice remote feeling. We love walking along the base of Twin Buttes here. We find them very interesting and beautiful. From the base of Twin Buttes you could not imagine that it is possible to get to the top, but you can do it on the **Twin Buttes Trail.**

At about 1.0 miles you have curved around the end of Twin Buttes going easterly. You will come to a gate. Go through the gate. Just beyond the gate you will be at the foot of **Chicken Point**, which will be to your left. Chicken Point is a slickrock saddle between red buttes. The jeep tours drive there frequently so don't be surprised if you see people on top, towering above you. This is the end of the hike.

Actually you can get to the top of Chicken Point from trail's end. Look for a path along the right side of the canyon.

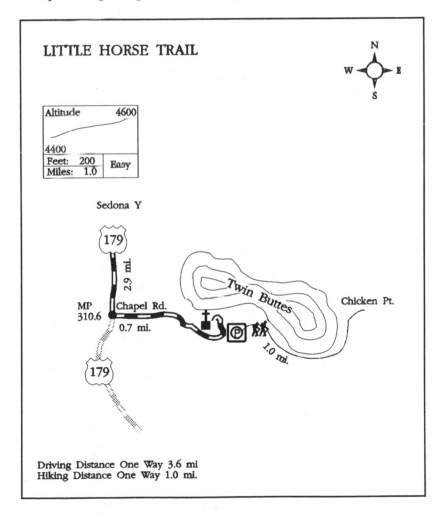

LITTLE HORSE TRAIL

Altitude	4600
Feet: 200	Easy
Miles: 1.0	

Sedona Y

179

2.9 mi.

MP 310.6 | Chapel Rd.

0.7 mi.

Twin Buttes

Chicken Pt.

1.0 mi.

179

Driving Distance One Way 3.6 mi
Hiking Distance One Way 1.0 mi.

LITTLE PARK HEIGHTS

General Information
Location Map F4
Sedona USGS Map
Coconino Forest Service Map

Driving Distance One Way: 5.6 miles (Time 15 minutes)
Access Road: All cars, All paved
Hiking Distance One Way: 1.0 miles (Time 40 minutes)
How Strenuous: Hard
Features: Views

NUTSHELL: Located across the highway from Bell Rock, just south of Sedona, this tall butte rewards your steep climb with great views.

DIRECTIONS:
From the Sedona Y Go:
        South on Highway 179 (toward Phoenix) for a distance of 5.6 miles (MP 308) to Bell Rock Vista. There is a parking place for several cars at the vista. Pull in and park.

TRAILHEAD: There are no signs. A trail marked with cairns starts just south of the outhouse at Bell Rock Vista.

DESCRIPTION: On the south end of the parking area at Bell Rock Vista there is a public toilet. This is set back from the highway. Just south of this you will find two trails leading away from the highway. Take the trail that is farthest south. It dips down at its start. Look carefully for cairns as you start this hike. Many false trails meander through this area as a result of cattle grazing so it is important to use the cairns for guides.
        You will climb constantly on this hike. The climb is gradual for the first quarter of a mile and then steep.
        Your destination will be obvious from the beginning. It is the saddle in the high butte located west of Bell Rock Vista. **Bell Rock** merits its fame, as it is an interesting place. It is listed in this book and makes for a fine hike. Its neighbor across the highway, the subject of this hike, is not well known but deserves to be. When you begin the hike it will seem as if it is an impossible task, that, "You can't get there from here." Then you will see how the trail makes use of the terrain and will realize that it is not only possible but that you are going to do it.
        As you climb up to the saddle you will reach two major benches before you come to the top. Each of these benches becomes a natural resting place and

a good observation point. From the benches you can see Bell Rock, Courthouse Butte and the colorful country between them and the Chapel of the Holy Cross.

Above the second bench you will have a hard steep haul and then you will reach the saddle. The saddle is at 1.0 miles. From there you can go to knobs on either the north or south ends of the butte. There is also an extension to the West where the main trail leads you onto a bare finger of rock from which you get excellent views. Depending on how much you roam around on the top, you can easily add another mile to this hike.

Once you are on top you can see to the West. There you will have views down on the Verde Valley School and the Red Rock Loop Road areas.

Some hikers report finding fossils on top of this butte. We were there on a windswept January day when it was so cold that we did not take time to look for fossils but the rock certainly did appear to be a fossil bearing stratum.

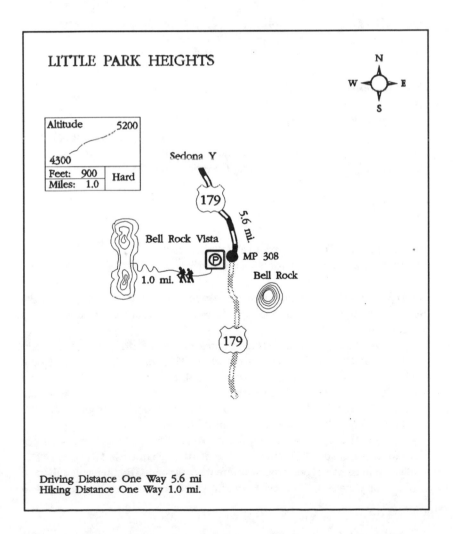

LITTLE PARK HEIGHTS

Driving Distance One Way 5.6 mi
Hiking Distance One Way 1.0 mi.

LONG CANYON

General Information
Location Map C3
Wilson Mt. USGS Map
Coconino Forest Service Map

Driving Distance One Way: 6.7 miles (Time 15 minutes)
Access Road: All cars, All paved
Hiking Distance One Way: 3.0 miles (Time 2 hours)
How Strenuous: Moderate
Features: Views, Great cliffs

NUTSHELL: Located 6.7 miles northwest of uptown Sedona, this trail takes you right up against the base of gorgeous red cliffs. This is one of the best trails for viewing rock formations. **A personal favorite.**

DIRECTIONS:
From the Sedona Y Go:
Southwest on Highway 89A (toward Cottonwood) for a distance of 3.2 miles (MP 371) to the Dry Creek Road, FR 152C. Turn right onto Dry Creek Road and follow it to the 6.1 mile point, where there is a stop sign. The paved road to your right is the Long Canyon Road. Take it to the 6.7 miles point, where you will see an unpaved road to your left. The entrance to the road is blocked with boulders. There is a parking area in front of the boulders. Park there.

TRAILHEAD: This is a marked and maintained trail. There is a rusty sign where you park reading, "Long Canyon #122."

DESCRIPTION: The trail begins as a wide jeep road. In fact, the Forest Service has moved several boulders across the road at its entrance to keep vehicles from using it.
At 0.30 miles you will come to a 3-pronged fork. Take the left fork. At 0.60 miles you will come to a big gate. This marks the entrance to the Redrock-Secret Mt. Wilderness Area. Go through the gate. The trail is a footpath from this point. At 1.0 miles you will reach another fork. Here one trail goes left parallel to a power line and the other trail goes right. Take the right fork. The left fork goes to Boynton Canyon.
For the first 1.5 miles on this trail you will be walking in open country with almost no shade. This part of the trail isn't much fun in hot weather. After that you will enter a cypress forest where there is shade. By then you will have moved fairly close to Maroon Mountain which is to your right (north). You

Earth Angel Spire from Brins Mesa

Front Cover: *View from The Shooting Range West Trail*

Reflection of Mitten Ridge

Soldier Pass Arches

Bear Mountain from Doe Mountain

Bear Mountain

Steamboat Rock and Spires

Sinagua Cliff Dwelling

Red Canyon

Silhouette of Kushman's Cone

Sinagua Petroglyphs

Sunset on Schnebly Hill

will catch glimpses through the trees of the magnificent red and white sculptured cliffs of Maroon Mountain as you hike.

Beyond the 2.5 mile point the vegetation becomes more alpine and less desert-like. Here you will encounter many oaks and huge alligator bark junipers. Some of the junipers are many centuries old.

At 3.0 miles the trail, which has been generally following a northwest course parallel to the base of the mountain, turns and goes straight north, climbing steeply. This is the stopping point for this hike. Here you will find genuine alpine conditions with pines and firs and a carpet of green on the forest floor. The canyon walls are nearer to you now and you get tremendous views.

The trail continues but becomes difficult. It plays out completely at 4.0 miles in a side canyon, in a place that is one of the wildest in the Sedona area. It really feels remote. The path narrows there to a barely discernible game trail where you are totally out of sight of the works of man. It is a perfect location for wild animals such as bear and mountain lions.

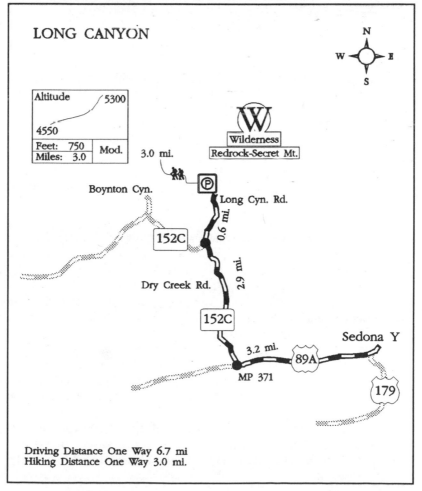

LOST CANYON

General Information
Location Map C4
Wilson Mt. USGS Map
Coconino Forest Service Map

Driving Distance One Way: 7.7 miles (Time 25 minutes)
Access Road: High clearance car best, Last 2.5 miles unpaved
Hiking Distance One Way: 2.2 miles (Time 80 minutes)
How Strenuous: Moderate, one short stretch is strenuous
Features: Scenic canyon, Indian ruins, Cave

NUTSHELL: This little known destination is reached by a trail that branches off the **Brins Mesa West Trail** on the road to Vultee Arch a few miles northwest of Sedona. **A personal favorite.**

DIRECTIONS:
From The Y in Sedona Go:
     Southwest on Highway 89A (toward Cottonwood) a distance of 3.2 miles (MP 371) to the Dry Creek Road. Turn right on Dry Creek Road, also known as FR 152C, and follow it to the 5.2 mile point where FR 152 branches to the right. Take FR 152. Follow the road to the 7.7 miles point, where you will see a sideroad to the right. Turn right and park in the cleared area.

TRAILHEAD: At the parking area you will see a rusty sign saying, "Brins Mesa #119."

DESCRIPTION: Start this hike by taking the **Brins Mesa West** trail. From the rusty sign walk up the trail 210 feet. At this point you will see a minor trail going off to the right marked by a cairn. Take it.
     You must watch for cairns to guide you. You will cross one wash and go across country to an arroyo that cuts across a redrock ledge. Here you turn left and hike up the arroyo for a short distance to a point where the trail branches off to the right. The trail is very steep here.
     At 0.40 miles you will come to the top of a ledge where you will have spectacular views. Beyond that you have another short climb to the top of a higher ledge. The trail follows the rim of this higher ledge. Before you is a giant red reef marking the toe of Lost Canyon. The trail takes you around the toe and into the canyon.
     When you get into Lost Canyon you will find that the canyon walls are tall and sheer. At times the trail comes very close to the edge of the rim. It you aren't bothered by heights this is one of the finest canyon hikes. The

ledge you walk on is made of harder stone than the layers of rock above it. The upper layers have weathered and receded leaving the ledge rather like a balcony all around the canyon. Above you are beautiful red cliffs topped with cream stone. Below are sheer drops.

At 0.75 miles you will see above you to your left a long narrow cave about half way up the cliff wall. There is a ruin in the cave. Cairns mark the place where you turn off the trail to go up to the ruin. It is a scramble.

From the ruin come back down to the ledge and continue on the trail to the head of the canyon. Look down into the bottom and you will see another ruin. You can reach the lower ruin by taking the **Lost Canyon Ruin** hike.

If you want a one mile hike the head of the canyon is a good place to stop. However, the trail goes on. It follows back out to the canyon mouth and then curves around another toe and goes into the canyon where the natural arch called **Devil's Bridge** is located. You can keep going to the 2.2 mile point, where the trail vanishes before it gets to the head of that canyon.

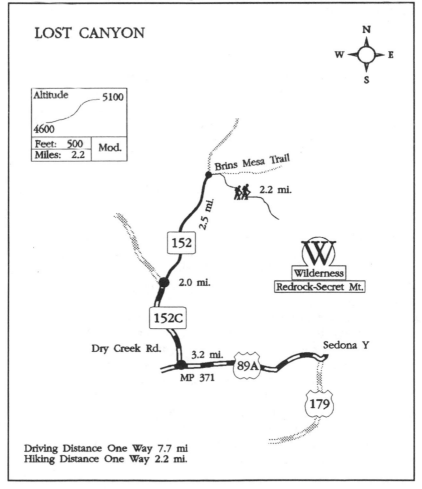

LOST CANYON RUINS

Driving Distance One Way: 7.1 miles (Time 25 minutes)
Access Road: High clearance car preferable, Last 1.9 miles rough dirt road
Hiking Distance One Way: 0.60 miles (Time 30 minutes)
How Strenuous: Easy
Features: Indian ruins

NUTSHELL: On this easy hike you bushwhack up a canyon bottom to a hidden Indian ruin.

DIRECTIONS:
From The Y in Sedona Go:
     Southwest on Highway 89A (toward Cottonwood) a distance of 3.2 miles (MP 371) to the Dry Creek Road. Turn right on Dry Creek Road, also known as FR 152C, and follow it to the 5.2 mile point where FR 152 branches to the right. Take FR 152. Follow the road to the 7.1 miles point, where you will see a canyon from your right cutting across the road. Turn right and park in the mouth of the canyon.

TRAILHEAD: There is no marked trail. You walk the canyon bottom to the head of the canyon.

DESCRIPTION: The Sedona area has so many remarkable land features, monuments, spires, buttes, etc., that naming them all was a real chore. We have never been able to find a name for this charming little canyon with its gem of an Indian ruin, so we decided to bestow a name upon it and have called it Lost Canyon.
     We have taken many hikes in the Sedona area that require hiking a streambed in the bottom of a canyon. Some of these are quite difficult because of brush and obstacles in the watercourse. This hike is one of the nicest, easiest streambed hikes. The actual floor of the canyon is redrock, with most of the soil washed off, so nothing grows in its middle, leaving it clear for walking. There are a couple of places where the channel is blocked, one by a boulder and the other by fallen trees. Both are easy to detour.
     The canyon is forested with Arizona cypresses, one of the prettiest stands in the region. They are of all ages and sizes, making for an interesting mixture. We love cypress forests. They are quiet and pleasant. The trees often

take fantastic shapes. Some are twisted while neighbor trees of the same age are straight as an arrow.

The canyon climbs gently. At the mouth, as you begin the hike, look high up to your left and you will see a cave. This contains the Indian ruin you visit on the **Lost Canyon** hike. Some of the smaller caves "upstairs" show signs of rock work too and are probably Indian ruins.

As you go farther up the canyon, the middle cliffs fill the horizon and you can't see the tallest cliffs. At the end of the canyon you enter a box. The ruin is under an overhang to your right. You have an easy climb of about 20 feet to get to it. It has been pothunted but is fairly intact. Enjoy it and then walk up to the very end of the canyon and look up. The water has undercut the cliff so that it projects over you. This would be a terrific sight when a gentle waterfall was running. If much water was running, however, you probably could not make this hike.

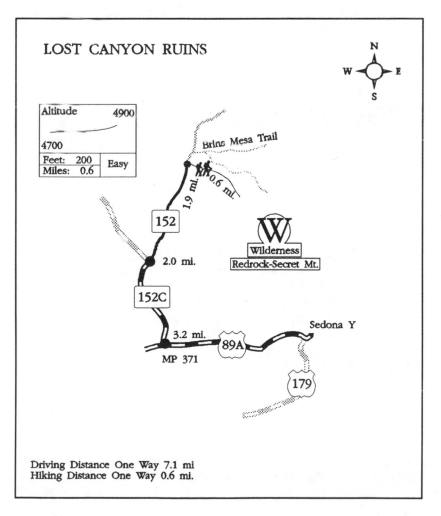

LOST CANYON RUINS

Altitude 4900

4700

Feet: 200 | Easy
Miles: 0.6

Brins Mesa Trail

0.6 mi.

1.9 mi.

152

Wilderness
Redrock-Secret Mt.

2.0 mi.

152C

3.2 mi.

89A

Sedona Y

MP 371

179

Driving Distance One Way 7.1 mi
Hiking Distance One Way 0.6 mi.

LOST WILSON MOUNTAIN

General Information
Location Map C4
Wilson Mt. USGS Map
Coconino Forest Service Map

Driving Distance One Way: 7.8 miles (Time 30 minutes)
Access Road: High clearance car preferable, Last 2.6 miles rough dirt road
Hiking Distance One Way: 1.3 miles (Time 45 minutes)
How Strenuous: Easy
Features: Scenic canyon

NUTSHELL: Located 7.8 miles north of Sedona, this hike follows a closed road to the southwest face of Wilson Mountain.

DIRECTIONS:
From the Sedona Y Go:
      Southwest on Highway 89A (toward Cottonwood) a distance of 3.2 miles (MP 371) to the Dry Creek Road. Turn right on Dry Creek Road, also known as FR 152C, and follow it to the 5.2 mile point where FR 152 branches to the right. Take FR 152. Follow the road to the 7.8 miles point where you will see a dirt road marked FR 9919 branching off to the right. Park across the main road (to your left).

TRAILHEAD: This trail is neither marked nor maintained. Walk the road, FR 9919.

DESCRIPTION: FR 152 can be a very rough road. Sometimes the first mile is graded but it is seldom graded after that. There are many places on the road where the soil has washed away from the surface leaving sharp projecting rocks that compete for the honor of tearing out your oil pan. In other places exposed ledges make for very rough encounters and must be crawled over.
      If you have a high clearance vehicle you can enter FR 9919, but don't try to go more than 0.10 miles on it. There are places where the road has been so washed out by erosion that no vehicle could make it. Besides, you want to hike this road, not drive it.
      The road goes through a beautiful forest of Arizona cypress, juniper, manzanita, agave and cactus. The road ambles along, curving here and there to follow the terrain and you do not have a very good sense of its purpose. It primarily goes north, parallel to the base of Brins Mesa and then turns east toward Mt. Wilson. Just about the time you think that it is going to take you right to the mountain, it stops. The stopping point does not make any sense.

You will not feel that you have reached a destination. The road just ends. We explored all the likely routes from this point but could find none.

In spite of this strange end, the road provides a very easy pleasant walk, far from the crowds. We tried it on a warm day in March about three days after a snowfall and it was just right, warm, bright and dust-free.

At the 0.90 mile point where the road makes a hairpin turn there is a small clearing to the right. We walked over there and found a cairn that seemed to mark a trail down into a streambed. We tried to follow it but found no other cairns. Perhaps one can hike up the streambed and come to the gap between Brins Mesa and Mt. Wilson. We have enjoyed looking at this gap from above, at the north end of Brins Mesa, on the **Brins Mesa East** hike and we would like to find a way to get there on the ground. Maybe the streambed is it.

How do you lose a mountain? In this case the name Lost Wilson refers to a nub projecting from the northwest face of the main mass of Wilson.

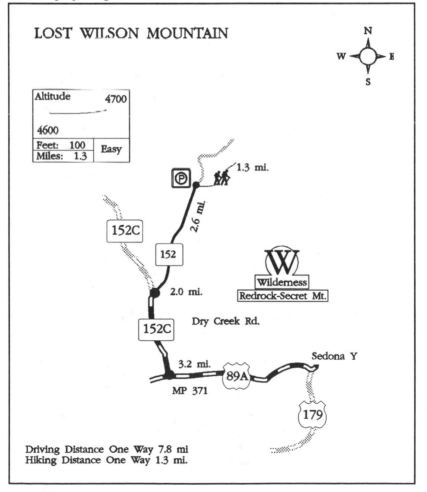

LOST WILSON MOUNTAIN

N
W — E
S

Altitude 4700

4600

Feet: 100 — Easy
Miles: 1.3

1.3 mi.

152C

2.6 mi.

152

W
Wilderness
Redrock-Secret Mt.

2.0 mi.

152C

Dry Creek Rd.

3.2 mi.

89A

Sedona Y

MP 371

179

Driving Distance One Way 7.8 mi
Hiking Distance One Way 1.3 mi.

LOY BUTTE

Driving Distance One Way: 19.9 miles (Time 45 minutes)
Access Road: All cars, Last 10.3 miles good dirt road
Hiking Distance One Way: 0.25 miles (Time 10 minutes)
How Strenuous: Easy
Features: Best Indian ruins in the Sedona area

NUTSHELL: Located about 20 miles northwest of Sedona, this is a short hike to excellent Indian ruins.

DIRECTIONS:
From The Y in Sedona Go:

Southwest on Highway 89A (toward Cottonwood) a distance of 9.6 miles (MP 364.5) to the Red Canyon Road. Turn right on Red Canyon Road, also known as FR 525, and follow it to the 12.4 mile point where FR 525C branches to the left. Stay on FR 525, the road to the right. Follow FR 525 to the 15.4 mile point, where it intersects the Boynton Pass Road, FR 152C. Stay on FR 525, the road to the left. At 15.6 miles you will reach an intersection with FR 795. Turn left here on FR 525. At 16.8 miles you will come to an intersection with FR 525D. Take a right, still on FR 525. At 19.5 miles you will reach the Hancock Ranch. Here the road goes through the ranch, which is private property. Take the left fork here, still on FR 525. At 19.9 miles you will come to the parking area for the ruins. Pull off to the right and park.

TRAILHEAD: This trail is not marked with a sign but you will see a distinct path heading toward the nearby cliff.

DESCRIPTION: Don't be alarmed by the Hancock Ranch signs as you drive into the region of the ruins. An easement for the road runs through the ranch and you are welcome so long as you stay on the road and abide by the rules: no shooting, no hunting, no wandering around on the private property, etc.

The ruins are located in a large cave in the cliff face. The official name for these ruins is The Honanki Ruins. In recent years the Forest Service has done some work to stabilize the ruins. There is no caretaker for them and over the years careless and malicious visitors have caused some damage. Even so, the ruins are well preserved and definitely worth a visit. You will see some names carved and painted on the walls. Some of them are fairly old. The

Smithsonian Institute did a survey of Indian ruins in northern Arizona in the 1920s, headed by an archaeologist named Jesse Fewkes. He spent some time at this ruin and thought that it was a major find. In spite of his glowing reports, the government did little about the ruins except to preserve public access to them. They were little known and not very frequently visited until lately. Now they seem to be on the menus for all the jeep tours.

It is fun to explore the ruins and walk along the cliff face on both sides of the ruins. Try to imagine yourself as an occupant of the place centuries ago when the tribe of Indians lived there and picture the life you would have led. There is a small streambed running along the cliff bottom but it seldom carries water. Maybe in the days when these ruins were inhabited water ran in the stream year around.

This is a gentle little excursion for the whole family. If you want a full-blooded hike in the nearby area, try the **Loy Canyon Trail**.

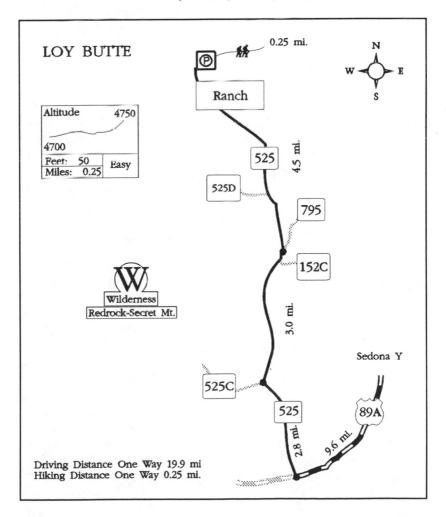

LOY CANYON

Driving Distance One Way: 19.2 miles (Time 40 minutes)
Access Road: All cars, Last 9.6 miles good dirt road
Hiking Distance One Way: 5.0 miles (Time 2.5 hours)
How Strenuous: Moderate. Last mile strenuous
Features: Indian ruins, Scenic canyon, Views

NUTSHELL: Located 19.2 miles northwest of Sedona, this trail takes you through a pleasant canyon containing Indian ruins to the top of the Mogollon Rim.

DIRECTIONS:
From The Y in Sedona Go:
Southwest on Highway 89A (toward Cottonwood) a distance of 9.6 miles (MP 364.5) to the Red Canyon Road. Turn right on Red Canyon Road, also known as FR 525, and follow it to the 12.4 mile point where FR 525C branches to the left. Stay on FR 525, the road to the right. Follow FR 525 to the 15.4 mile point, where it intersects the Boynton Pass Road, FR 152C. Stay on FR 525, the road to the left. At 15.6 miles you will reach an intersection with FR 795. Turn left here on FR 525. At 16.8 miles you will come to an intersection with FR 525D. Take a right, still on FR 525. At 19.2 you will reach a fence. Park on either side of the road at the fence.

TRAILHEAD: You will see a rusty sign marked, "Loy Canyon #5" on the right side of the road in front of the fence.

DESCRIPTION: Since you are so close, drive on down the road another 0.7 miles and visit the Honanki Indian ruins located at **Loy Butte** if you haven't seen them. They are the Sedona area's finest Indian ruins.

The Loy Canyon trail was built as a cattle trail in the late 1890s. Like many other cattle trails that are now used for hiking, the purpose of this trail was to provide access to drive cattle to the top of the Mogollon Rim. The cattle would be kept in the warm low country during the winter and then driven to the cool high country for the summer. The rim is over a thousand feet high in most places, so it was difficult to find spots where a trail could be built.

You start this hike by skirting the fence around a ranch for about half a mile. Once you are by the ranch you begin to walk up the canyon bottom.

Look for a small Indian ruin set in a cave at 0.75 miles. It is in a cliff face to your left.

The trail rises gradually through a forest for 4 miles. It meanders across the creekbed a few times, so you don't want to make the hike when water is running high. Because the trail gains in altitude the vegetation along the trail also changes. It is very desert-like at the beginning, with cactus and low shrubs. As you progress, you enter a pine forest and stay in it to the top.

At the end of the 4 mile approach to the final climb it is clear that the character of the trail changes. It is now at the base of the cliffs forming the rim and some serious work begins to get to the top. The trail becomes much steeper and you climb about one thousand feet in a mile. Some hikers may prefer to end their hike at the 4 mile point and eschew the hard haul to the top.

If you do decide to make the final climb, you will come out on top of the Mogollon Rim at Secret Mountain, as described in our book, *Flagstaff Hikes.*

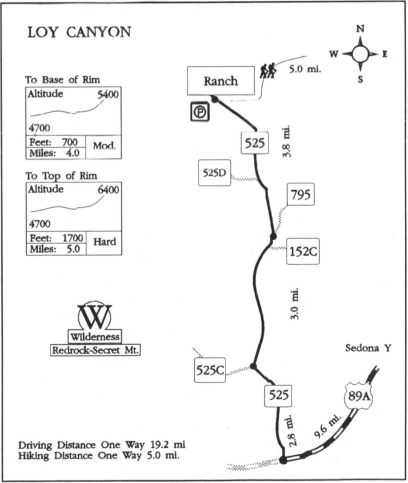

LOY CANYON

To Base of Rim

Altitude	5400
4700	

Feet: 700	Mod.
Miles: 4.0	

To Top of Rim

Altitude	6400
4700	

Feet: 1700	Hard
Miles: 5.0	

Wilderness
Redrock-Secret Mt.

Ranch   5.0 mi.

525   3.8 mi.

525D

795

152C

3.0 mi.

Sedona Y

525C

525   89A

2.8 mi.   9.6 mi.

Driving Distance One Way 19.2 mi
Hiking Distance One Way 5.0 mi.

MARG'S DRAW

General Information
Location Map E5
Sedona USGS Map
Coconino Forest Service Map

Driving Distance One Way: 1.1 miles (Time 10 minutes)
Access Road: All cars, All paved
Hiking Distance One Way: 1.0 miles (Time 40 minutes)
How Strenuous: Easy
Features: Views

NUTSHELL: Marg's Draw is a beautiful area in Sedona's backyard, being a bowl surrounded by the Crimson Cliffs, Munds Mountain, Lee Mountain and Twin Buttes. This short hike takes you into the center of the area.

DIRECTIONS:
From the Sedona Y Go:
    South on Highway 179 (toward Phoenix) for a distance of 0.9 miles (MP 312.8) to Sombart Lane, which is just beyond a Circle K store. Turn left onto Sombart Lane and follow it to the 1.1 mile point, where there is an unpaved parking area. Park there.

TRAILHEAD: You will see no trail signs. You will see a footpath. Follow it uphill through the wooden gate.

DESCRIPTION: You will climb uphill a bit to get through the wooden gate and then you will reach a flat. There are several paths and trails through the area. Follow directions carefully so that you don't take the wrong trail. At 0.27 miles you will reach a fork. Take the left fork. At 0.35 miles the trail splits three ways. Take the middle trail. At 0.375 miles the Marg's Draw Trail goes to the right along a redrock shelf. You will know you are on the right trail if it swings away from the red cliff and heads south. Another trail described in this book, **The Schnebly-Marg's Connection**, takes you around the base of the cliffs and to the north. **The Snoopy Rock Trail** heads straight for the cliff.
    This is an easy walk, being quite level. You will feel at times that you are in a remote area and then a view will open up allowing you to look at Sedona, reminding you that you are just a stone's throw from it. How nice to have such an area so close to town.
    The story goes that the Thompsons, a family of early settlers in the area, had a mule named Marg. They used her to perform arduous hauling tasks. One of the toughest jobs was pulling a wagon up the steep road to Flagstaff.

Mules are pretty intelligent animals and Marg learned how to tell when the family was about to go somewhere when she saw them get out the wagon, harness and tack. When she saw such activity she would gallop away into a draw to hide. But Marg wasn't smart enough, because the natural bowl shape of the draw made it easy to box her in and catch her. The family referred to the area as Marg's Draw and the name stuck.

The draw is accessible from the north end by the route covered in this article. The south end can be reached easily by taking Morgan Road. There is no connection in the middle. We have tried to bushwhack through the middle a couple of times. We would find what seemed to be a trail and follow it only to have it play out.

Your trail will end at about the one mile point, where you are standing on a large redrock shelf. Notice the strange quartz bubbles imbedded in the surface of the rock. Walk out to the end of the shelf. There are great views of the cliffs on three sides from this point.

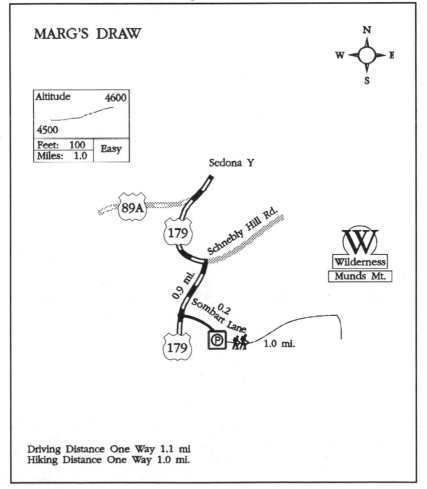

MARG'S DRAW

Altitude   4600

4500

Feet: 100   Easy
Miles: 1.0

Sedona Y

89A

179

Schnebly Hill Rd.

0.9 mi.

Sombart Lane   0.2

179

1.0 mi.

Wilderness
Munds Mt.

Driving Distance One Way 1.1 mi
Hiking Distance One Way 1.0 mi.

MERRY-GO-ROUND

General Information
Location Map D5
Munds Mt. and Munds Park USGS Maps
Coconino Forest Service Map

Driving Distance One Way: 5.0 miles (Time 30 minutes)
Access Road: All cars, Last 3.7 miles good gravel road
Hiking Distance, Complete Loop: 1.0 miles (Time 45 minutes)
How Strenuous: Moderate
Features: Historic road, Redrocks, Views

NUTSHELL: This hike takes you to a prominent landmark on the Schnebly Hill Road just east of Sedona, where you climb a rock formation and then hike part of an historic road.

DIRECTIONS:
From the Sedona Y Go:
        South on Highway 179 (toward Phoenix) for a distance of 0.3 miles (MP 312.8) to the Schnebly Hill Road. It is just across the bridge past Tlaquepaque. Turn left onto the Schnebly Hill Road. It is paved for the first mile and then turns into a gravel road that is all right for any car unless the road is muddy. At 5.0 miles you will see a gate made of very thick steel pipes. This is used to close the road in winter. You will see a parking area on the left side of the road just before the gate. Park here.

TRAILHEAD: The trail starts at the parking place. It is unmarked and unsigned.

DESCRIPTION: At the parking place you will see a line of three boulders blocking what looks like a road going uphill to a couple of redrock spires just above your head. This hike has two levels. First take the uphill portion of the path, making a mental note of the fork downhill to the left (south).
        The uphill path takes you on a steep but short climb to the base of the two spires. It is fun to explore these. If you are adventuresome, you can climb them. This whole area on top is a good viewpoint from which to enjoy the eye-filling delights of the area. We sat here one memorable evening and watched a thrilling sunset.
        After you have finished enjoying the top, go back downhill and take the lower path. Although unmarked, it is well worn and you will have no trouble following it. In about 0.10 miles you will intersect the old Schnebly Hill Road. Take the left fork first and follow the old road about 0.05 miles,

around the bend of a small arroyo that cuts it. When you look to your right here you will see the red butte whose top you just climbed. Circling the butte is a layer of rusty mauve stone about 12 feet thick. This is the Ft. Wingate formation, a harder stone than the redrock above and below it. There are a couple of small windows in this layer. The old road followed this circular ledge around the butte and was referred to as the Merry-Go-Round.

Now go back to the trail fork and take the Merry-Go-Round. Step away from the road and go to the lip of the ledge all along the way to enjoy the many fine views into some of the most scenic areas around Sedona.

You will soon have girdled the butte. Keep following the old road uphill. You will see how the Merry-Go-Round was an ideal natural road, being flat and sandy, while the road above and below it was steep and rocky. You will intersect the present Schnebly Hill Road in about 0.25 miles from the butte. From there walk back down the present road to your car. To hike the old road to the top of the rim see the **Old Schnebly Hill Road** hike.

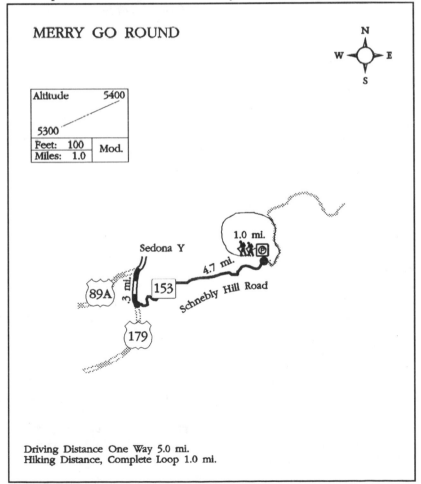

MERRY GO ROUND

Driving Distance One Way 5.0 mi.
Hiking Distance, Complete Loop 1.0 mi.

MESCAL MOUNTAIN

General Information
Location Map C3
Wilson Mt. USGS Map
Coconino Forest Service Map

Driving Distance One Way: 6.7 miles (Time 15 minutes)
Access Road: All cars, All paved
Hiking Distance One Way: 2.5 miles (Time 90 minutes)
How Strenuous: Moderate
Features: Views, Indian ruins

NUTSHELL: Mescal Mountain is a small mesa at the mouth of Boynton Canyon 6.7 miles northwest of Sedona. It takes a bit of scrambling to get to the top but it is worthwhile.

DIRECTIONS:
From the Sedona Y Go:
> Southwest on Highway 89A (toward Cottonwood) a distance of 3.2 miles (MP 371) to the Dry Creek Road, FR 152C. Turn right on Dry Creek Road and follow it to the 6.1 mile point, where there is a stop sign. The paved road to the right is the Long Canyon Road. Take it to the 6.7 miles point where you will see an unpaved road to your left. The road's entrance is blocked with boulders. There is a parking area in front of the boulders. Park there.

TRAILHEAD: You will begin this hike on a marked and maintained trail. There is a rusty sign where you park reading "Long Canyon #122."

DESCRIPTION: Start the hike by taking the **Long Canyon Trail**, which begins as a wide jeep road. In fact, the Forest Service has moved several boulders across the road at its entrance to keep vehicles from using it.
> At 0.30 miles you will come to a 3-pronged fork. Take the leftmost fork. At 0.60 miles you will come to a big gate. This marks the entrance to the Redrock-Secret Mt. Wilderness Area. Instead of going through the gate, stay outside it and walk along the fence. At the 1.0 mile point you will reach a butte. Here the trail begins to climb sharply.
> You will see a cave to your right that looks large enough to contain an Indian ruin. It is large enough but there is no ruin due to a large crack in the cave roof that allows water to pour into the cave when it rains. There is a side trail over to this cave and it is worth taking for the fun of exploring.
> From the cave the trail zigzags to a saddle on Mescal Mountain. Just below the saddle you will see a shallow cave containing a rudimentary Indian

ruin.

From this point the trail gets steeper. You will see a distinct footpath marked with cairns going up to the south. A few yards above the saddle there is the ruin of a pit house. Beyond it the trail winds right up to the face of the highest point on Mescal Mountain and then curves, hugging the cliff at its base. It is fairly easy hiking, though steep, until you get to a point just below the top. There you will have to do some climbing if you want to go to the top.

We don't do any rock climbing. We are risk-averse and climbing scares the hell out of us. The small climb involved here is no worse than climbing a high ladder, though. Once you are on top, walk around the perimeter to enjoy the view. The distance to the top is 1.5 miles. Fully exploring the top you can add another mile to the hike.

When you see Mescal Mountain from a distance you think that the top will be empty slickrock, bare as a bald man's head. In fact, however, erosion has created soil and the soil supports much vegetation.

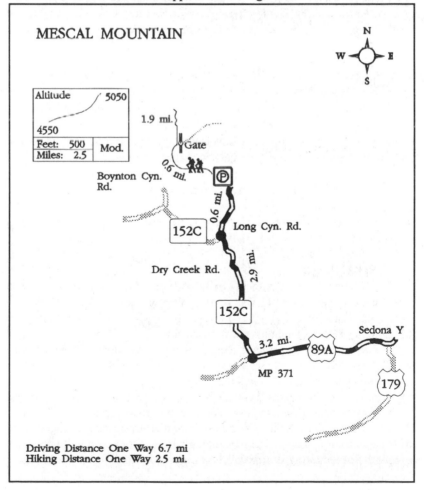

MESCAL MOUNTAIN

Altitude 5050
4550
Feet: 500   Mod.
Miles: 2.5

1.9 mi.
Gate
0.6 mi.
Boynton Cyn. Rd.
0.6 mi.
152C
Long Cyn. Rd.
Dry Creek Rd.
2.9 mi.
152C
3.2 mi.
89A
Sedona Y
MP 371
179

Driving Distance One Way 6.7 mi
Hiking Distance One Way 2.5 mi.

MITTEN RIDGE

General Information
Location Map D5
Munds Mt. and Munds Park USGS Maps
Coconino Forest Service Map

Driving Distance One Way: 3.8 miles (Time 20 minutes)
Access Road: All cars, Last 2.5 miles good gravel road
Hiking Distance One Way: 2.5 miles (Time 2 hours)
How Strenuous: Moderate
Features: Views, Fascinating rock formations and sculptures, Vortex

NUTSHELL: Just a mile east of Sedona as the crow flies, the Schnebly Hill Road is enjoyed by thousands of people. The hike takes you part way up the road, then across Bear Wallow Canyon to explore the redrock buttes on the west side of the canyon.

DIRECTIONS:
From the Sedona Y Go:
        South on Highway 179 (toward Phoenix) for a distance of 0.3 miles (MP 312.8) to the Schnebly Hill Road. It is just across the bridge past Tlaquepaque. Turn left onto the Schnebly Hill Road. It is paved for the first mile and then turns into a gravel road that is all right for any car unless the road is muddy. At the 3.8 mile point, pull over and park. There is an area off the road to your right for parking and there are some spaces on the shoulder.

TRAILHEAD: There are no signs. You will see a trail going over the left side of the road (to the west). Follow it.

DESCRIPTION:
        As you drive up Schnebly Hill Road you will become conscious of a deep streambed to your left. This is Bear Wallow Canyon. You will also be aware of a big butte between the road and Sedona. This is Mitten Ridge, one of the major Sedona landmarks and it is your goal on this hike.
        At the parking place you can park on the shoulder or drive up onto a slickrock shelf. Then you walk across the road and look for the trail. It dips down and heads toward Mitten Ridge.
        In about 200 yards you will come to a redrock shelf that was capped with a very thin layer of gray lava. This cap has broken up into small stones. This place is one of the Sedona Vortex spots and believers have arranged some of these gray stones into a huge medicine wheel. Often you will encounter people there meditating, drumming, holding vigils, and so forth. Spend a little

time in the center of the circle if you can to see how you react to a vortex.

Thus far you are following the same trail that we have described for the **Cow Pies** hike. At 0.50 miles, the paths split. You will go straight instead of turning left as you would for the Cow Pies hike. You will walk toward ledges at the base of Mitten Ridge. Cairns usually mark the trail. It goes across several lower ledges to get up near the base of the cliffs. Once there you work your way west, at times ascending to a higher ledge. At first you will be walking through brush but at 1.5 miles you will break out onto clear slickrock.

Here you will find an upper and lower trail. Try the lower one. You will soon see a saddle above you to the right. The saddle is a great viewpoint. You probably will not find a regular trail going to the saddle but it is easy and fun to walk up the sloping redrock face of the ridge to the saddle.

From the saddle you can continue to work your way down toward the south end of Mitten Ridge. We were unable to go all the way to the end because the trail thinned out at the 2.5 mile point and became dangerous.

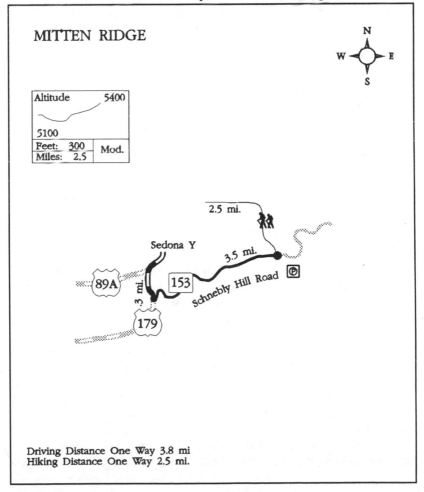

MITTEN RIDGE

N
W — E
S

Altitude   5400

5100

Feet: 300   Mod.
Miles: 2.5

2.5 mi.

Sedona Y

3.5 mi.

89A   153

Schnebly Hill Road

179

Driving Distance One Way 3.8 mi
Hiking Distance One Way 2.5 mi.

MOONEY TRAIL

General Information
Location Map C1
Loy Butte USGS Map
Coconino Forest Service Map

Driving Distance One Way: 18.1 miles (Time 30 minutes)
Access Road: All cars, Last 8.5 miles good dirt road
Hiking Distance One Way: 3.75 miles (Time 2.5 hours)
How Strenuous: Hard
Features: Views

NUTSHELL: This cattle trail starts at Black Tank 18.0 miles southwest of Sedona and climbs to the base of the Mogollon Rim (or, alternatively, to the top)

DIRECTIONS:
From the Sedona Y Go:
        Southwest on Highway 89A (toward Cottonwood) a distance of 9.6 miles (MP 364.5) to the Red Canyon Road. Turn right on Red Canyon Road, also known as FR 525, and follow it to the 12.4 mile point where FR 525C branches to the left. Turn left onto FR 525C. Follow it to the 18.1 mile point, where FR 551 branches to the right. Pull in on FR 551 and park.

TRAILHEAD: This is a marked and maintained trail. You will see a rusty sign near the road reading, "Mooney Trail #12."

DESCRIPTION: You will know you are near the trailhead when you see the red earth bank of a dam with fence posts on top on your right. This is Black Tank. Just as you curve around the tank there is a road to your right into the tank. This is FR 551. You will see the trail's rusty sign as you pull in.
        Park near the tank. If you have a high clearance vehicle you can drive about 1.0 mile on FR 551, parking just before the road crosses a gully. The gully is Spring Creek.
        If you park at the tank, then walk through the fenced area toward the pumphouse, a small brick building. When you exit the gate at the other end of the tank area, turn right. You will see a profusion of trails because cattle are still run here and everywhere they wander they leave false trails. Follow the most heavily travelled jeep trail for 0.25 miles, to a point where the road forks. The left fork is marked FR 551A, and this is the fork to take.
        The trail goes along foothills, gradually climbing to a ridge top. Then you walk along the top of the ridge. The ridge is javelina country and you will

see plenty of sign. It is hard to see these critters, as they are shy. Sometimes you may get a whiff of them. The javelina odor smells just like a cow barn. From the ridge top you get good distant views, particularly to the north of the Mogollon Rim, but there isn't much to see close at hand. In fact, this is a rather drab trail.

You will reach another cattle tank called Sebra Tank. Beyond Sebra Tank you will come to the base of the Mogollon Rim, where the trail begins a steep ascent. There is an arch located in the cliff face here.

The trail to the top is hard. It is a severe climb and most of it is in the open exposed to full sunlight. You wouldn't want to do this on a hot sunny day. At the top you will come out on a ridge at a place where the Mooney Trail, Taylor Cabin Trail and Casner Mountain trails all converge. If you turn left here, you will go to Casner Mountain; if you turn right, you will go to the top of the rim.

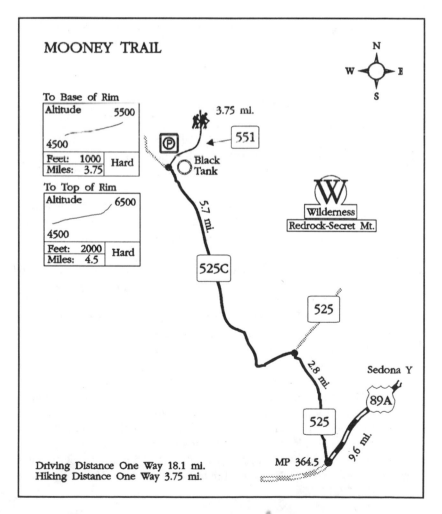

MUNDS MOUNTAIN NORTH

General Information
Location Map D5
Munds Mt. and Munds Park USGS Maps
Coconino Forest Service Map

Driving Distance One Way: 6.6 miles (Time 30 minutes)
Access Road: All cars, Last 5.3 miles good gravel road
Hiking Distance One Way: 3.4 miles (Time 2.5 hours)
How Strenuous: Hard
Features: Views

NUTSHELL: This hike takes you to the top of the north end of Munds Mountain. The approach goes 2.9 miles over easy country. Then you make a final steep 0.5 mile ascent to the top, from where you have glorious views.

DIRECTIONS:
From the Sedona Y Go:
South on Highway 179 (toward Phoenix) for a distance of 0.3 miles (MP 312.8) to the Schnebly Hill Road. It is just across the bridge past Tlaquepaque. Turn left onto the Schnebly Hill Road. It is paved for the first mile and then turns into a gravel road that is all right for any car unless the road is muddy. At 5.0 miles you will see a gate made of very thick steel pipes. This gate is locked across the road in winter, usually about mid-November to mid-April. (Call the Sedona Forest Service Ranger Station to find out whether it is open.) Drive to the top, 6.6 miles from the Y, where you will find the Schnebly Hill Vista with a big parking area to your left. Park there.

TRAILHEAD: Your approach to the trailhead is over old jeep roads. From the parking area walk up the main road about 100 paces, where you will see a dirt road to your right (south). Take it. If you are in a high clearance vehicle with stout tires, you can drive this road about 1.25 miles and make this an easier hike. The road is the Old Schnebly Hill Road, following the alignment it had from 1902 until the 1930s. At 0.88 miles on this road you come to a fork. Go left (south) here. You will soon see a small microwave tower. At 1.2 miles you will come to a fork. Here the old road goes right, on the hike we call the **Old Schnebly Hill Road.** Go left (northeast) here. At 1.25 miles you will reach the remains of a cattle guard, the end of the line if you are driving. Go through the gate here on foot. At 1.35 miles you come to a fork. Go right (south) through a gate framed by tall poles and follow that road to the 2.38 mile point, where you meet another road. Turn right (west) here. At 2.5 miles you will reach Committee Tank. Follow the road to the left along a fence. The road ends at

2.67 miles at the corner of the fence. Here you will find a Wilderness sign, and a gate. Go inside and follow the foot trail downhill. The trail goes out on a thin ridge connected to Munds Mt. At 2.9 miles you will find the trailhead sign, "Munds Mt. Trail 77," just beyond the point where the **Jacks Canyon Trail** meets the ridge.

DESCRIPTION: From the trailhead walk uphill about 20 yards. Here you will see the trail split with no markers. The left fork is the **Munds Mountain South** trail. Take the right fork instead. It is in a sandy groove. The footing on this trail is not good, as you encounter innumerable small white rocks that tend to slip when you step on them. The trail is hard to see as there are white rocks everywhere and cairns don't stand out. The trail goes to the top by switchbacks and gets better about halfway up. Here you will begin to get thrilling glimpses into the Mitten Ridge area. At the top you emerge onto a rather bare park. Move around its perimeter for unsurpassed views.

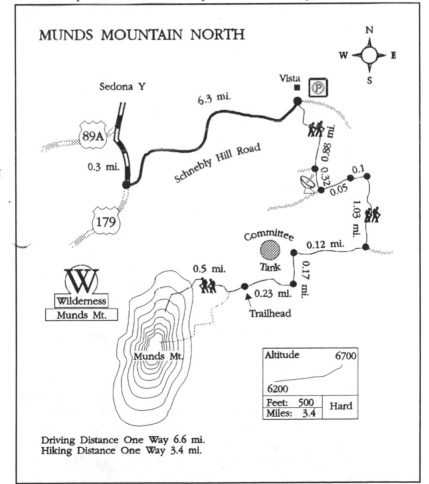

MUNDS MOUNTAIN NORTH

Driving Distance One Way 6.6 mi.
Hiking Distance One Way 3.4 mi.

MUNDS MOUNTAIN SOUTH

General Information
Location Map D5
Munds Mt. and Munds Park USGS Maps
Coconino Forest Service Map

Driving Distance One Way: 6.6 miles (Time 30 minutes)
Access Road: All cars, Last 5.3 miles good gravel road
Hiking Distance One Way: 3.75 miles (Time 2.5 hours)
How Strenuous: Hard
Features: Views

NUTSHELL: This hike takes you to the high point of Munds Mountain. The approach goes 2.9 miles over easy country; then you have a final steep 0.85 mile ascent to the top. From there you have tremendous views.

DIRECTIONS:
From the Sedona Y Go:
 South on Highway 179 (toward Phoenix) for a distance of 0.3 miles (MP 312.8) to the Schnebly Hill Road. It is just across the bridge past Tlaquepaque. Turn left onto the Schnebly Hill Road. It is paved for the first mile and then turns into a gravel road that is all right for any car unless the road is muddy. At 5.0 miles you will see a gate made of very thick steel pipes. This gate is locked across the road in winter, usually about mid-November to mid-April. Call the Sedona Forest Service Ranger Station to find out whether it is open. Drive to the top, 6.6 miles, where you will find the Schnebly Hill Vista with a big parking area to your left. Park there.

TRAILHEAD: Your approach to the trailhead is over old jeep roads. From the parking area walk up the main road about 100 paces, where you will see a dirt road to your right (south). Take it. If you are in a high clearance vehicle with stout tires, you can drive this road about 1.25 miles and make this an easier hike. The road is the Old Schnebly Hill Road, following the alignment it had from 1902 until the 1930s. At 0.88 miles on this road you come to a fork. Go left (south) here. You will soon see a small microwave tower. At 1.2 miles you will come to a fork. Here the old road goes right, on the hike we call the **Old Schnebly Hill Road.** Go left (northeast) here. At 1.25 miles you will reach the remains of a cattle guard, the end of the line if you are driving. Go through the gate here on foot. At 1.35 miles you come to a fork. Go right (south) through a gate framed by tall poles and follow that road to the 2.38 mile point, where you meet another road. Turn right (west) here. At 2.5 miles you will reach Committee Tank. Follow the road to the left along the fence. The road ends at 2.67 miles at the corner of the fence. Here you will find a Wilderness sign, and a gate. Go inside and follow the foot trail downhill. The trail goes out on a thin ridge connected to Munds Mt. At 2.9 miles you will find the trailhead sign, "Munds Mt. Trail 77," just beyond the point where the **Jacks Canyon Trail** meets the ridge.

DESCRIPTION: From the trailhead walk uphill about 20 yards. Here you will see the trail split with no markers. The right fork is the **Munds Mountain North** trail. Take the left fork instead. This trail is difficult. It is steep in places, hard to see and the footing is slippery. Every footfall comes down on rocks. There were pink ribbons tied to branches to guide us. Without these, the trail is only for experienced hikers. It tops out at the high point on Munds Mt. in difficult brush. From here you have good panoramic views and a look down onto Lee Mt. and some interesting lower plateaus that invite exploration by those who are energetic enough.

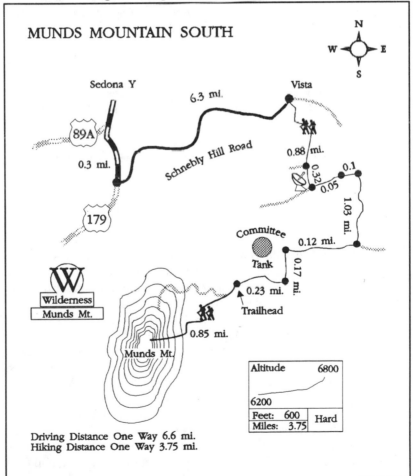

MUSHROOM ROCK

General Information
Location Map C3
Wilson Mountain USGS Map
Coconino Forest Service Map

Driving Distance One Way: 8.0 miles (Time 20 minutes)
Access Road: All cars, All paved
Hiking Distance One Way: 2.25 miles (Time 90 minutes)
How Strenuous: Hard
Features: Gorgeous canyon, Indian Ruins, Vortex

NUTSHELL: A hike in **Boynton Canyon** 8.0 miles from Sedona. You branch off the main trail into a side canyon for a clifftop hike of eye-popping beauty.

DIRECTIONS:
From the Sedona Y Go:
        Southwest on Highway 89A (toward Cottonwood) a distance of 3.2 miles (MP 371), where you take a right turn onto Dry Creek Road (FR 152C) Follow it to the 6.1 mile point, where it joins Long Canyon Road. Take a left here, staying on FR 152C. At the 7.7 mile point, you reach another junction. Go right. At 7.9 miles, just before the gatehouse to the Enchantment Resort, is a parking area to the right. Park there.

TRAILHEAD: It is marked at the parking area by a sign reading, "Boynton Canyon #47."

DESCRIPTION: Hike the Boynton Canyon Trail for 1.3 miles, where the trail is a corridor through a thicket of head-high mazanitas. Take an unmarked but distinct trail to the right (east) going downhill into a wash here, on the other side of which is a canyon full of Arizona cypress trees.
        On the far side of the wash the trail turns left (north), leaves the forest and climbs to a saddle on a ridge. At the saddle you will find that the ridge forms the south wall of yet another canyon. Go east, toward the head of the canyon, where you will find a walkable ledge along a ten foot high groove in the redrock. This groove is a magic place. Plants in natural "baskets" hang on its wall and we saw one pictograph there. Some hikers will want to stop at the groove's end.
        For the robust, who are unafraid of heights and don't mind some redrock scrambling, deeper magic lies ahead. Follow cairns that take you up a steep path. About half way up you will see a side path to your left. Take it to a pristine cliff dwelling in a large cave, then return to the main trail for a

stiff climb to the next top.

You will emerge onto a terrace. Below you are ridges. Above you are ledges crowned with sheer cliffs. There are more ruins in a grooved ledge high above. You see into two canyons. Standing in this glorious place, we were transfixed with beauty and thought of the Navajo Night Chant:

With beauty before me I walk. With beauty behind me I walk.
With beauty above me I walk. With beauty below me I walk.
With beauty all around me I walk.

Following cairns, you will hike west along the north wall of the canyon, climbing up and down to use walkable ledges. Some are wide as a street and some are narrow and scary. You come around the corner of a giant reef at 2.0 miles and, bang!, there is Mushroom Rock at the head of a steep V-shaped gorge, perfectly framed by giant rippling walls of stone. The trail goes on another 0.25 miles, pinching down to an irreducible end where you stand on the tip of a finger ridge out over a deep immensity of echoing chasms.

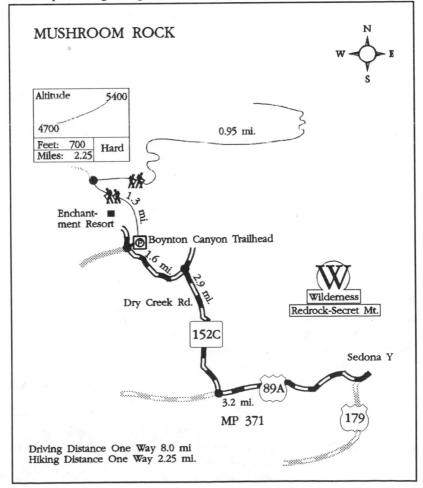

OAK CREEK & VERDE CONFLUENCE

General Information
Location Map G1
Cornville USGS Map
Coconino Forest Service Map

Driving Distance One Way: 22.2 miles (Time 40 minutes)
Access Road: All cars, Last 4.0 miles good dirt road
Hiking Distance One Way: 2.0 miles (Time 1 hour)
How Strenuous: Easy
Features: Indian ruins, River confluence

NUTSHELL: Located 22.0 miles southwest of Sedona, this hike has no trail but offers interesting exploration along a river bank to see a river confluence and an Indian ruin.

DIRECTIONS:
From The Y in Sedona Go:
Southwest on Highway 89A (toward Cottonwood) a distance of 17.2 miles (MP 357), to a point where the Cornville Road intersects Highway 89A. A sign identifies this as Cornville and I-17 access. Turn left on the Cornville Road and follow it one mile, to the 18.2 point. Turn right there onto FR 671, an unpaved road. Follow this road to the 21.5 mile point, where there is a three-pronged fork. Take the left fork onto an unmarked dirt road. Follow this road to the 22.1 mile point, where there is a two-pronged fork. Take the left fork here. At 22.2 miles you will be near the Indian ruin at the rim of Oak Creek canyon. Park here.

TRAILHEAD: No trail. You will see Indian ruins to your left at the parking spot. View them and then hike to the confluence.

DESCRIPTION: The Indian ruin is a two-story structure located on a prominent knob of land near the riverbank. Unfortunately it is located on private land and protected by a fence festooned with "No Trespassing" signs. You can get close enough for a good look without going onto the land. This is an unusual ruin for the area, as it is neither a pit house nor a cliff dwelling. Instead it is a freestanding "apartment building." It is built with distinctive round boulders from the river, which add to its unusual appearance.

From the ruin you can walk along the riverbank overlooking the river back to the confluence or you can drive there. To drive to the confluence just go back to the last fork in the road and turn left, from where it is about 0.40 miles to the spot where the rivers converge.

The two streams meet at a V-shaped point overlooked by a high white bluff. This bluff provides a natural perch, a place to sit and watch the meeting of the waters. As you sit on the point looking forward, downstream, Oak Creek is to your left and the Verde River is to your right. After a rain, Oak Creek runs red, while the Verde (true to its name, which means "green" in Spanish) runs green. It is fascinating to watch the waters mix. Oak Creek seems to run faster than the Verde.

This is not a wilderness experience. Right across the river is a big trailer and RV park and there are several ranches in the area. You could actually make this trip with no hiking at all. It is an excellent hike, though, if you explore along the river bank for a couple of miles as we did.

Look sharp as you are walking and you may find pottery sherds and arrowheads along the river rim, as this area was inhabited by Indians for hundreds of years. Leave them in place. Never take artifacts from an historic site.

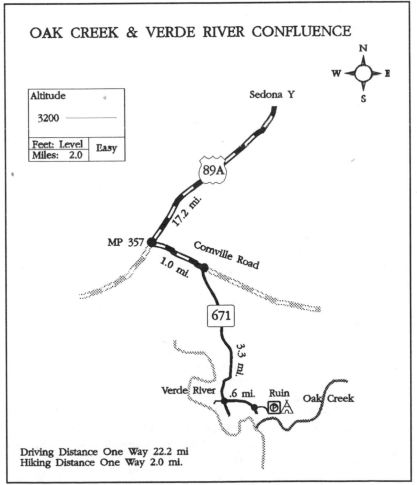

OAK CREEK & VERDE RIVER CONFLUENCE

N
W — E
S

Sedona Y

Altitude

3200

| Feet: Level | Easy |
| Miles: 2.0 | |

89A

17.2 mi.

MP 357   Cornville Road

1.0 mi.

671

3.3 mi.

Verde River   .6 mi.   Ruin   Oak Creek

Driving Distance One Way 22.2 mi
Hiking Distance One Way 2.0 mi.

OAK CREEK VISTA

General Information
Location Map F3
Mountainaire USGS Map
Coconino Forest Service Map

Driving Distance One Way: 15.8 miles (Time 30 minutes)
Access Road: All cars, All paved
Hiking Distance, Complete Loop: 0.20 miles (Time 30 minutes)
How Strenuous: Easy
Features: Sightseeing spot, Signs explaining flora and fauna

NUTSHELL: More of a stroll than a hike, this easy trail is located 15.8 miles north of Sedona on the rim of Oak Creek Canyon. A good place to take relatives to show them Oak Creek Canyon.

DIRECTIONS:
From The Sedona Y Go:
North on Highway 89A (toward Flagstaff). You will drive the entire length of Oak Creek Canyon, climbing up the switchbacks. When you get to the top of the canyon, at the 15.8 mile point (MP 390), you will see Oak Creek Vista to your right. It has a paved entrance with many parking places and public toilets.

TRAILHEAD: The trail is paved, of all things. Pick it up from the parking lot at any point. It makes a loop, so you can join it anywhere you like and come back to where you started.

DESCRIPTION: The Forest Service has made an attractive viewpoint out of the old highway alignment, which used to go through here. On a busy weekend when the weather is good, you will find Indians selling jewelry on blankets they have laid out along the sides of the path.

The path follows around a bend in the canyon rim. Several stand-points have been established along the rim with signs at each point. The signs explain the history, biology, zoology and geology of the area. You will get some impressive views into the canyon depths from these standpoints.

The canyon is very deep below this part of the rim, probably one thousand feet or more. The area directly below the viewpoints is actually **Pumphouse Wash**, a tributary of Oak Creek Canyon, rather than Oak Creek Canyon itself. You will pass over Pumphouse Wash when you drive through Oak Creek Canyon. It is spanned by a bridge just below the Sterling Springs Fish Hatchery, where the switchbacks start.

At the canyon rim, the rock you see is a thick cap of gray basalt (lava) at the top with white or buff sandstone cliffs below the gray. The redrock for which Sedona is famous occurs in lower strata. The basalt cliff faces here are favorite spots for rope climbers. Look for them on the cliff faces to the east (on your left) on the same wall of the canyon you are standing on.

An interesting sight is Highway 89A corkscrewing around the toe of a fin as it works its way downhill and comes out onto the floor of Oak Creek Canyon.

This is a very gentle and satisfying walk, an easy stroll for Aunt Maude or other visiting relatives. Kids even seem to like it. It gives an appreciation of the size and depth of Oak Creek Canyon and you just might pick up a jewelry bargain at the same time. It isn't worth the drive just for the hike, but for an outing combining a nice drive and a chance to see the whole canyon with explanatory signs, it is a satisfying experience.

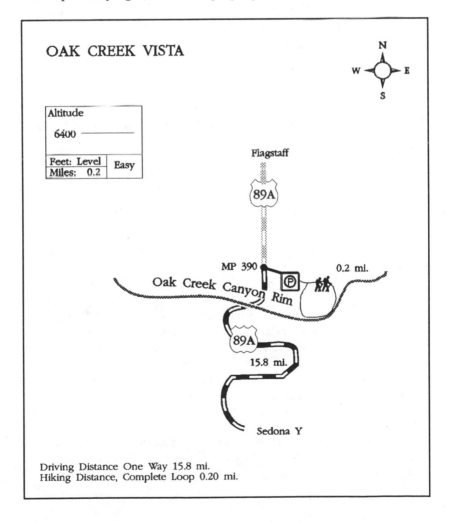

OLD HIGHWAY 79

General Information
Location Map F2
Page Springs and Sedona USGS Maps
Coconino Forest Service Map

Driving Distance One Way: 8.5 miles (Time 15 minutes)
Access Road: All cars, All paved
Hiking Distance One Way: 2.5 miles (Time 75 minutes)
How Strenuous: Moderate
Features: Views

NUTSHELL: This old dirt road has been replaced by the present Highway 89A. It provides a pleasant stroll from a point on Highway 89A to a point on the lower Red Rock Loop Road.

DIRECTIONS:
From the Sedona Y Go:
Southwest on Highway 89A (toward Cottonwood) for a distance of 8.2 miles (MP 366), to a point where you see a dirt road going through a gate on the left (east) side of the highway. Turn left and go through the gate, which is unlocked. Drive on the old road about 0.30 miles and park.

TRAILHEAD: No signs posted. You walk the old road.

DESCRIPTION:
From Highway 89A you can see the unlocked gate to your left. Go through it and drive down the dirt road for about 0.30 miles. The road is good to this point and any car can make it that far. If you want to try to shorten the hike, you can drive farther if you have a high clearance vehicle. You will reach a bad place in the road at about 0.50 miles where the road dips down into the Dry Creek streambed. The road is steep here and suffers lots of damage from washouts. Most vehicles, even with high clearance, should park here, at the hilltop. Don't go down to the river unless you are a hardy soul and are equipped with a high clearance four-wheel drive vehicle.
In the old days this road was the main road south of Sedona. It was the only wagon road connecting Sedona to the Verde Valley, Cottonwood and Jerome. The right of way was a good one and might have been preserved except for the fact that it crosses Dry Creek at creek level. Dry Creek isn't always dry. It carries water every spring when the snow in the high country is melting, and after hard rains, and at such times may be impassable. Every now and then a real gully-washer comes along and rips things up, requiring a rebuilding. The

present location of Highway 89A crosses Dry Creek on a good high bridge, thereby avoiding the flooding problem.

The scenery along the road is not very interesting, but the road provides a good stroll as it is open, flat and wide. You get some good views.

The road ends on the Lower Red Rock Loop Road, which was paved in 1990. There are horse stables here and you will run into a profusion of horse trails near the end of the hike. The main old road is obvious because it is so much bigger than the horse trails, so if you stay on it, you will have no trouble finding your way.

The area where Old Highway 79 meets the Lower Red Rock Loop Road used to be called Elmerville, a name that has now faded into disuse. There was and is a collection of small homes at the site and it may even have had its own post office at one time. It was a natural way station on the old road. After doing this hike, you can impress your friends by casually mentioning that you went to Elmerville last weekend.

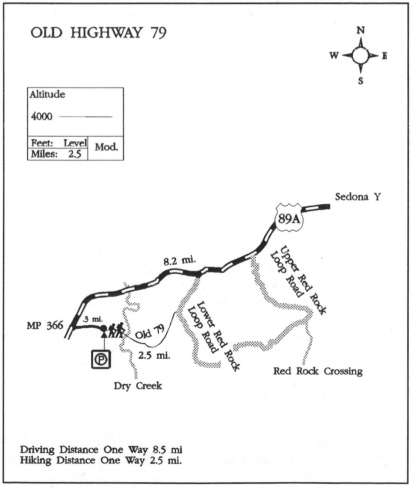

OLD HIGHWAY 79

N
W — E
S

Altitude

4000 ————

| Feet: Level | Mod. |
| Miles: 2.5 | |

Sedona Y

89A

8.2 mi.

Upper Red Rock Loop Road

Lower Red Rock Loop Road

MP 366   .3 mi.

Old 79

2.5 mi.

Red Rock Crossing

Dry Creek

Driving Distance One Way 8.5 mi
Hiking Distance One Way 2.5 mi.

OLD JIM THOMPSON ROAD

General Information
Location Map D4
Munds Park and Wilson Mt. USGS Maps
Coconino Forest Service Map

Driving Distance One Way: 1.2 miles (Time 10 minutes)
Access Road: All cars, Last 0.2 miles good gravel road
Hiking Distance One Way: 3.5 miles (Time 2 hours)
How Strenuous: Moderate
Features: Rock formations, Views

NUTSHELL: Located in uptown Sedona's backyard, this old road takes you from a point near the end of Jordan Road to Wilson Canyon at Midgley Bridge.

DIRECTIONS:
From the Sedona Y Go:
North on Highway 89A (toward Flagstaff) for a distance of 0.3 miles to Jordan Road. Turn left onto Jordan Road. Follow it to the end. You will run out of paving and see signs indicating that the road ends, but do not be bothered by that, as the paving simply changes into a good gravel road. Drive toward the Shooting Range. You will see a sign for it. At 1.1 miles you will reach an intersection. The road to your right is a private drive. Go left here toward the Shooting Range. Before you get to the Shooting Range, at 1.2 miles, you will come to a closed road on your right marked FR 633. Park here.

TRAILHEAD: Not marked as a hiking trail. You hike the closed road, FR 633.

DESCRIPTION: You will walk along the old wagon road built by Jim Thompson in the early 1900s. The entrance to the old road is blocked by a row of boulders. Fools every now and then drive around this blockade and try their macho skills on FR 633. We would not take any truck we ever owned over FR 633. We have seen a couple of full-sized pickups high center on giant rocks on this road and tear up their undercarriages getting loose.

You will come to an unlocked metal gate across the road at about the 0.50 mile point. There are good views down onto Sedona as you walk along the road. You also have fine views back toward Brins Mesa. The road goes along the base of Wilson Mountain and winds around the bottom of **Steamboat Rock**.

At 1.0 miles, just beyond a powerline, you will find a weather-beaten sign, with a trail forking off to your right. This path to the right is the only private hiking trail that we know of in Sedona. It goes 1.0 miles down to the Red Rock Lodge, a motel on the north side of Sedona on Highway 89A. It was built by the people at the lodge for their guests.

Just beyond this trail junction you will walk around the base of Steamboat Rock, a favorite Sedona landmark. It really does look like a steamboat with a tall "funnel" rising above a "deck." At 2.0 miles you will reach Steamboat Tank, (worth a visit) uphill to your left.

The road ends where it comes down to **Wilson Canyon**. There are many trails around Wilson Canyon and things can be confusing. It helps to think of the terrain. Wilson Canyon is deep and building a bridge across it in the old days would have been much too expensive. Therefore the road went to the head of the canyon where it pinches into a narrow V and then went back out to the mouth. You can see abutments where the original Highway 89A bridged the canyon near the narrow point of the V. Midgley Bridge was constructed years later to span Wilson Canyon at its mouth.

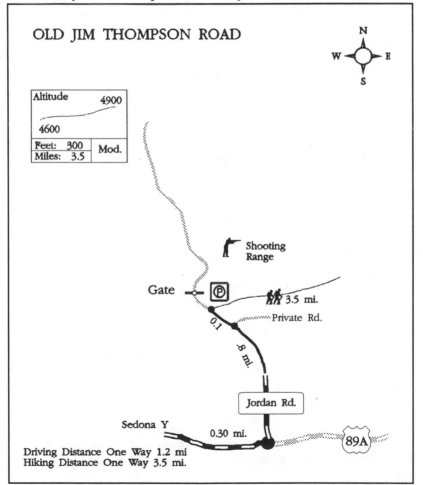

OLD JIM THOMPSON ROAD

N
W — E
S

Altitude 4900
4600
Feet: 300 | Mod.
Miles: 3.5

Shooting Range

Gate — P

3.5 mi.

0.1

Private Rd.

.8 mi.

Jordan Rd.

Sedona Y
0.30 mi.
89A

Driving Distance One Way 1.2 mi
Hiking Distance One Way 3.5 mi.

OLD SCHNEBLY HILL ROAD

General Information
Location Map D5
Munds Mt. and Munds Park USGS Maps
Coconino Forest Service Map

Driving Distance One Way: 5.5 miles (Time 30 minutes)
Access Road: All cars, Last 4.2 miles good gravel road
Hiking Distance One Way: 1.1 miles (Time 45 minutes)
How Strenuous: Moderate
Features: Historic road, Views

NUTSHELL: This is a scrambling, bushwhacking experience just off the Schnebly Hill Road, only a mile east of Sedona as the crow flies.

DIRECTIONS:
From the Sedona Y Go:
        South on Highway 179 (toward Phoenix) for a distance of 0.3 miles (MP 312.8) to the Schnebly Hill Road. It is just across the bridge past Tlaquepaque. Turn left onto the Schnebly Hill Road. It is paved for the first mile and then turns into a gravel road that is all right for any car unless the road is muddy. At 5.0 miles you will see a gate made of very thick steel pipes. This is used to close the road in winter. Half a mile above this gate you will see a knoll to your left with a parking area big enough for four cars. Park there.

TRAILHEAD: To get onto the old road, walk down the present road about twenty yards from where you have parked. You will see what looks like a drainage ditch coming down. Clamber up the bank and you're on your way. The old road is unmistakable from here.

DESCRIPTION: The present road was realigned at the point where you parked to curve around a promontory and goes to the top now by a gentler grade. There is nothing subtle about the old road. It just climbs up in a straight line.
        As you walk along the old road you will have fascinating and ever changing views to the west. First you will look down into the Bear Wallow-Mitten Ridge area. As you move farther south (uphill) you will begin to see around the south end of the ridge into Sedona. At the top you can see right through a natural corridor into the Verde Valley. There are many superb vista points.
        Look at the soil and rocks as you ascend and you will get a mini-geology lesson. First you are in the familiar red sand. Then you reach gray basalt. Then an outcrop of buff-colored sandstone, then more basalt. It's a real

layer cake.

At 0.80 miles, near the top, you reach a grove of trees. Farther along is a beautiful stand of oaks through which the road carves a tunnel. There are some fine lava cliffs and boulders here too. Near where the power line crosses overhead the road divides, having an inside-outside lane. Grandfather's idea of a freeway? Look for a line of flat stones across the road there and you can appreciate the difficulties of early roadbuilding when builders didn't have the equipment and resources we have today. The stones make a culvert.

At the 1.0 mile point look to your right just at the top of the grade and you will see the ruins of an old stone chimney and the stem wall of a cabin. Traveler's hut? Sheepherder's cabin?

At the top the road swings north and the trees thin out. It's relatively bare there, giving some great viewpoints along the rim. The road connects to the present Schnebly Hill Road just above Schnebly Hill Vista, 1.2 miles away.

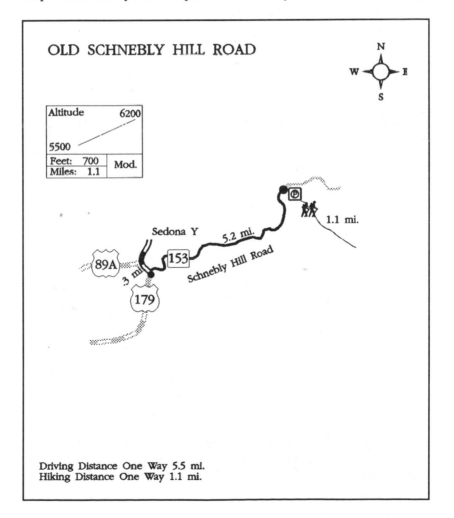

PARSONS TRAIL

General Information
Location Map F1
Clarkdale and Sycamore Basin USGS Maps
Coconino Forest Service Map

Driving Distance One Way: 34.3 miles (Time 1 hour)
Access Road: All cars, Last 10.5 miles good dirt road
Hiking Distance One Way: 4.0 miles (Time 2 hours)
How Strenuous: Moderate
Features: Tremendous canyon, Year around stream

NUTSHELL: This trail enters the south end of Sycamore Canyon, 34.3 miles southwest of Sedona. It is the easiest trail into the canyon.

DIRECTIONS:
From The Y in Sedona Go:
Southwest on Highway 89A a distance of 19.4 miles, which will take you into the town of Cottonwood. Go straight through Cottonwood on Main Street and then on Broadway, headed toward Tuzigoot National Monument. At 23.4 miles you will reach the road to Tuzigoot. Turn right onto it and follow it to the 23.8 mile point, just over the bridge. You will see signs there for the Verde Valley Country Club and Sycamore Canyon Wilderness. Turn left on this dirt road, which is FR 131. Stay on FR 131 to the 34.3 mile point, which is a parking area at the top of Sycamore Canyon.

TRAILHEAD: The trail is well marked at the parking area. A rusty sign reads, "Parsons Trail #144."

DESCRIPTION: On this hike you enter the south end of Sycamore Canyon at a point where the canyon walls are not as tall as they are upstream. The walls display interesting rock formations. The hue of the red stone is rosier than the rock in Sedona. It is mixed with white rock and is very rough, grainy and chunky. Basalt is blended in, rather than being a cap as it is in Sedona.
The trail follows along Sycamore Creek, usually on the right bank, though it does cross the creek twice. It is fairly level. In all but extremely dry years, water runs year around up to Parsons Spring at 4.0 miles, so you have the pleasant experience of walking beside running water. The vegetation is lush. Cows often graze through the area.
The canyon for the first two miles seems wide and spacious. At 1.3 miles you will reach Summers Spring. It usually seeps water across the trail. Although the water looks clear and pure, the Forest Service advises not to drink

it unless you treat it. Also be careful about eating the watercress growing there.

Upstream from Summers Spring the trail gets rough. A heavy flood in 1980 tore out a lot of the trail and the Forest Service has lacked funds to restore it. In spots you have to scramble over boulders. Keep moving near the streambed and you will pick up the surviving parts of the trail every time you pass one of the washouts. You will encounter several large pools that hold fish.

Sycamore Canyon is in a mineralized zone and before it became a Wilderness Area some mining occurred there. You will pass the entrance to an agate mine at 2.7 miles. It has been plugged but bits of hardware are still around.

The canyon narrows and the walls get steeper as you work your way up the canyon. You will reach Parsons Spring at 4.0 miles. Above this point the stream is only intermittent. This is the place to stop for a day hike. The trail continues but becomes very difficult and is for experienced prepared hikers only.

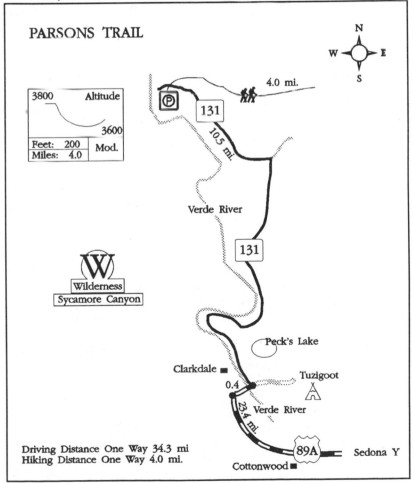

PINK SAND CANYON

General Information
Location Map B5
Mountainaire USGS Map
Coconino Forest Service Map

Driving Distance One Way: 12.7 miles (Time 20 minutes)
Access Road: All cars, All paved
Hiking Distance One Way: 0.25 miles (Time 30 minutes)
How Strenuous: Easy
Features: Scenic canyon

NUTSHELL: Starting at the Pine Flat Campground in upper Oak Creek Canyon, this hike takes you across the creek and up an unusual narrow canyon, the floor of which is covered with pink sand.

DIRECTIONS:
From the Sedona Y Go:

North on Highway 89A (toward Flagstaff) for a distance of 12.7 miles (MP 386.9) to the Pine Flat Campground. On your left at the upper end of the campground on the shoulder of the highway, you will see a structure about 5 feet high and 4 feet square made of round stones that houses a spring. Park anywhere near here. There are wide aprons on both shoulders in this area.

TRAILHEAD: Go into the campground at the north entrance just below the standpipe. A roadway branches to the right as you enter. Take it. It becomes unpaved and goes down to Oak Creek, where you will find a concrete driveway going across the creek. This is the trailhead. It is unmarked.

DESCRIPTION: The water in the spring at the Pine Flat campground is pure. You will see many people stop off here and fill bottles and jugs for drinking water. We do this ourselves every time we go into Oak Creek Canyon. Caution: with any spring water, even though it tests pure, there are natural microbes in the water. Local residents are used to these microbes and their immune systems can handle them. This may not be true of visitors; so be careful. Just because you see someone drinking from a spring doesn't mean that the water is good for *you.*

From creekside, walk across the concrete pad and follow the old sunken road you will find on the other side. After walking it a short distance you will come to a three-way fork. Take the center road here, which is still a sunken lane. In about 0.1 mile this road will wind around to a point under a power line, where you will see it turn into a footpath heading west into a canyon.

Follow this trail into the canyon. Although the trail is not posted, it is distinct at the entrance to the canyon. It goes up on the top of the bank until it is about half way up the canyon. There it reaches a place where it is better to hike down into the canyon bottom and follow it the rest of the way.

You will find the bottom of this attractive canyon covered with an unusual pink sand, almost a coral color. The canyon is narrow, getting narrower as it goes. A thousand feet above your head are soaring white cliffs, though you will be walking in redrock.

At a point 0.25 miles from the beginning, the canyon becomes a narrow slot choked with boulders. It would take a lot of effort to scramble over these boulders, so most hikers will want to quit in this spot, where you can see the canyon end in a few hundred yards ahead of you in a beautiful box.

This hike is shaded all the way and would be cool even in summer. It is a little known but delightful adventure.

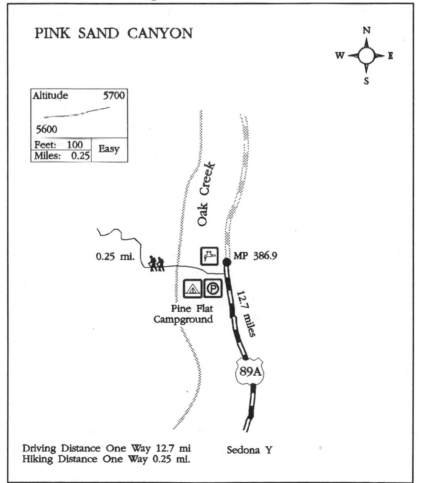

PINK SAND CANYON

Altitude	5700
5600	
Feet: 100	Easy
Miles: 0.25	

0.25 mi.

Oak Creek

MP 386.9

12.7 miles

Pine Flat
Campground

89A

Driving Distance One Way 12.7 mi
Hiking Distance One Way 0.25 mi.

Sedona Y

PUMPHOUSE WASH

General Information
Location Map B5
Mountainaire USGS Map
Coconino Forest Service Map

Driving Distance One Way: 13.5 miles (Time 20 minutes)
Access Road: All cars, All paved
Hiking Distance One Way: 1.5 miles (Time 1.5 hours)
How Strenuous: Moderate
Features: Scenic canyon

NUTSHELL: Pumphouse Wash is a tributary canyon meeting Oak Creek at the bottom of the Highway 89A switchbacks. There is no trail. You rock hop along the canyon bottom, enjoying the sight of immense towering cliffs, redrock sculptures and a get-away-from-it-all feeling.

DIRECTIONS:
From the Sedona Y Go:
　　　　North on Highway 89A (toward Flagstaff) for a distance of 13.5 miles (MP 387.7) to the bridge that spans Pumphouse Wash. It is posted. Below (south) of the bridge there is a wide apron that will hold a couple of cars on the right hand side of the road (east), or you can cross the bridge and park on a wide apron on the left side of the road (south).

TRAILHEAD: There is no marking or official trail. Look for a way down into the bottom of the wash. There are paths from both parking areas.

DESCRIPTION: Once you are in the canyon bottom, you walk along the streambed in an upstream direction, away from Oak Creek. The bottom is strewn with large boulders and you have to jump from rock to rock. As a result of this, the hike is harder than the mileage and altitude would seem to indicate.
　　　　Pumphouse Wash does not carry water year around. During the spring snowmelt it can run high, but after the first of June it is usually dry except for a few pools. The trick is to make the hike when there is enough water in the wash to add to the enjoyment of the hike but not so much as to make it impassable. Try mid-May. If you see water running under the bridge, there is too much water to make the hike.
　　　　Soon after you enter the canyon, your attention will turn from the boulders under your feet to the vertical dimension. The walls of the canyon are extremely high and sheer, giving the hiker a real awestruck feeling of just how small humans are in the scale of things.

At about 0.3 miles you will reach the first of a chain of half a dozen pools. These are situated so that you cannot bypass them, but must go through them. Depending on how much water is present, this can mean anything from walking, wading or swimming. When the water is low, an old pair of tennies is good gear. You just wade through and keep on going, walking in wet shoes. If the water is deep enough, there are some good swimming holes.

You will be out of the pool zone in about 0.6 miles and soon after will see a transition. The rock you hike on changes from white to red. We love this middle part of Pumphouse Wash. It seems virgin and primitive. Oak Creek Canyon itself must have looked like this before it was developed. The cutting action of the water has carved chutes and swirls and all kinds of fascinating sculptures in this red stone. You will see evidence of beaver activity.

We think that the 1.5 mile point is a good place to stop the hike, the place where the redrock disappears and you get into a region of basalt, the gray caprock.

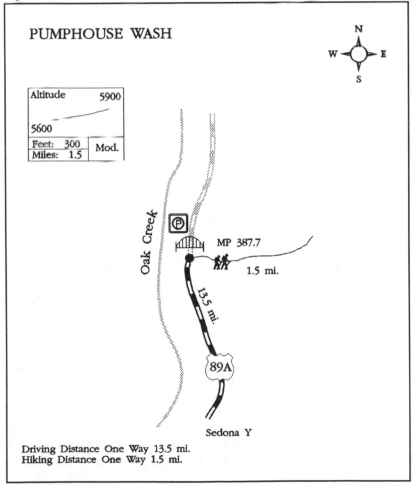

PUMPHOUSE WASH

N
W — E
S

Altitude   5900

5600

Feet: 300   Mod.
Miles: 1.5

Oak Creek

MP 387.7

1.5 mi.

13.5 mi.

89A

Sedona Y

Driving Distance One Way 13.5 mi.
Hiking Distance One Way 1.5 mi.

PURTYMUN TRAIL

General Information
Location Map B5
Munds Park and Wilson Mt. USGS Maps
Coconino Forest Service Map

Driving Distance One Way: 8.4 miles (Time 20 minutes)
Access Road: All cars, All paved
Hiking Distance One Way: 1.0 miles (Time 1 hour)
How Strenuous: Hard
Features: Views

NUTSHELL: This hard hike climbs the east wall of Oak Creek Canyon from a point directly across Highway 89A from the Junipine Resort in the upper canyon, 8.4 miles north of Sedona. The trail is in poor condition.

DIRECTIONS:
From the Sedona Y Go:
North on Highway 89A (toward Flagstaff) for a distance of 8.4 miles (MP 382.6) to the entrance to the Junipine Resort, which is on your left (west). There are some public parking spaces at the north end of the property, adjacent to the highway.

TRAILHEAD: There are no markings for this trail. Go across the highway to the Fire Station. The trail starts there.

DESCRIPTION: The people at Junipine have created a parking lot at the north end of their property that has space for several cars. If it is full then park along the road shoulder nearby. The trailhead is not conspicuous. You will see a Fire Station across the highway from the resort. The trail starts at the south side of the Fire Station where there is a yellow fire plug.
This trail was built by the Purtymun family, which homesteaded the Junipine property in the late 1800s. Like other families in the canyon they needed a way to get to the rim so that they could go to Flagstaff, so they built this trail. They did not have sophisticated equipment, just picks, shovels, crowbars and maybe a little dynamite. Their practice was to leave a wagon at the top. When they wanted to go to town they would walk a horse to the top, hitch it to the wagon and then drive to Flagstaff. In town they would load the wagon with goods, perhaps bartering some of the vegetables and fruits they had grown for flour and coffee. They would then drive the wagon back to Oak Creek Canyon and chain it to a tree at the top of the trail. After that they would carry the goods down in saddlebags. Such a trip could take three or four days.

In spite of the hardships of using the trail, the alternative was worse. There was no convenient wagon road from Sedona to Flagstaff until the Schnebly Hill Road was built in 1902. Before that the only wagon road was the old **Beaverhead** route several miles farther south. Highway 89A did not come onto the scene until much later. It was built in phases starting in the early 1920s, and it took a decade to complete.

This trail is so steep and so rough that we don't see how the Purtymuns could ever have gotten a horse up and down it. It is hard climbing for a human, who can grab onto trees for support. We rate this the worst kept and most difficult trail in the book. We do not recommend this hike but we include it as an historic trail.

If you want a good hike up the east rim of upper Oak Creek Canyon try **Cookstove**, **Harding Spring** or **Thomas Point**. They are all decent trails and though they are steep they show some signs of care and a bit of engineering.

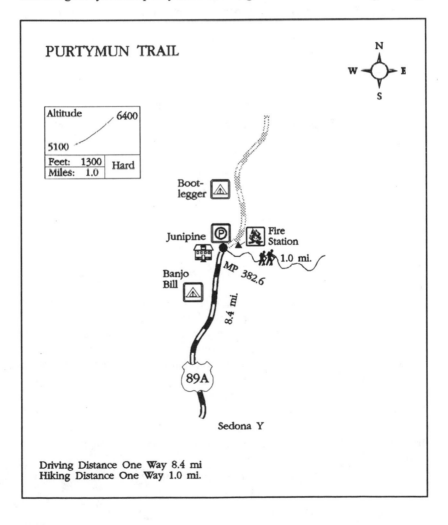

PURTYMUN TRAIL

Altitude 6400
5100
Feet: 1300 Hard
Miles: 1.0

Boot-legger

Junipine

Fire Station

1.0 mi.

MP 382.6

Banjo Bill

8.4 mi.

89A

Sedona Y

Driving Distance One Way 8.4 mi
Hiking Distance One Way 1.0 mi.

RATTLESNAKE CANYON

General Information
Location Map G5
Munds Mt. USGS Map
Coconino Forest Service Map

Driving Distance One Way: 23.0 miles (Time 45 minutes)
Access Road: All cars, Last 1.0 miles medium gravel
Hiking Distance One Way: 0.75 miles (Time 30 minutes)
How Strenuous: Moderate
Features: Remote scenic canyon

NUTSHELL: This trail takes you to the bottom of Rattlesnake Canyon, a little known beautiful spot.

DIRECTIONS:
From the Sedona Y Go:
    South on Highway 179 (toward Phoenix) for 14.7 miles, to the I-17 Interchange. Turn north and head toward Flagstaff on I-17. At the 22.0 mile spot you will see Exit 306 "Stoneman Lake" (MP 306.1). Make this exit. Go under I-17 into the lane marked south, to Phoenix, but look for a dirt road to your right (west), FR 647, just beyond the underpass. Turn off onto FR 647. For the first 0.75 miles it is in good condition except for one gully. At the 22.75 mile point you reach a T. Turn right here. The road becomes much worse, bare dirt with lots of ruts and rocks. Most cars should be able to make it to the 23.0 mile point, beyond which the road is too rough. Pull off the road and park.

TRAILHEAD: There are no signs. You walk the road to the canyon rim and then hike down to the bottom.

DESCRIPTION: If you park at the 23.0 mile point as we recommend, then you will have to walk about one-quarter of a mile to get to the canyon.
    You won't have to ask *what* canyon. As you near the rim you can see it plainly. This is one of those hidden canyons that you don't see from anywhere unless you fly over it. But it is a deep and interesting canyon. The walls are quite sheer and are made of successive layers of columnar-jointed basalt. There are many such canyons in northern Arizona, but this one has more color and character than most.
    At the canyon rim you will see that the road goes down into the canyon but that no one drives it. Walk down the road. The road will disappear in about 0.10 miles.
    Beyond this point you will find a footpath in good condition. It is a

real walking path, with erosion control and other improvements and you can see that a lot of work has been done on it. It is not a recreational trail, but is used to provide access to the gaging station that you will find at the bottom.

We think the rock walls you pass by are interesting and have some beautiful markings, including accents made by lichens and mosses.

At the bottom you will find a cable strung across the canyon and the gaging station, which is a sort of tall corrugated tube with a box on top. There is a depth gauge on the front of the tube showing depths as high as ten feet.

Beyond this there is a waterfall with a thirty foot drop. Water was running over it while we were there and it seemed dangerous to climb. Other sources indicate that one can climb down it, but we do not recommend dangerous climbing. From this point, Rattlesnake Canyon joins **Woods Canyon** in about 2.25 miles. It is a satisfying hike just to sit at the waterfall. If you want to explore the canyon, go upstream. It is interesting for about 0.5 miles. It joins I-17 about 1.5 miles from the waterfall.

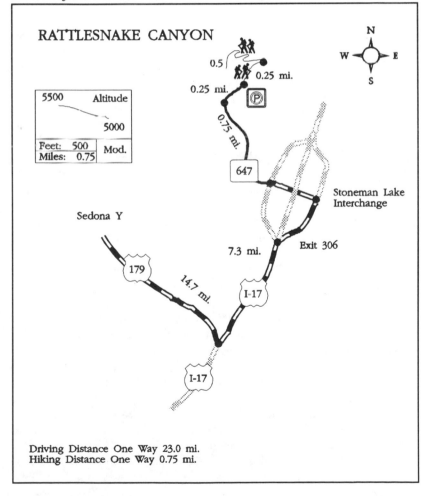

RATTLESNAKE CANYON

RATTLESNAKE RIDGE TRAIL

General Information
Location Map F3
Sedona USGS Map
Coconino Forest Service Map

Driving Distance One Way: 8.6 miles (Time 15 minutes)
Access Road: All vehicles, All paved
Hiking Distance, Complete Loop: 0.25 miles (Time 15 minutes)
How Strenuous: Easy
Features: Easy access, Red Rock State Park, Views

NUTSHELL: This easy trail is located in Red Rock State Park 8.6 miles southwest of Sedona. It takes you part way up a hill at a picnic site for views of the park area.

DIRECTIONS:
From the Sedona Y Go:
    Southwest on Highway 89A (toward Cottonwood) for a distance of 5.5 miles (MP 368.6) to the Lower Red Rock Loop Road. Turn left on the Lower Red Rock Loop Road and follow it to the 8.5 miles point, where you will see the entry to Red Rock State Park. Turn right into the park. You will come to a toll booth where an admission is charged. From that point, drive into the park 0.1 miles to the Twin Cypress Picnic Area. Turn left into the picnic area and drive over to the ramada (the roof-covered picnic tables) where you park.

TRAILHEAD: You will see the trailhead straight ahead of you about twenty yards at the base of a low hill. The trail goes up this hill.

DESCRIPTION: Soon after you begin hiking up the hill you will reach a fork. You can go either left or right here; it doesn't matter, because you are entering a loop.
    The high point of the loop is a viewpoint with a bench. The trail doesn't even go to the top of the hill, so the views are not sweeping. From the viewpoint you descend and are back to the ramada *tout suite.*
    There isn't much to this trail, it's just a leg stretcher, a good way to work off a little of the food that you ate while enjoying the picnic area.
    There are scary signs about rattlesnakes, and the name itself would put you on guard. Don't panic. Rattlers are in the area all right, but it's not as if there is one under every rock. Our motto in this regard, as in all areas around Sedona is, "Be watchful but not paranoid."
    Red Rock State Park is a tremendous addition to public recreation

around Sedona. The property began as a number of small ranches. Several decades ago, one of the high officials in TWA, Jack Frye, an aviation pioneer, and his wife Helen fell in love with the place as a retreat. They bought some of the ranches and consolidated them. They are the people who built the House of Apache Fire. The couple was later divorced and Helen received the property, together with another ranch down the road. She lived in the area until her death and was a noted patron of the arts. She left the land to Eckankar in her will. The State of Arizona acquired the land and added to it some of the other ranches, finally putting it all together in the park that you can enjoy today.

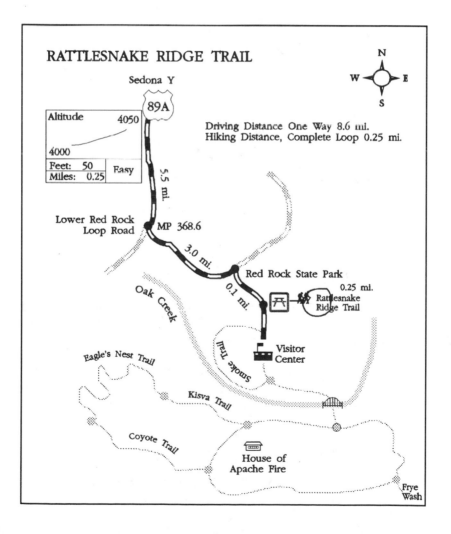

RED CANYON RUINS

General Information
Location Map C2
Loy Butte and Page Springs USGS Maps
Coconino Forest Service Map

Driving Distance One Way: 17.4 miles (Time 30 minutes)
Access Road: All cars, Last 7.8 miles good dirt road
Hiking Distance One Way: 1.5 miles (Time 1 Hour)
How Strenuous: Easy
Features: Indian ruins, Pictographs, Caves

NUTSHELL: This adventure takes you to the Palatki Indian Ruins 17.4 miles northwest of Sedona for a short jaunt to cliff dwellings and a meander along the base of Bear Mountain to see pictographs and caves.

DIRECTIONS:
From the Sedona Y Go:
Southwest on Highway 89A (toward Cottonwood) a distance of 9.6 miles (MP 364.5) to the Red Canyon Road. Turn right on Red Canyon Road, (FR 525) and follow it to the 12.4 mile point where FR 525C branches to the left. Stay on FR 525, the road to the right. Follow FR 525 to the 15.4 mile point, where it intersects the Boynton Pass Road, FR 152C. Stay on FR 525, the road to the left. At 15.6 miles you will reach an intersection with FR 795. Turn right here on FR 795. At 17.4 miles you will come to the parking area.

TRAILHEAD: There are signs at the parking area.

DESCRIPTION: At the parking area you will see three signs. You will also find a box that contains a self-guiding trail brochure. The middle trail is the one to the main ruins. You will walk through the yard of a ranch house toward red cliffs. In about 0.20 miles you will reach the main ruins. These are in two shallow caves. The first ruin is the smaller one, containing two chambers on the first level. It appears to have had a second story for a total of eight rooms. The second ruin is larger and also contained eight chambers. The walls of the ruins are well preserved even to the juniper poles that supported doors and windows. The view to the south across the Verde Valley and over to the Black Hills is superb. If the light is right you can see Jerome.
Retrace your path to the bottom where the path began its short climb to the ruins. To the right you will see another path hugging the same cliff face. If you follow this you will find a couple of small caves. One contains a six-room ruin and the other contains some farm equipment, lumber, etc.

This is a short easy trip so far. Since you are here you should take one of the other paths. We recommend the one that was to the left from where you parked. It goes up to the base of the red cliffs to the left of the ranch house. This trail takes you to a series of caves at the base of a butte. In the first cave you will find what appears at first to be an ancient ruin but is really a 1920s dwelling made on the premises before the ranch house was built. A string of caves continues for about a mile. The caves contain the largest collection of rock art in the Verde Valley area, ranging from art of the ancient Sinagua to the more modern Apaches. They also contain a few inscriptions by Anglo pioneers. This cave exploring ends in a black cave that has the inscription "M. F. Farrell 1900" written high on its wall.

Modern occupation of the site began in the mid-1920s when Charles Willard, a pioneer of Cottonwood, decided to try fruit ranching and farming at Red Canyon. He had over two thousand fruit trees here in the late 1930s. He gave up and returned to Cottonwood after an almost fatal accident.

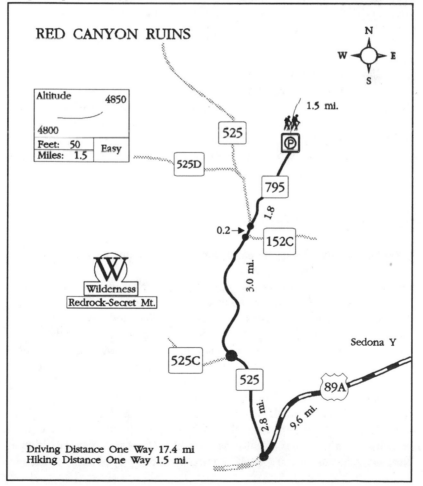

RED TANK DRAW

General Information
Location Map G6
Apache Maid and Casner Butte. USGS Maps
Coconino Forest Service Map

Driving Distance One Way: 16.1 miles (Time 30 minutes)
Access Road: All cars, Last 1.4 miles good gravel road
Hiking Distance One Way: 0.9 miles (Time 1 hour)
How Strenuous: Moderate
Features: Intermittent stream, Picturesque cliffs

NUTSHELL: This hike follows the course of Red Tank Draw, 16.1 miles southeast of Sedona, in the Wet Beaver Creek country. You walk along the streambed enjoying a beautiful little canyon.

DIRECTIONS:
From the Sedona Y Go:
　　South on Highway 179 (toward Phoenix) for 14.7 miles, to the I-17 Interchange. Instead of going onto I-17, go underneath it onto the dirt road. At 15.2 miles, you will come to a junction. The right fork goes to Montezuma Castle. Take the left fork (FR 618). It is a good dirt road. At 16.1 miles, you will see a sign reading, "Red Tank Draw" located just in front of a small bridge. There is a dirt road to the left here. Pull in on it and park.

TRAILHEAD: There is no designated or marked trail. You go down into the streambed and walk the canyon upstream (north).

DESCRIPTION: From the parking place, you simply walk down to the streambed at any place you choose. It is easy to enter it anywhere in this area because the canyon walls are low. Farther upstream the walls become higher.
　　The best time we found for this hike was in late April, when the stream was carrying just enough water to be interesting. We tried it in early April and the runoff waters were too high for hiking. You can hike it when it is dry also, which is most of the year, but we think a little running water adds interest.
　　At the place where you go into the canyon there are two forks. It doesn't much matter which fork you choose to hike, as they will merge upstream. This is a rock hopping hike, as the bottom of the draw is boulder strewn. Such hikes can be fun but they are hard on the feet.
　　As you move upstream, the canyon will deepen. At about 0.6 miles you come to a narrow spot with sheer red walls, not tremendously high as Northern Arizona canyons go, about thirty feet, but very pleasing to the eye.

The area is one of geologic uplifts, the result of which has been to twist the rock into some very interesting angles. Look for swallows' nests throughout this area. The birds make their nests by cementing countless beakfuls of mud dabs into globular nests that hang from the underside of rock shelves. They are about the size of a baseball.

You will move out of the most scenic part of Red Tank Draw soon afterwards. At 0.9 miles you will come to an old barbed wire fence with a gate. We think this is a good stopping place for the hike, though we have gone much farther.

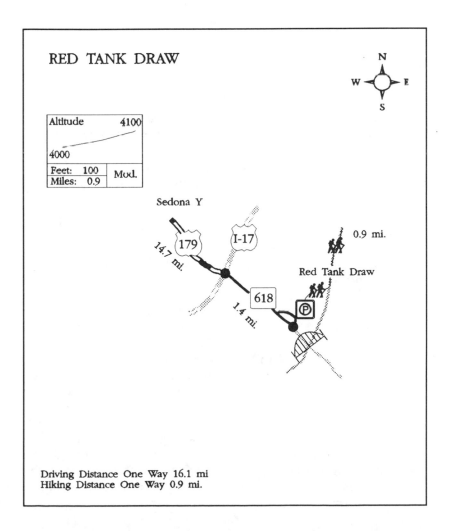

RED TANK DRAW

N
W — E
S

Altitude   4100
4000
Feet: 100   Mod.
Miles: 0.9

Sedona Y

14.7 mi. 179   I-17   0.9 mi.

618   Red Tank Draw

1.4 mi.   ⓟ

Driving Distance One Way 16.1 mi
Hiking Distance One Way 0.9 mi.

ROBBERS ROOST

General Information
Location Map C1
Loy Butte and Page Springs USGS Maps
Coconino Forest Service Map

Driving Distance One Way: 19.2 miles (Time 30 minutes)
Access Road: All cars, Last 9.6 miles good dirt road
Hiking Distance One Way: 1.5 miles (Time 45 minutes)
How Strenuous: Easy
Features: Fascinating cave with unique window

NUTSHELL: This is a short hike to an interesting cave in a red butte located 19.2 miles northwest of Sedona.

DIRECTIONS:
From the Sedona Y Go:
      Southwest on Highway 89A (toward Cottonwood) a distance of 9.6 miles (MP 364.5) to the Red Canyon Road. Turn right on Red Canyon Road, also known as FR 525, and follow it to the 12.4 mile point where FR 525C branches to the left. Turn left on FR 525C and follow it to the 19.2 miles point. There you will see a rough road branching to the right marked FR 9530. Take this but drive it only a short distance to the top of the hill, where you will park.

TRAILHEAD: You walk up the road, FR 9530, for 1.1 miles. There you will see the trail going down into a ravine to your right. It is not signed.

DESCRIPTION: If you have a high clearance vehicle and tough tires you can drive right up to the trailhead and save a mile of walking, but don't try to make it in an ordinary passenger car.
      As you walk up the road you approach Casner Mountain. Your object is the muffin shaped red butte just in front of and on the right hand side of the mountain. Robbers Roost is located on the far side of that butte.
      At the trailhead you will see an area to your left where the vegetation is matted down because of cars parking there. Look for the trail to your right. Usually there are cairns marking the beginning of the trail. The trail goes straight downhill into the bottom of a ravine, then goes up the other side.
      The trail, after rising from the bottom of the ravine, curls around to the far side of the butte and climbs about two-thirds of the way to the top of it. At 0.35 miles from the beginning of the trail, the trail forks. The right fork goes to the top. Ignore it for now and take the left fork. This will require that you walk out on the face of the butte on the slickrock (a misnomer, as the rock

actually gives very good traction, like sandpaper). As you go around the bend of the rock you will see two metal rods five feet high sticking vertically out of the rock face.

After that you will see the cave. Rock walls have been built at the mouth of the cave to support some dirt fill that was placed there to make the floor of the cave level. There are even steps to the "door" of the cave.

The cave looks out to the Northeast, toward Bear Mountain and Maroon Mountain. Down below it there is a cattle tank.

There is a circular window in the cave that looks more to the south. This window is unique. There is nothing else like it in the Sedona area. The cave gets its name, Robbers Roost, from the fanciful notion that this would be a good hideout for robbers, who could use the window as a lookout without revealing themselves.

On your way back out it is worthwhile to go to the top of the butte. It is an easy climb and the views are excellent.

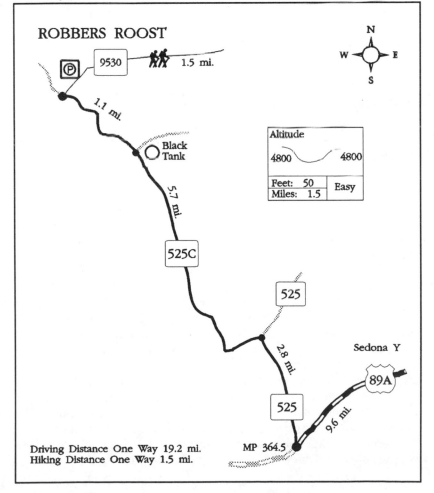

SACRED MOUNTAIN

General Information
Location Map G6
Casner Butte USGS Map
Coconino Forest Service Map

Driving Distance One Way: 18.0 miles (Time 30 minutes)
Access Road: All cars, Last 3.3 miles good dirt road
Hiking Distance One Way: 0.35 miles (Time 30 minutes)
How Strenuous: Moderate
Features: Indian ruins, Views

NUTSHELL: Located 18.0 miles southeast of Sedona, this special mountain takes moderate effort to climb. At the top are pueblo ruins and fine views.

DIRECTIONS:
From the Sedona Y Go:
　　　　South on Highway 179 (toward Phoenix) for 14.7 miles, to the I-17 Interchange. Instead of going onto I-17, go underneath it onto the dirt road. At 15.2 miles, you will come to a junction. The right fork goes to Montezuma Castle. Take the left fork (FR 618). It is a good dirt road. At 17.3 miles you will reach a three-way fork. Take the middle road here, which is FR 618. At 17.8 miles as the road is curving right, you will see a dirt road, FR 9201A, to your left. Pull off on this. You will see that the road leads to a fence. Try to get as close to the fence as you can (it's about 0.2 miles) and park.

TRAILHEAD: You will not see a trail sign. Go through the gate and turn right and walk parallel to the fence. The path is obvious.

DESCRIPTION: The mountains that are constantly on the northern horizon as you drive through the Beaver Creek area are all part of the Mogollon Rim, a giant uplift that runs from Silver City, New Mexico to Ashfork, Arizona. As you come around a curve in the road, Sacred Mountain comes into sight. It is really more of a butte than a mountain in this country full of mountains, and it stands alone in front of the rim. It is set apart by its color. It is white, against the darker colors of the rim, which are gray, black and red. At times, when the low evening sun hits Sacred Mountain, the mountain seems to glow.
　　　　We saw a beautiful example of this one March evening when we were at the nearby Montezuma's Well (a recommended visit). From the top of the well we looked northwest and saw Sacred Mountain as if it were isolated by a spotlight, and it did seem to be something special. One can well understand why the ancient Indians thought that the mountain was sacred.

At the fence surrounding Sacred Mountain there is a small sign indicating that the ruins are protected by Federal law. Go through the gate and immediately turn right, walking along parallel to the fence. You will pick up the trail there and will see it going up the toe of the mountain that faces the road. The trail will take you to a sign with a register to add your name to. At the top of the mountain you will find extensive ruins that have been partially excavated. They have also been thoroughly pothunted, more's the pity. Please do not disturb them.

The site has not been restored, just investigated. The remains of many walls have been uncovered so that you can see the outline of the pueblo. It was a fairly large site, perhaps as large as Tuzigoot. A ranger at the visitor center at Tuzigoot told us that ruins have been found on a number of hills and buttes that formed a chain throughout the Verde Valley and the Beaver Creek country. These were in sight of each other, leading archaeologists to speculate that the Indians communicated by smoke signals or other means.

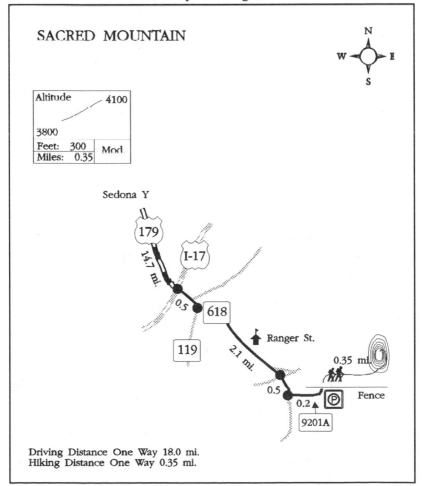

SACRED MOUNTAIN

Altitude 4100
3800
Feet: 300   Mod
Miles: 0.35

Sedona Y

179

14.7 mi.

I-17

0.5 618

Ranger St.

119

2.1 mi.

0.35 mi.

0.5 Fence

0.2 9201A

Driving Distance One Way 18.0 mi.
Hiking Distance One Way 0.35 mi.

SCHNEBLY HILL BUTTES

General Information
Location Map D5
Munds Mt. and Munds Park USGS Maps
Coconino Forest Service Map

Driving Distance One Way: 5.5 miles (Time 20 minutes)
Access Road: All cars, Last 4.2 miles good gravel road
Hiking Distance One Way: 0.60 miles (Time 45 minutes)
How Strenuous: Moderate
Features: Views, Fascinating rock formations and sculptures

NUTSHELL: This is a scrambling, bushwhacking experience just off the Schnebly Hill Road, only a mile east of Sedona as the crow flies.

DIRECTIONS:
From the Sedona Y Go:
 South on Highway 179 (toward Phoenix) for a distance of 0.3 miles (MP 312.8) to the Schnebly Hill Road. It is just across the bridge past Tlaquepaque. Turn left onto the Schnebly Hill Road. It is paved for the first mile and then turns into a gravel road that is all right for any car unless the road is muddy. At the 5.0 mile point, you will see a gate and a half mile beyond that a knoll to your left fronted by an apron big enough to hold three or four cars. Park on this apron.

TRAILHEAD: At the parking place.

DESCRIPTION: You park at the foot of a knoll. There you will see a footpath going straight up to the top of the knoll. Take it. On top you will see some fine views and you will find several paths heading toward the cliffs to the west.
 Look straight ahead to the west and you will see a tall butte across the valley. Pick out the main trail going toward the butte. As you reach the base of the butte, one trail will go to your left (south) skirting the base, while the other goes up. Go up. The trail is pretty easy except for one place where you must climb up a red stone ledge. You need to find the gap that makes this climb easy.
 You will top out on a saddle. To your left (south) you can go to a point jutting out into Bear Wallow Canyon. The right hand trail goes up to a taller butte.
 Try the south trail first. The point is narrow and has several stages or landings. You can walk around it for magnificent views. This is a real "Ah!" experience.
 If you are afraid of heights, adjust your comfort level as to how far out

on the point you want to go. Daredevils can walk right out to the cantilevered tip of a "diving board" where it's 1200 feet straight down to join Elvis. Sissies can stay well back on solid footing and still get great views.

It's fun to watch cars coming up the Schnebly Hill Road from this point. If they see you they will wonder how you got there and why you're foolishly risking your neck.

From the diving board it's on to the higher butte. It is an easier climb than you would expect from its appearance. The main path is quite distinct and gentle. The views are not as good as you would hope because another butte to the west partially blocks southward sights. You do have good views to the north.

Coming down is easy. The only trick is to find an easy-to-descend crevice in the sandstone ledge about halfway down.

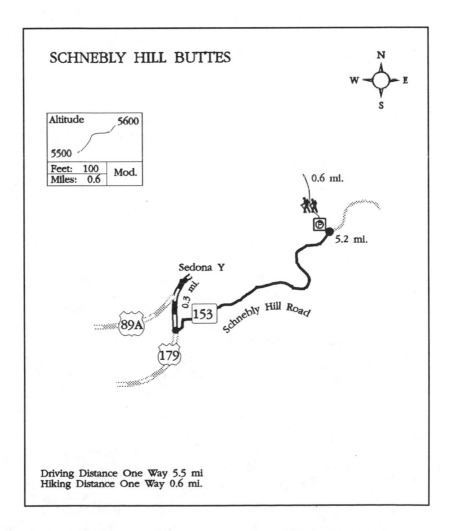

SCHNEBLY TO-MARG'S DRAW

General Information
Location Map E5
Sedona and Munds Mt. USGS Maps
Coconino Forest Service Map

Driving Distance One Way: 1.1 miles (Time 10 minutes)
Access Road: All cars, All paved
Hiking Distance One Way: 1.3 miles (Time 40 minutes)
How Strenuous: Easy
Features: Views

NUTSHELL: Marg's Draw is a beautiful area in Sedona's backyard, being a bowl surrounded by the Crimson Cliffs, Munds Mountain, Lee Mountain and Twin Buttes. This short hike takes you around the base of the Crimson Cliffs and out on the Schnebly Hill Road.

DIRECTIONS:
From the Sedona Y Go:
          South on Highway 179 (toward Phoenix) for a distance of 0.9 miles (MP 312.8) to Sombart Lane, which is just beyond a Circle K store. Turn left onto Sombart Lane and follow it to the 1.1 mile point, where there is an unpaved parking area. Park there.

TRAILHEAD: You will see no trail signs. You will see a footpath. Follow it uphill through the wooden gate.

DESCRIPTION: You will climb uphill a bit to get through the wooden gate and then you will reach a flat. There are several paths and trails through the flat area, so follow these directions carefully. At 0.27 miles you will reach a fork with two trails. Take the left fork At 0.35 miles the trail splits three ways. Take the left trail. At 0.375 miles the **Marg's Draw Trail** goes to the right along a redrock shelf. The Schnebly-Marg's Connection forks to the left and takes you around the base of the Crimson Cliffs and to the north, linking up with the Schnebly Hill Road. The **Snoopy Rock Trail** is the middle fork. It heads straight for the cliff. You want to take the left fork.
          Once you get the trails sorted out and get started on the Schnebly-Marg's Connection, this trail is easy to follow. It proceeds along the contour of the Crimson Cliffs, not too close to the base, and heads north toward the Schnebly Hill Road. The Crimson Cliffs are beautiful and walking along so near to them is a wonderful experience. At 0.48 miles you will reach another fork. Take the path to the right. A few paces beyond that a trail comes in from

the right. Ignore it.

At 0.53 a trail to the left takes off downhill. Ignore it. Just beyond that is a trail to the right. Ignore it.

At this point you are at a place where you can look to your left (west) and see into uptown Sedona. This is an unusual vantage point from which to see the town. Beyond this place a trail goes left. Ignore it. You are a little closer to the cliffs here but never get right up to them.

At 0.73 miles the forest begins to change to a cypress forest and the trail crosses several drainages coming down from the cliffs.

At 1.2 miles a faint trail to the left goes down into a gully and then it goes up to join the Schnebly Hill Road. The main path goes on a bit farther, then branches left to join the road. The place is marked by a small cairn. The point where you come onto the Schnebly Hill Road is located about 0.80 miles from the stop sign where the Schnebly Hill Road joins Highway 179.

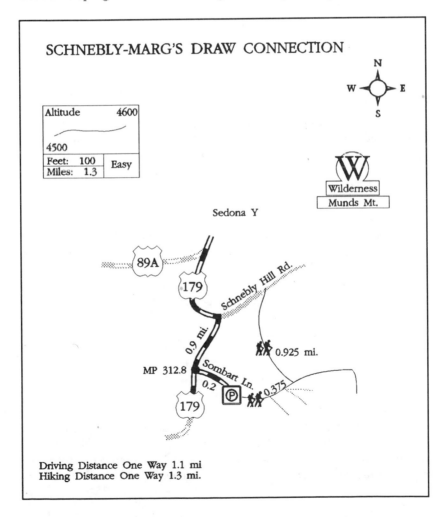

SCHNEBLY-MARG'S DRAW CONNECTION

Altitude 4600

4500
Feet: 100
Miles: 1.3   Easy

Wilderness
Munds Mt.

Sedona Y

89A

179

Schnebly Hill Rd.

0.9 mi.

0.925 mi.

MP 312.8

Sombart Ln.

0.2

0.375

179

Driving Distance One Way 1.1 mi
Hiking Distance One Way 1.3 mi.

SCHUERMAN MOUNTAIN

General Information
Location Map E3
Sedona USGS Map
Coconino Forest Service Map

Driving Distance One Way: 5.55 miles (Time 15 minutes)
Access Road: All vehicles, All paved
Hiking Distance One Way: 1.0 miles (Time 40 minutes)
How Strenuous: Moderate
Features: Views

NUTSHELL: This sprawling mountain 5.55 miles southwest of Sedona is rather drab but is a platform for great views.

DIRECTIONS:
From the Sedona Y Go:
      Southwest on Highway 89A (toward Cottonwood) for a distance of 5.3 miles (MP 368.9) to the Upper Red Rock Loop Road. Turn left on the Upper Red Rock Loop Road and follow it to the 5.55 miles point, where you will see an unpaved road branching off to your right. Turn off onto this dirt road and park.

TRAILHEAD: This is a marked and maintained trail. You will see a rusty sign reading, "Trail #56, Scheurman Mountain" at the fence.

DESCRIPTION: If you are driving a low clearance vehicle you will want to park near the paved road. If you are in a high clearance vehicle you can drive right up to the fence.
      Schuerman Mountain is a low but wide mountain southwest of Sedona. The trail zigzags up to a saddle on the mountain, reaching the top in about 0.50 miles.
      At the top you will find three trails. One goes left, one goes straight ahead and the other goes right. We recommend that you take the left trail. It goes out onto an overlook that gives you good views of **Cathedral Rock** and Oak Creek. This viewpoint is about 0.20 miles from the saddle.
      The middle path goes out into the basin of the mountain. The right path goes out to the west face.
      Schuerman Mountain is a shield volcano like **House Mountain, Windmill Mountain** and others in the area. This means it is rather shallow and sprawling with a center that is not very deep. You can walk around the rim of the mountain to get views in different directions. The walking is fairly

easy, but the ground is stony and there is a lot of cactus growing there. We pretty well walked all around the rim, taking about 2 miles to make the loop.

There are no sights of interest on the mountain top itself. In fact, it is quite drab. The payoff is the views that you get. You will see that horse riders use the mountain top. They also have a network of trails around the base of the mountain. There is a large horse stable located on the Lower Red Rock Loop Road.

The mountain is named after a Sedona pioneer, Henry Schuerman. He was a German who spelled his name Schürman. The standard way to Americanize that spelling is to place an e after the ü, making the correct spelling Schuerman. For some unknown reasons the persons who prepared the government map spelled the name Scheurman and this has been picked up and used in other places. Perhaps it is quixotic of us to use the original spelling but that is an author's prerogative. Other German immigrants solved the ü problem by changing the name to Sherman.

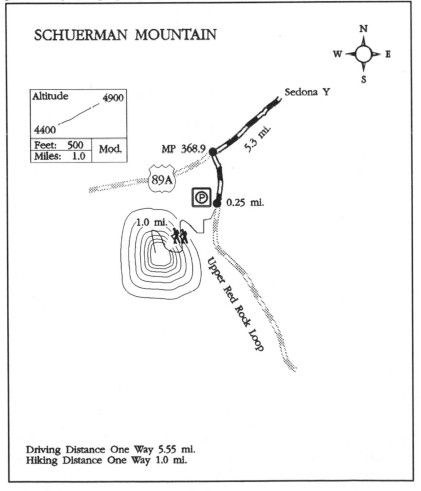

SCHUERMAN MOUNTAIN

N
W — E
S

Sedona Y

Altitude 4900

4400

Feets: 500   Mod.
Miles: 1.0

MP 368.9

5.3 mi.

89A

Ⓟ 0.25 mi.

1.0 mi.

Upper Red Rock Loop

Driving Distance One Way 5.55 mi.
Hiking Distance One Way 1.0 mi.

SECRET CANYON

General Information
Location Map C4
Loy Butte and Wilson Mt. USGS Maps
Coconino Forest Service Map

Driving Distance One Way: 8.6 miles (Time 30 minutes)
Access Road: High clearance vehicles, Last 3.4 miles rough dirt
Hiking Distance One Way: 2.5 miles (Time 90 minutes)
How Strenuous: Moderate
Features: Views, Remote canyon

NUTSHELL: This beautiful canyon, 8.6 miles northwest of uptown Sedona, provides a delightful hike but the access road is very rough. Leave the Cadillac at home and borrow a pickup.

DIRECTIONS:
From the Sedona Y Go:
Southwest on Highway 89A (toward Cottonwood) for 3.2 miles (MP 371) to the Dry Creek Road. Turn right on Dry Creek Road and follow it to the 5.2 mile point, where FR 152 (the Vultee Arch Road) branches off to the right. Turn right and follow FR 152 to the 8.6 mile point. There you will find a short half hidden road to your left. A rusty sign at the roadside says, "Secret Canyon #121." Pull in on this road and park.

TRAILHEAD: There is a rusty sign at the roadside where you turn in reading, "Secret Canyon #121."

DESCRIPTION: The access road to this hike, FR 152, is one of the roughest roads in the Sedona area. In many places the soil has washed away from the road surface leaving exposed rocks and ledges that threaten your car's undercarriage. We frequently see people in ordinary passenger cars driving this road but they don't seem very happy about it. If you can, get a high clearance vehicle for this drive. You won't need four-wheel drive unless the road is muddy, but the high clearance is definitely recommended.
Watch carefully for the turnoff to the Secret Canyon trailhead. The road in this area is lined with a screen of brush and trees and the entry is a brief opening in this screen. The trail sign is small and rusty. It is hard to see.
The parking space is limited. It can hold only about five cars.
From the parking spot the trail goes immediately to Dry Creek and then turns right and runs along the bottom of Dry Creek, going up toward its headwater. If water is running in Dry Creek you may not be able to make this

hike as the trail winds back and forth across the creek several times.

The trail takes you through some beautiful back country, winding through some impressive redrocks. At 0.60 miles you will see the **H S Canyon** trail taking off to the left.

At about 2.25 miles you come up out of the canyon bottom and walk along the side of the canyon. At 2.5 miles you will enter a pine forest. Up to this time the hike has been unshaded, but from this point the pines provide ample shade.

For the purposes of this book, which features day hikes, we have you stop here in the cool pines at 2.5 miles. The trail goes farther. If you are a real iron-man bushranger, you can even whack your way to the top of the Mogollon Rim, coming up in the Dave Joy Point area. We have not tried this, so we can't give the mileage figure but from its appearance, this would be a long hard hike. We have been at the Dave Joy Point, accessing it by driving there on the top of the rim. From the point you can see into Secret Canyon. It is very rugged.

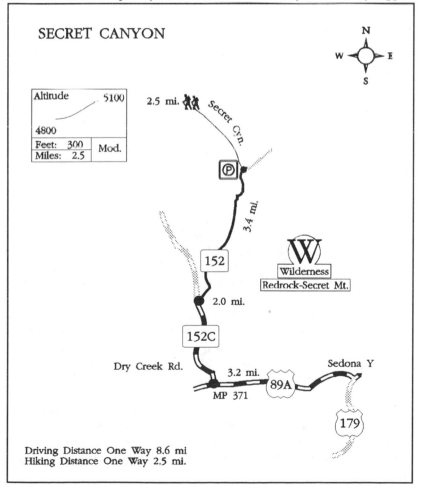

SECRET CANYON

Altitude	5100
4800	
Feet: 300	Mod.
Miles: 2.5	

2.5 mi. — Secret Cyn.

3.4 mi.

152

W Wilderness
Redrock-Secret Mt.

2.0 mi.

152C

Dry Creek Rd.

3.2 mi.

89A

Sedona Y

MP 371

179

Driving Distance One Way 8.6 mi
Hiking Distance One Way 2.5 mi.

SHOOTING RANGE RIDGE EAST

General Information
Location Map D4
Wilson Mountain USGS Map
Coconino Forest Service Map

Driving Distance One Way: 1.5 miles (Time 10 minutes)
Access Road: All cars. Last 0.40 miles gravel, in medium condition
Hiking Distance One Way: 0.7 miles (Time 40 minutes)
How Strenuous: Moderate
Features: Easy to reach, Good views

NUTSHELL: You climb to the top of a 300 foot high ridge for excellent views.

DIRECTIONS:
From the Y in Sedona Go:
　　　　North on Highway 89A (toward Flagstaff) a distance of 0.30 miles, to Jordan Road, a main street in uptown Sedona. Follow Jordan Road to its end, beyond the point where the paving disappears. At 1.1 miles, you reach a junction with a private drive, turn left here and follow the road to the former Sheriff's Shooting Range, at 1.5 miles. Park outside the gate.

TRAILHEAD: This is not a signed trail. The trail starts on a sideroad located just in front of the gate to the shooting range.

DESCRIPTION: Just before you reach the gate to the old shooting range you will see a road to your left (west). Park and walk back to this road, then follow it. You will find that it is a jeep trail. Keep following it uphill as far as it goes. It soon ends and a foot path starts. This path was marked by cairns when we hiked it in February 1992 and was easy to follow.
　　　　On the way up you will begin to enjoy views that are even better at the top. You will reach a well-defined trail on the top of the ridge at 0.46 miles. From here turn to the left and follow the trail out to its end, which is on the toe of the ridge. Along the way you will enter an area where there are steep redrock cliffs to either side. We enjoy looking down on these. The trail ends at a great viewpoint. You look down on upper Sedona. To your left you have fine views of Wilson Mountain. To your right you see into the Capitol Butte and Coffee Pot Rock areas.
　　　　After you have had your fill of the views you can go back the way you came or you can check out the balance of the ridge. From the point where you came up to the ridgetop trail, you walk along the top for a short distance. Then the trail dips down to a saddle, and rises again, taking you to a fence at 0.1 miles.

From there the trail generally follows the fence line. You will come to a gate at 0.23 miles, where the **Shooting Range Ridge West Trail** takes off downhill to your left.

Go beyond this point about five paces, where you will see a trail in a deep groove going downhill to your right. This is the trail to take on the way back. It intersects the Brins Mesa Trail at 0.4 miles, at a point that is only 0.05 miles from the gate.

If you want to go on out to the far end of the ridge, you will get to it at 0.5 miles. From there you will have exceptionally fine views of Brins Mesa and Wilson Mountain.

This is a nice little hike, a good choice when the backroads are too muddy or you don't have time to drive far out into the country.

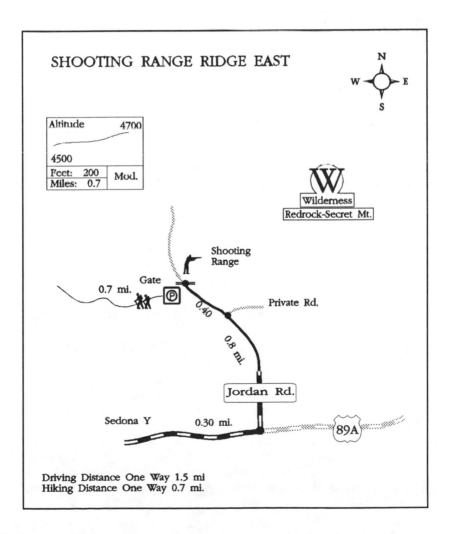

SHOOTING RANGE RIDGE EAST

SHOOTING RANGE RIDGE WEST

General Information
Location Map D4
Sedona and Wilson Mt. USGS Maps
Coconino Forest Service Map

Driving Distance One Way: 1.55 miles (Time 10 minutes)
Access Road: All cars, All paved
Hiking Distance One Way: 1.35 miles (Time 45 minutes)
How Strenuous: Moderate
Features: Views

NUTSHELL: Starting from Devil's Kitchen in the Soldier Pass area, this moderate hike takes you to a scenic ridge dividing Soldier Pass from the upper Jordan Road area of Sedona.

DIRECTIONS:
From the Sedona Y Go:
    Southwest on Highway 89A (toward Cottonwood) for a distance of 1.2 miles (MP 372.8) to Soldier Pass Road. Turn right onto Soldier Pass Road and follow it to the 1.4 mile point, where it intersects Rim Shadows Drive, where you turn right. Follow Rim Shadows a short distance, to the 1.45 miles spot, where it intersects Canyon Shadows Drive. There you turn left onto Canyon Shadows and follow it to the 1.5 miles point. There you will see a sign saying "Forest Service Access." Take the road to your left at the sign. At 1.55 miles you will come to the parking area. Park there.

TRAILHEAD: You will see a rusty sign at the parking area reading, "Soldier Pass Trail #66."

DESCRIPTION: This trail is an old jeep road and is still used by jeep tours. Walk down the road 0.10 miles, where you will see a road branching off to your right marked FR 904B. Take this road. You will climb uphill a short distance, reaching **Devil's Kitchen** at 0.35 miles. See the entry for Devil's Kitchen for information about it. It is the largest sinkhole in the Sedona area.
    The jeep road to Devil's Kitchen appears to continue around the sinkhole. Follow it to the point where the road ends, which is about two hundred yards beyond the sinkhole.
    Keep walking at roughly the same level as the road, staying near the base of the cliff. As you come to the end of a slickrock ledge you will see some cairns marking the trail you are to take. Look carefully for them, as the trail is rather faint and you need the cairns to guide you. Farther along, two cairn-

marked trails fork to the right. The second trail that you will reach is better than the first one. Here you will go to the right, down into a gully. You will walk up out of the gully on the other side, then cross a second ravine. From there you will turn left and walk up a small canyon.

At 0.60 miles you will join another trail. Take the fork to the left. At 0.70 miles another trail joins in. Here you are walking along a streambed. You will see a path to your right going up the ridge. Take it. You will reach an intermediate top at 0.90 miles. There is a fence at this point. Uphill a few feet from this place there is a gate in the fence. Go through the gate, then turn right and follow the fence to the true top of the ridge.

You will come out onto red slickrock, where you get great views. To the east is Wilson Mountain, Brins Mesa, Mormon Canyon and the Shooting Range. To the west is the Soldier Pass area. To your right is uptown Sedona in the Jordan Road area. We really love the views from this place, especially in evening light.

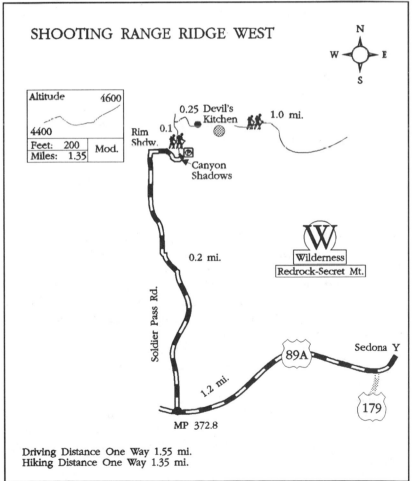

SHOOTING RANGE RIDGE WEST

Driving Distance One Way 1.55 mi.
Hiking Distance One Way 1.35 mi.

SLIDE ROCK

General Information
Location Map C4
Wilson Mt. USGS Map
Coconino Forest Service Map

Driving Distance One Way: 6.9 miles (Time 15 minutes)
Access Road: All cars, All paved
Hiking Distance One Way: 0.5 miles (Time 30 minutes)
How Strenuous: Moderate
Features: Slide Rock State Park

NUTSHELL: You enjoy two hiking trails in Slide Rock State Park 6.9 miles north of Sedona, one at water's edge and the other on the cliffs above Oak Creek.

DIRECTIONS:
From The Y in Sedona Go:
North on Highway 89A (toward Flagstaff) a distance of 6.9 miles (MP 381.1) to the entrance to Slide Rock State Park. The park is well marked and signed and you will have no trouble finding it. Pull in to the park (there is an entry fee) and park on the large lot.

TRAILHEAD: From the parking lot, walk upstream along a paved walkway. When you get to the Apple Packing Shed, you will be at the place where the two hiking trails start.

DESCRIPTION: (1) **Creekside Trail:** At the Packing Shed you will see a flight of steps going down to Oak Creek. Take the steps. You will emerge onto a long redrock ledge going upstream. It is easy and fun to walk along the ledge, enjoying the water and the redrock cliffs on either side. This is a favorite place for visitors and is likely to be crowded. You will see a place where the creek has cut a channel into the bedrock. This is the slide of Slide Rock and you will probably see people using it, as they sit in the water at the beginning of the channel and let the current sweep them down to its end in a deep pool.

There are well-worn trails at the base of the cliffs and also at the edge of the water. When the water is low, you can walk across the creek on a duckboard bridge, but we think the best sights are on the west bank, the side you start on. The trails end at an interesting old shed built of rock in front of an irrigation flume at about 0.5 miles. From there you can rock hop upstream for a considerable distance depending on the depth of the water and your desire to explore.

(2) **Clifftop Trail**: Now go back to the top of the stairs. There you will see a sign for the Cliff Top Trail. The trail runs along the top of the cliffs parallel to the creek, providing several places where you can step off the trail and go over to the cliff tops to look down on Slide Rock. The Cliff Top Trail ends at about 0.10 mile at the ruins of a concrete gatehouse that controlled the flow of water in the irrigation ditch. You can go a few paces beyond this for a view of the irrigation flume winding its way around the face of cliffs, but can go no farther due to a *No Trespassing* sign.

Slide Rock has been a popular spot for years, but its use soared when the state bought it and improved the access and parking. In the height of the tourist season, it can be so crowded as to be annoying. We like to visit it in the off season in order to avoid the throngs.

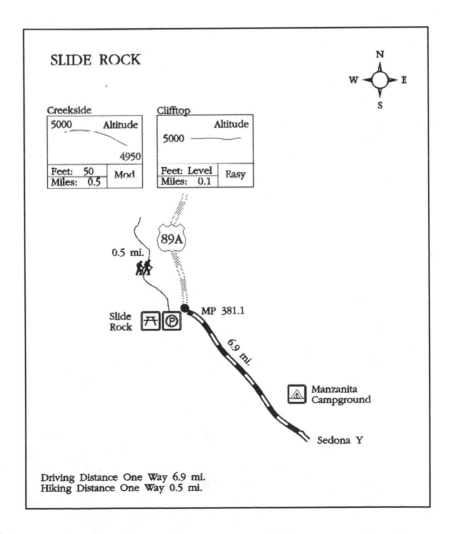

SMOKE TRAIL

General Information
Location Map F3
Sedona USGS Map
Coconino Forest Service Map

Driving Distance One Way: 8.8 miles (Time 15 minutes)
Access Road: All vehicles, All paved
Hiking Distance One Way: 0.35 miles (Time 15 minutes)
How Strenuous: Easy
Features: Creekside shady walk

NUTSHELL: This easy trail, located in Red Rock State Park 8.8 miles southwest of Sedona, takes you from the Visitor Center down to the creek bank, where you take a leisurely walk to the Cottonwood Picnic Area.

DIRECTIONS:
From the Sedona Y Go:
      Southwest on Highway 89A (toward Cottonwood) for a distance of 5.5 miles (MP 368.6) to the Lower Red Rock Loop Road. Turn left on the Lower Red Rock Loop Road and follow it to the 8.5 miles point, where you will see the entry to Red Rock State Park. Turn right into the park. You will come to a toll booth where an admission is charged. From that point, drive to the Visitor Center and park there, at 8.8 miles. On your way you will see the turnoff to the Cottonwood Picnic Area to your right; don't go there now, but keep it in mind.

TRAILHEAD: This is a marked and maintained trail, part of the network of seven trails planned for the park. Go down through the Visitor Center. Though the center is not marked as the trailhead for this hike, it is the starting point for it.

DESCRIPTION: Enjoy the Visitor Center and then walk through it, turning right on the paved trail. At 0.08 miles you will come to the first trail junction. Here the Smoke Trail forks to the right, where Sentinel Crossing is located. Turn right here and go down to the creek. At creekside you will find a small lecture area, where a few seats have been set up around a lectern. There is a nice bench facing the creek where you can sit and watch the water. You will also find the Sentinel Trail crossing, which is not really a trail in its own right, just a low floating bridge across the creek to give the hiker trail access. The bridge is hinged so that it will swing downstream when the creek floods rather than being washed away. The Smoke Trail turns to the right and follows downstream along the creek bank.

A lot of work has been done on this trail to define it and make it comfortable. It is easy to walk and very relaxing with its shade and the water of Oak Creek sliding by.

In 0.3 miles the trail swings away (to your right) from the creek and goes up to the Cottonwood Picnic Area. From the Visitor Center to the Cottonwood Picnic Area is 0.35 miles.

On the way back you have an option. You will see a side trail going uphill to your left less than one-tenth of a mile from Cottonwood. This trail winds up to the parking lot at the Visitor Center. It is 0.68 miles to the top. Back to the center from there is a distance of 0.14 miles.

The dedicated hiker will find this trail too short and simple to be of much interest but we noted a number of elderly people who were obviously enjoying it, demonstrating the value of having different trails for people of different tastes and abilities.

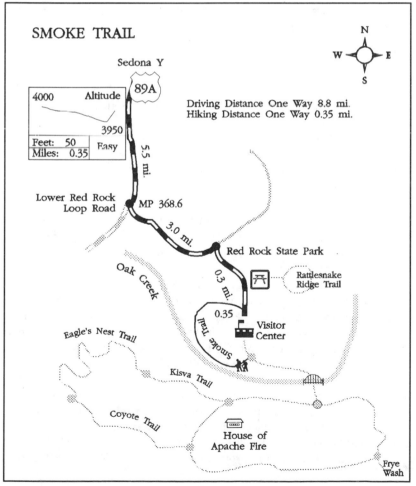

SNOOPY ROCK

General Information
Location Map E5
Sedona and Munds Mt. USGS Maps
Coconino Forest Service Map

Driving Distance One Way: 1.1 miles (Time 10 minutes)
Access Road: All cars, All paved
Hiking Distance One Way: 1.1 miles (Time 60 minutes)
How Strenuous: Moderate
Features: Views, Favorite rock formation

NUTSHELL: This short hike takes you to Snoopy Rock, which is located on the Crimson Cliffs at the north end of Marg's Draw, only 1.1 miles from the Y. This hike is fun and easy to reach.

DIRECTIONS:
From the Sedona Y Go:
      South on Highway 179 (toward Phoenix) for a distance of 0.9 miles (MP 312.8) to Sombart Lane, which is just beyond a Circle K store. Turn left onto Sombart Lane and follow it to the 1.1 mile point, where there is an unpaved parking area. Park there.

TRAILHEAD: You will see no trail signs. You will see a footpath. Follow it uphill through the wooden gate.

DESCRIPTION: From the parking lot you will see a trail going uphill to a wooden gate. Go through the gate. The trail will take you to a flat area where you will see several other trails. Follow the directions carefully so that you do not get off on the wrong trail.
      The easiest way to stay on the right trail is to know what your objective is. If you know Snoopy Rock, then it is simple. If not, look to your left (north). You will see large red cliffs. To your farthest left is a lower formation with a couple of comparatively short red columns rising from it. This is your goal.
      At 0.27 miles you will reach a fork. Take the left fork. At 0.35 miles the trail splits three ways. Take the middle trail. At 0.375 miles the **Marg's Draw Trail** goes to the right along a redrock shelf. Don't take it. Stay on the left trail. You will know you have the correct trail if it brings you closer to the cliff. Another trail mentioned in this book, the **Schnebly-Marg's Connection**, takes you around the base of the cliffs and then heads north. Only the Snoopy Rock trail aims at the cliff.
      From about 0.40 miles you can see how Snoopy Rock gets its name.

If you use your imagination you can see Snoopy sleeping on top of his doghouse. The column to your left is his feet, while the column to the right is his nose. Sometimes it is one main feature about a rock formation that gives it its name. In this case it is the bulb on the end of Snoopy's nose. Otherwise you have to use a lot of imagination to see Snoopy. There is a distinct mauve rock on the top of the nose, making the bulb. The stomach is caved in instead of bulging out as it should be with a well-fed Snoopy.

At about 0.50 miles the trail begins to climb the cliff. It is a good trail, zigzagging its way up to moderate the grade. The trail tops out at 1.1 miles, at a saddle just below Snoopy's head. You can see over the other side of the saddle to the West, right down into uptown Sedona.

Back in Sedona, look at Snoopy Rock and congratulate yourself. From there it looks unclimbable; so you can impress people: "Snoopy Rock? Oh, yes, it's over there. I climbed it an hour ago."

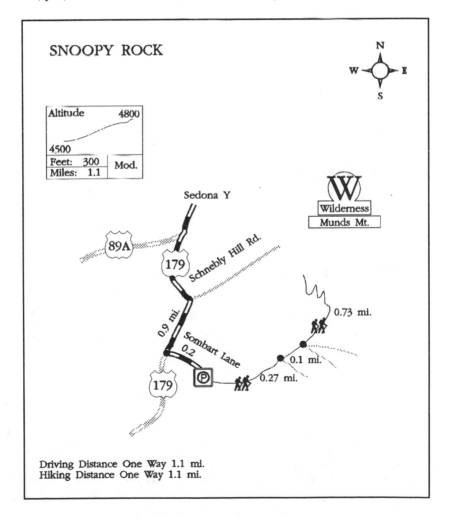

SNOOPY ROCK

Altitude   4800

4500
Feet: 300   Mod.
Miles: 1.1

Sedona Y

Wilderness
Munds Mt.

89A

179   Schnebly Hill Rd.

0.73 mi.

0.9 mi.

Sombart Lane
0.2

0.1 mi.

179

0.27 mi.

Driving Distance One Way 1.1 mi.
Hiking Distance One Way 1.1 mi.

SOLDIER PASS ARCHES

General Information
Location Map D4
Sedona and Wilson Mt. USGS Maps
Coconino Forest Service Map

Driving Distance One Way: 1.55 miles (Time 10 minutes)
Access Road: All cars, All paved
Hiking Distance One Way: 1.1 miles (Time 60 minutes)
How Strenuous: Moderate
Features: Views, Arches

NUTSHELL: Located off of Soldier Pass Road, the trailhead for this hike is only 1.55 miles from the Y. The hike follows an old jeep road most of its way, then climbs up to a trio of interesting arches.

DIRECTIONS:
From the Sedona Y Go:
          Southwest on Highway 89A (toward Cottonwood) for a distance of 1.2 miles (MP 372.8) to Soldier Pass Road. Turn right onto Soldier Pass Road and follow it to the 1.4 mile point, where it intersects Rim Shadows Drive, where you turn right. Follow Rim Shadows a short distance, to the 1.45 miles spot, where it intersects Canyon Shadows Drive. There you turn left onto Canyon Shadows and follow it to the 1.5 miles point. There you will see a sign saying "Forest Service Access." Take the road to your left there. At 1.55 miles you will come to the parking area. This is well defined and spacious. Park there.

TRAILHEAD: You will see a rusty sign at the parking area reading "Soldier Pass Trail #66."

DESCRIPTION: This trail is an old jeep road. As you walk up the road you will see a sideroad at 0.10 miles going off to the right. It is marked FR 904B. This is the way to the **Devil's Kitchen**. It is not part of this hike but if you haven't seen it, it is only 0.25 miles away and is worth a detour.
          Keep walking up the main road. You will see some side paths forking off here and there but don't take them. At 0.85 miles you will reach a stone barrier where there is a sign reading, "Road Closed. Wilderness Boundary Ahead."
          The road forks here. Do not take the left fork. Instead, step over the stones. Walk up the larger wash. You will see the that the road follows the wash, comes out of it and then goes back down into the wash. Soon after that

you come out of the wash for good. Beyond the wash you will come out onto a large red slickrock ledge, which provides good views in all directions. You are in a box canyon at this point, with interesting and colorful cliffs on all sides except east (toward Sedona). Walk up to the left edge of the ledge. If you look up at the cliffs to your left from this spot you will see one arch.

From there the trail is narrow and steep up to the arch, but it is a short climb. When you arrive you will see that there are two arches. You can walk under the first one. It is fun to explore, as it forms a sort of cave. There is a third arch that you can't see. You can reach it by walking along the cliff face on a faint trail. The third arch is the smallest and least interesting. Just above you on top of the rim is the **Brins Mesa Trail**.

This is a good hike to take when the roads are muddy because the access road is all paved and it is near town. The first time we hiked this trail it seemed that it was way out in the country. Now the trailhead is in the middle of a subdivision. That kind of encroachment is unsettling. Adios, wilderness.

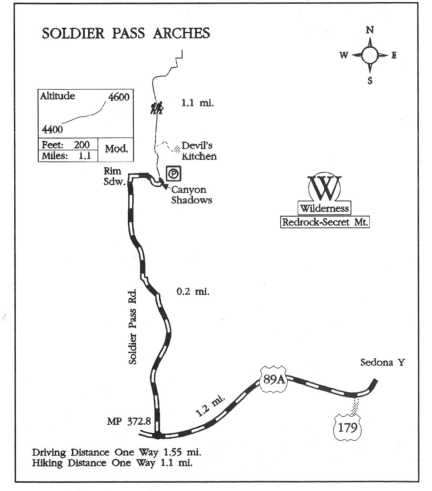

SOLDIER PASS ARCHES

N
W — E
S

Altitude   4600
4400
Feet: 200   Mod.
Miles: 1.1

1.1 mi.

Devil's Kitchen

Rim Sdw.

Canyon Shadows

Wilderness
Redrock-Secret Mt.

0.2 mi.

Soldier Pass Rd

Sedona Y

89A

1.2 mi.

MP 372.8

179

Driving Distance One Way 1.55 mi.
Hiking Distance One Way 1.1 mi.

SOLDIER PASS TRAIL

General Information
Location Map D4
Sedona and Wilson Mt. USGS Maps
Coconino Forest Service Map

Driving Distance One Way: 1.55 miles (Time 10 minutes)
Access Road: All cars, All paved
Hiking Distance One Way: 1.5 miles (Time 60 minutes)
How Strenuous: Moderate
Features: Views

NUTSHELL: Located off Soldier Pass Road, the trailhead for this hike is easily reached. The hike follows an old jeep road most of its way, then climbs to the top of Brins Mesa, a Sedona landmark.

DIRECTIONS:
From the Sedona Y Go:
Southwest on Highway 89A (toward Cottonwood) for a distance of 1.2 miles (MP 372.8) to Soldier Pass Road. Turn right onto Soldier Pass Road and follow it to the 1.4 mile point, where it intersects Rim Shadows Drive, where you turn right. Follow Rim Shadows a short distance, to the 1.45 miles spot, where it intersects Canyon Shadows Drive. There you turn left onto Canyon Shadows and follow it to the 1.5 miles point. There you will see a sign saying "Forest Service Access." Take the road to your left at the sign. At 1.55 miles you will come to the parking area. This is well defined and spacious. Park there.

TRAILHEAD: You will see a rusty sign at the parking area reading, "Soldier Pass Trail #66."

DESCRIPTION: This trail is an old jeep road. As you walk up the road you will see a sideroad to your right at the 0.10 mile point. This is marked FR 904B. This fork goes to **Devil's Kitchen**, which is only 0.25 miles away and is well worth a detour if you haven't seen it.
Keep walking up the main road. You will see some side paths forking off but don't take them. At 0.85 miles you will reach a stone barrier where there is a sign reading, "Road Closed, Wilderness Boundary Ahead."
The road forks at this point. Do not take the left fork, as it ends in a loop about 0.20 miles from here. Instead, step over the stones. Walk up the larger wash. You will see the road follow the wash, come out of the wash, then dip into it again. Soon after that, it splits, with the right hand fork going up

to the **Soldier Pass Arches**.

Stay on the lower trail, which goes into the wash for the third time. Look for a sign to your left that reads, "National Forest Wilderness. Closed to Vehicles and Motorized Equipment." This sign marks the path that you want to take. This is at 0.90 miles.

At about 1.0 miles, look to your right and you will see the three Soldier Pass Arches clearly. The trail from here follows along the top of a low ridge in the canyon bottom. At 1.25 miles the trail begins a fairly steep ascent up to **Brins Mesa**. You are high enough there to get some great views.

At 1.3 miles you will reach a gate in a barbed wire fence. You top out at 1.4 miles. From this point you can follow the trail to link up with the Brins Mesa Trail at 1.5 miles. This connection makes some other hikes possible. You could take the left fork and follow the **Brins Mesa West Trail** coming out on the road to **Vultee Arch**. Or you could go right and come out on the Jordan Road access to **Brins Mesa East**.

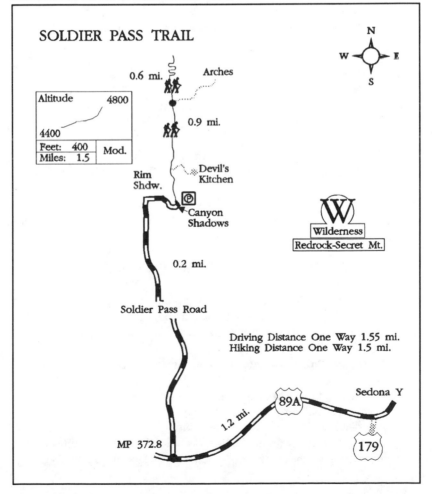

STEAMBOAT ROCK

General Information
Location Map D5
Munds Park USGS Map
Coconino Forest Service Map

Drive Distance One Way: 1.1 miles (Time 5 minutes)
Access Road: All cars, All paved
Hiking Distance One Way: 1.5 miles (Time 1.5 hours)
How Strenuous: Hard
Features: Views

NUTSHELL: Located 1.1 miles north of Sedona, Steamboat Rock is one of the area's most famous landmarks. This hike takes you near the top, just below the "funnel" for breathtaking views and an unforgettable adventure. *For experienced hikers only.*

DIRECTIONS:
From the Sedona Y Go:
North on Highway 89A (toward Flagstaff) for a distance of 1.1 miles (MP 375.9). Go just across Midgley Bridge and turn left into the parking area.

TRAILHEAD: You will see a rusty sign at the parking lot. It reads, "Wilson Canyon #49." Start this hike by taking the **Wilson Canyon Trail** for 0.5 miles.

DESCRIPTION: The trailhead is as easy as pie to locate. Just walk toward the picnic tables at the end of the parking lot. There you will find the Wilson Monument, a bronze plaque set in stone, and two rusty signs. The sign to the left marks **Wilson Canyon #49** and is the one you want for this hike. The other sign marks an uphill trail, Wilson Mountain #10, which is called **Wilson Mountain South** in this book.

Take note of how far it is to the first point where the trail crosses the streambed (0.25), which is just beyond the old bridge abutment. Walk another 0.25 miles along the trail to a point where you will see an old road coming down from your left. This road is badly eroded, with rocks sticking out everywhere. It is a piece of the **Old Jim Thompson Road.** Turn left (west) here and go uphill on the old road.

You will top out at 0.75 miles. Go left on the road you find here. In about 20 yards you will reach another intersection. Avoid both of the wide trails here and instead take the narrow footpath going right, uphill toward the nearest red butte. Look carefully for the trail, as it is rather faint and you must follow it to take advantage of the only two approaches on the face of the butte that allow you to go to the top.

As you begin to come onto the slickrock, watch for cairns. They will lead you up the east face of Steamboat Rock. After a short stretch of scrambling, you will emerge onto the top of the butte, where the walking is easy and the trail is wide. Ahead of you is the towering "funnel" of the "steamboat." Approach it and you will find a talus slope going up to a band of mauve Ft. Wingate sandstone forming a ledge (the "deck") at the funnel's base. Here you must make a decision. If you are afraid of heights, stop here. If not, scale the slope; it is steep but short. You will find that the Wingate layer is too thick to climb. Work your way west (to your right) and you will find a four-rung ladder made of rebar giving access to the top. The ladder is not perfectly stable. There is danger involved in climbing it. If you do climb it, you will be rewarded with sublime views. If it breaks off with you...well, this is a beautiful place to die. You can walk almost all the way around the "deck." You will even find a small Indian ruin there. This is one of the best viewpoints in Sedona.

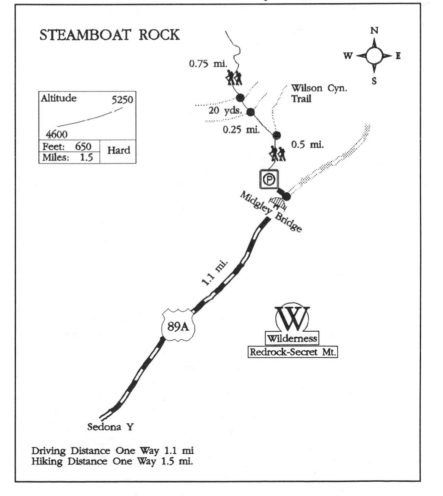

STEAMBOAT ROCK

Altitude 5250
4600
Feet: 650 Hard
Miles: 1.5

0.75 mi.

20 yds.

0.25 mi.

Wilson Cyn. Trail

0.5 mi.

Midgley Bridge

1.1 mi.

89A

Wilderness
Redrock-Secret Mt.

Sedona Y

Driving Distance One Way 1.1 mi
Hiking Distance One Way 1.5 mi.

STERLING PASS

General Information
Location Map C5
Munds Park and Wilson Mt. USGS Maps
Coconino Forest Service Map

Driving Distance One Way: 6.2 miles (Time 10 minutes)
Access Road: All cars, All paved
Hiking Distance One Way: 1.65 miles (Time 60 minutes)
How Strenuous: Hard
Features: Views, Great rock formations

NUTSHELL: Located 6.2 miles north of Sedona, just above the north end of Manzanita Campground, and just below Slide Rock Lodge, this steep but beautiful hike climbs through a heavy forest to a mountain pass.

DIRECTIONS:
From the Sedona Y Go:
North on Highway 89A (toward Flagstaff) for a distance of 6.2 miles (MP 380.4). Park anywhere you can along the roadside in this area.

TRAILHEAD: There is a rusty sign in a little alcove marking this maintained trail. The sign reads, "Sterling Pass #46."

DESCRIPTION: There is very little parking at the roadside near the trailhead. You have to pick out a wide spot on the shoulder and do your best.
This trail rises steeply, climbing all the way. For the first portion you parallel a little side canyon, which may contain running water during spring thaw. When it does, it creates a charming waterfall near the highway. The trail wanders back and forth over the streambed four times.
For those who think of the Oak Creek area as sunswept expanses of redrock dotted with cactus, this trail will be an eye-opener. It goes through a cool pine forest. While you will cross over a bit of red slickrock at the beginning and will see some gorgeous red cliffs and buttes as you progress, the soil underfoot will be a rich brown loam. The forest is heavy. In addition to the familiar ponderosa pine you will see some Douglas fir and a few spruces. After about the first quarter mile you are far enough away from the road so that you can no longer hear its sounds and can see no signs of human activity. The area feels primeval and is truly delightful.
Because the forest is so heavy, you can't see much until you have gone about 1.25 miles. Until then you get glimpses of giant white cliffs ahead of you (west) and red cliffs on your right and left. Then you rise above the trees and

get great views across Oak Creek Canyon and nearby. The cliffs here are a treat to the eye, highly sculptured, with many interesting lines and angles. You will find a viewpoint at a bend of the trail where you can look over into an adjacent canyon to your left for views of soaring white cliffs.

The crest is at about 1.65 miles, where you come onto a saddle. There is a heavy stand of trees here with oaks on the east side and oaks and maples on the west wide. Because of these trees the views are not as good at the top as they are just below the top. This is a true mountain pass, there being a decided gap in the cliffs here.

The trail continues down the other side, another 0.75 miles, to intersect the **Vultee Arch Trail.** If you do go down the west side you might as well go on to Vultee Arch, which is only 0.20 miles from the trail junction. Many hikers will stop at the saddle and go back the way they came.

You can do a two-car shuttle. Park one car at Vultee Arch trailhead and the other at the Sterling Pass trailhead.

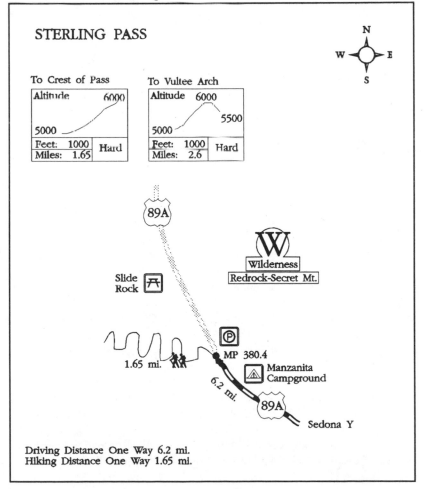

SUBMARINE ROCK

General Information
Location Map E5
Sedona USGS Map
Coconino Forest Service Map

Driving Distance One Way: 2.0 miles (Time 10 minutes)
Access Road: All cars, All paved
Hiking Distance One Way: 1.0 miles (Time 30 minutes)
How Strenuous: Easy
Features: Rock formation, Views

NUTSHELL: Located only a couple of miles southeast of uptown Sedona, this interesting rock formation is fun to climb and pretend that you are Captain Nemo.

DIRECTIONS:
From the Sedona Y Go:
South on Highway 179 (toward Phoenix) for a distance of 1.4 miles (MP 312.1), to Morgan Road. Turn left onto Morgan Road. Follow it to the 2.0 mile point where you will see a cattle guard and the paving ends. Drive just beyond the cattle guard and park.

TRAILHEAD: The jeep road, FR 179F, is the trail.

DESCRIPTION: Walk down the jeep road. You will see a sign at the cattle guard reading "Trail Walk-Through." We suggest that you disregard the walkthrough and just stay on the road. The road is widely used by the jeep tours that have proliferated in Sedona, so the road is well maintained, although you may have to share it with motor vehicles, which detracts from the back-to-nature qualities of the experience.

As you walk the road, you will reach a spot at 0.32 miles where a sunken road goes off to the right (south). This is the trail to the **Devil's Dining Room**, a large sinkhole. It is a short jaunt and worth seeing.

At 0.4 miles, the road splits but it doesn't matter which fork you take, as the roads converge on the other side of a hill. The high road gives better views. At 0.67 miles you reach a T fork. Go straight here. The right fork goes up to a nice viewpoint, again worth a short detour. At 0.71 miles you come to a Y fork. The left branch goes down into a gully and up to Submarine Rock. The right fork goes to **Chicken Point**.

Submarine Rock is well named. It looks like a submarine lying on the floor of the valley. It is a low rounded redrock formation that stands alone.

The jeep tours love to drive the tourists up the face of Submarine Rock and in doing so they have unfortunately left unsightly black tire marks behind them. The marks make it easy to follow the path, however.

Submarine Rock is easy to climb and once you are on top of it you can have great fun walking around it, getting the views and clambering up to the top of the "conning tower."

When you are at Submarine Rock you are only about three-quarters of a mile from **Chicken Point** and may want to take that hike on the same trip.

Submarine Rock is located at the south end of **Marg's Draw**, a scenic bowl formed by the Crimson Cliffs on the north, Munds Mountain and Lee Mountain on the east and Twin Buttes on the south. This is a beautiful natural area and the home of several good hikes. Marg's Draw is remarkable, being unspoiled and yet close to developed parts of Sedona. Land barons would love to get their hands on it and subdivide it but—fortunately for outdoor lovers—part of it is protected by being included in the Munds Mt. Wilderness Area.

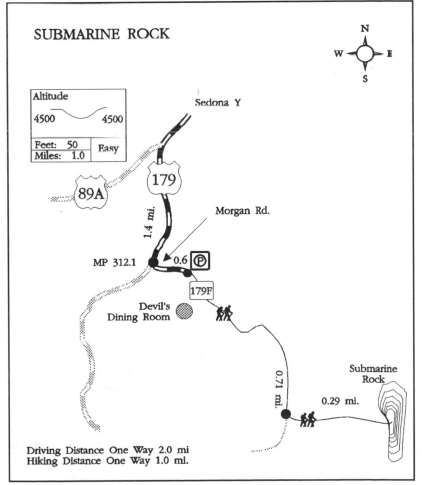

SUBMARINE ROCK

N
W — E
S

Altitude

4500   4500

Feet: 50   Easy
Miles: 1.0

Sedona Y

179

89A

1.4 mi.

Morgan Rd.

MP 312.1   0.6 Ⓟ

179F

Devil's
Dining Room

0.71 mi.

Submarine
Rock

0.29 mi.

Driving Distance One Way 2.0 mi
Hiking Distance One Way 1.0 mi.

SUGARLOAF AT BLACK MT.

General Information
Location Map C1
Page Springs and Sycamore Basin USGS Maps
Coconino Forest Service Map

Driving Distance One Way: 30.5 miles (Time 60 minutes)
Access Road: High clearance vehicles, Very rough roads
Hiking Distance One Way: 0.33 miles (Time 30 minutes)
How Strenuous: Moderate
Features: Ruins, Views

NUTSHELL: Located 30.5 miles southwest of Sedona, this small mountain is moderately easy to climb. There are Indian ruins at the top. Great views.

DIRECTIONS:
From the Sedona Y Go:
Southwest on Highway 89A (toward Cottonwood) a distance of 16.0 miles (MP 358) to FR 761, the unpaved Bill Gray Road. Turn right and take FR 761 to the 25.5 miles point, which is the junction of FR 761 and FR 258A, the Buckboard Road. Go right here, staying on FR 761. At 26.2 miles, you will see a road to your left marked FR 9761A, with a sign saying that it is a Forest Protection Road. Turn left onto this road. Up to this point, the road has been good, but now it gets quite rough. A high clearance vehicle with sturdy tires is recommended, and you should drive it only when the road is dry. At 28.3 miles, you reach a Y fork, with FR 9761A going right and FR 9761C going left. Drive FR 9761A, to the right. This is a very rough but spectacular road. Pick a good parking place in the area of the 30.5 mile point and park.

TRAILHEAD: No trail. You bushwhack up the mountain.

DESCRIPTION: Although this Sugarloaf (there are two others near Sedona) is a small mountain, the south face is not easy to climb because of some thick eroded ledges there. On the east face, where we have had you park, the access to the top is much easier.
You will have to contend with two ledges here, one of redrock and the other of buff colored stone, but they both narrow down on this face and it is easy to get around them.
At the top you will find a small ruin, just a short wall about three feet high filled with sand. Hikers have also built a cairn at the top. Add a stone to the cairn to show you've been here. There is another ruin on the west side of the crest, downhill a bit.

The area at the top is small, so you can easily walk around it and get good views in all directions. The views to the north, east and south are terrific.

Since you are so close to it, you should also visit the **Black Mountain Mystery House** while you are here.

The early settlers in Sedona were hard pressed to come up with names for the multitude of hills, mountains, rock formations and other land features they found and they used the name Sugarloaf three times. See **Sugarloaf in Sedona**.

One hundred years ago, people didn't buy granulated sugar as we know it today. Molasses was boiled down until it began to crystallize and was poured into cone-shaped molds, where it hardened. These "loaves" of sugar, about the size of a golf ball, were their sugar. The loaves became very hard as they aged and it was usually the job of the children in a family to break up the loaves with a hammer so that the sugar could be measured and used in cooking. A sugarloaf was a blunt-tipped cone and aptly describes these hills.

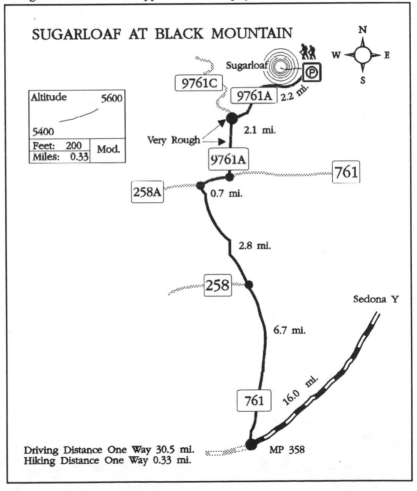

SUGARLOAF IN SEDONA

Driving Distance One Way: 2.6 miles (Time 10 minutes)
Access Road: All cars, All paved
Hiking Distance One Way: 0.70 miles (Time 30 minutes)
How Strenuous: Moderate
Features: Rock formation, Views

NUTSHELL: This ramp-shaped landmark located a couple of miles west of uptown Sedona can be climbed with moderate effort for great views.

DIRECTIONS:
From the Sedona Y Go:
Southwest on Highway 89A (toward Cottonwood) for a distance of 1.7 miles (MP 372.5), to Mt. Shadows Street. Turn right onto Mt. Shadows Street. Follow it to the 2.6 mile point where you will find a large water storage tank and a transmitter inside a chain link fence. The road intersects Fabulous Texan Way here (streets were named after movies filmed in Sedona). Drive across the street onto the dirt apron around the fenced area and park there.

TRAILHEAD: At the parking area. There are no signs, but you will see a crawl-through in the fence; it looks like a picture frame.

DESCRIPTION: Squeeze through the crawl-through and walk uphill along the fence. The path forks just past the fence. Take the left fork (west), which goes uphill. It circles the base of Sugarloaf and takes you around to the north side, where you will find the low point of the "ramp," which is the obvious place to begin the ascent to the top. You will find this in a clearing where the old road ended. There is a line of flat red rocks blocking the entrance to a road going up Sugarloaf. You want to walk this "ramp."
It is as if Sugarloaf was created to be a viewpoint, because you have the ramp to allow easy hiking to the top and natural forces have sheared off the east face of the mountain to give you unobstructed views once you reach the crest.
There is another Sugarloaf in the Sedona area, which we call **Sugarloaf at Black Mountain** in this book to distinguish the two. It is also a good hike.
The early settlers in Sedona were hard pressed to come up with names

for the multitude of hills, mountains, rock formations and other land features they found and they can be forgiven for using the name Sugarloaf more than once. There is yet a third Sugarloaf adjacent to the **Airport Hill Vortex** hike.

One hundred years ago, when these pioneers came, people didn't buy granulated sugar as we know it today. In those days molasses was boiled down until it began to crystallize and was poured into cone-shaped molds, where it hardened. These "loaves" of sugar, about the size of a golf ball, were their sugar. The loaves became very hard as they aged and it was usually the job of the children in a family to break up the loaves with a hammer so that the sugar could be measured and used in cooking. Eating a bit of the sugar was their reward. A sugarloaf was a blunt-tipped cone, a shape that aptly describes these buttes.

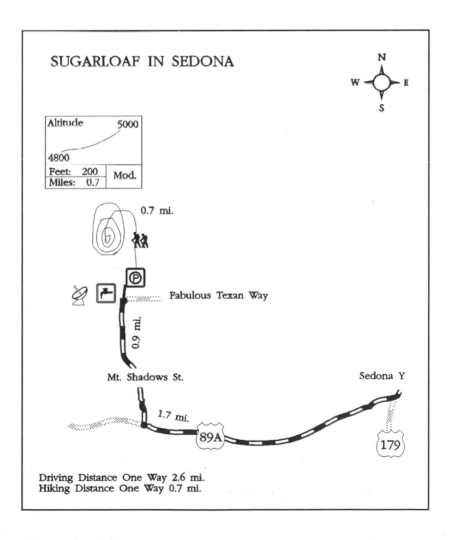

SUGARLOAF IN SEDONA

N
W — E
S

Altitude	5000
4800	
Feet: 200	Mod.
Miles: 0.7	

0.7 mi.

Fabulous Texan Way

0.9 mi.

Mt. Shadows St.

Sedona Y

1.7 mi.

89A

179

Driving Distance One Way 2.6 mi.
Hiking Distance One Way 0.7 mi.

TELEPHONE TRAIL

General Information
Location Map B5
Munds Park USGS Map
Coconino Forest Service Map

Driving Distance One Way: 10.9 miles (Time 20 minutes)
Access Road: All cars, All paved
Hiking Distance One Way: Unknown (Time Unknown)
How Strenuous: Unknown
Features: Unknown

NUTSHELL: This is a marked and posted trail. Maps indicate that it climbs the east wall of Oak Creek Canyon. We have found the trailhead and explored the trail on half a dozen occasions but have never been able to follow the trail beyond the first 0.20 miles. It is a mystery. We include it because it is a marked and numbered trail in the Forest Service's trail system. **We will pay a reward of $25.00 to the first person who can show us the way to the top.**

DIRECTIONS:
From the Sedona Y Go:
    North on Highway 89A (toward Flagstaff) for a distance of 10.9 miles (MP 385.1). Here you will see a wide apron on the right side of the highway under a twenty foot high cliff. Park here.

TRAILHEAD: From the parking place, walk up Highway 89A on the right shoulder about one hundred yards, looking into the screen of vegetation to your right. You will see the typical rusty metal trailhead sign off the highway a few feet. The sign reads, "Trail 72, Telephone."

DESCRIPTION: From the sign look sharp and you will see cairns marking the trail. The trail itself is hard to see because the trail is little used and is covered with pine needles.
    The trail runs along parallel to the highway for about 0.05 mile, then swings to the right, away from the road. You will begin walking toward the east wall of the canyon. If you look hard, you can see that you are walking along an old road bed, probably a construction road that was created while the telephone line was being installed.
    At 0.1 miles you will walk under the phone line. The trail here seems obvious and easy to follow. At 0.2 miles the trail ends in a little pocket at the base of the east wall. Here the cairns disappear and there are no markers or clues of any kind that we could find.

We have tried everything we could think of from this point. We followed the line itself in both directions. No good. We tried going up the east wall wherever it seemed to make sense. No good. We are baffled by this mysterious trail.

It would seem obvious to solve the mystery by calling the Forest Service. We tried. The only response of the person "who knew about hiking trails" was to deny that there is such a trail. When we described it and pointed out that it had their sign and a trail number, this person claimed still that it was not a Forest Service trail and that the sign must have been accidentally left behind by the phone company. No good.

Solve the mystery and win a prize.

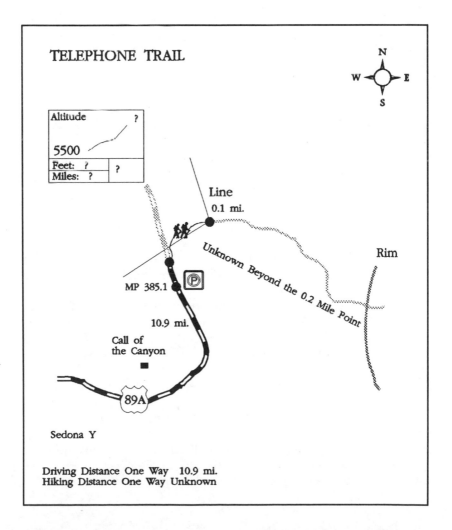

TELEPHONE TRAIL

N
W ← → E
S

Altitude ?

5500

Feet: ?   ?
Miles: ?

Line
0.1 mi.

Unknown Beyond the 0.2 Mile Point

Rim

MP 385.1   P

10.9 mi.

Call of
the Canyon

89A

Sedona Y

Driving Distance One Way   10.9 mi.
Hiking Distance One Way Unknown

THOMAS POINT

General Information
Location Map B5
Munds Park USGS Map
Coconino Forest Service Map

Driving Distance One Way: 10.3 miles (Time 20 minutes)
Access Road: All cars, All paved
Hiking Distance One Way: 1.00 miles (Time 60 minutes)
How Strenuous: Hard
Features: Views

NUTSHELL: This is a marked and posted trail that climbs the east wall of upper Oak Creek Canyon from a point almost directly across Highway 89A from the West Fork trailhead, 10.3 miles north of Sedona.

DIRECTIONS:
From the Sedona Y Go:
       North on Highway 89A (toward Flagstaff) for a distance of 10.3 miles (MP 384.5) There is no designated parking area. Park where you can.

TRAILHEAD: On the east side of the road twenty yards up Highway 89A from the entrance to the **West Fork Trail** you will see a rusty sign reading, "Thomas Point #142." The sign is set back about 20 feet from the highway.

DESCRIPTION: There is no official parking area for this hike. Cars park all along the shoulder of the highway here, mostly for the **West Fork** hike. You can go up the highway about a quarter of a mile and park off the road at the Call of the Canyon. It will be downhill to your left where the road makes a big curve to the right.
       You will probably see a multitude of people hiking the West Fork trail. Instead of following the horde, walk up the road on the right side of the highway about 20 yards north of the West Fork entrance. There you will see a groove worn into the soil bank and the trailhead sign at the head of the groove. Look sharp, for the sign is hard to see.
       Like the other trails that climb the east wall of the canyon, this trail goes nearly straight up, with little finesse. You start in a pine and spruce forest. The trail zigzags in such a way that it isn't a killer trail like the **Purtymun Trail** or **Thompson's Ladder**.
       After hiking a short distance you will climb high enough to get good views of the sheer white cliffs of the West Fork and East Pocket areas across the canyon. You can see the path of Oak Creek and glimpse bits of the highway.

At about the half mile point you wind around onto an unshaded south face of the canyon wall. Here the pines disappear and you are in the chaparral and juniper life zone. These plants are small compared to the pines so you have better views along this part of the trail. Near the top you come back into the pine and spruce forest again.

At the top pine needles may cover the trail and make it indistinct, so look for cairns. They mark an extension of the trail to a viewpoint to the north, where Thomas Point is located. Thomas Point is well named, for it is a peninsula or tongue pointing west. Standing at the tip of the point you will have good views north, west and south. Particularly good are the views of the San Francisco Peaks and the head of Oak Creek Canyon. As long as you are at the top of the rim, you might as well walk along the rim in both directions to find different viewpoints and places of interest.

This hike and the **Harding Spring** trail are our favorites for climbing the east wall of Oak Creek Canyon, with the **Cookstove** trail not far behind.

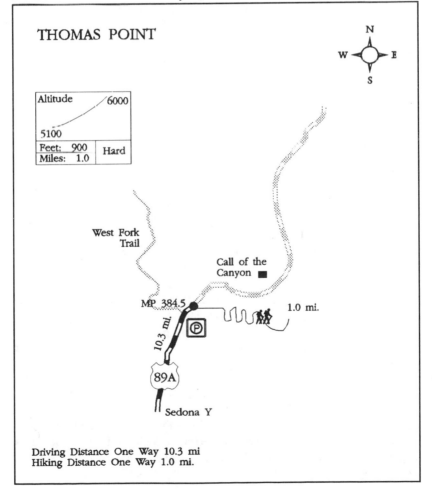

THOMAS POINT

N
W E
S

| Altitude | 6000 |
| 5100 | |

| Feet: 900 | Hard |
| Miles: 1.0 | |

West Fork Trail

Call of the Canyon ■

MP 384.5

1.0 mi.

10.3 mi.

Ⓟ

89A

Sedona Y

Driving Distance One Way 10.3 mi
Hiking Distance One Way 1.0 mi.

THOMPSON'S LADDER

General Information
Location Map C5
Munds Park USGS Map
Coconino Forest Service Map

Driving Distance One Way: 4.5 miles (Time 10 minutes)
Access Road: All cars, All paved
Hiking Distance One Way: 3.00 miles (Time 2 hours)
How Strenuous: Very Hard
Features: Views

NUTSHELL: This trail climbs the east wall of upper Oak Creek Canyon from a point near Indian Gardens, 4.5 miles north of Sedona.

DIRECTIONS:
From the Sedona Y Go:
North on Highway 89A (toward Flagstaff) for a distance of 4.5 miles (MP 378.7). There is no designated parking area. Park where you can.

TRAILHEAD: From the parking area you hike a closed road down to the creek, cross the creek on a disused concrete bridge and pick up the trail on the other bank. It is not signed.

DESCRIPTION: The entrance to the parking spot is hard to find, as you are suddenly upon it without any cues to its existence. It is located 0.04 miles south of the row of mailboxes at the entrance to the Creekside Trailer Park, and 0.10 miles south of the southernmost point on the Twin Oaks Cafe parking lot. It looks like a wide shoulder with a black gravel surface. In fact, it is the mouth of an old road. The road has been blocked off, leaving a space big enough for one car to park.

The road descends sharply to the creek where you walk across an old bridge. On the other side you walk about halfway up the paved remnant of the old road, about 0.13 miles from the parking place. Here you will see an unmarked trail going off to your right. This is your trail. It forks in a few feet. Take the left (uphill) fork.

The trail is hard to see because it is covered with oak leaves. Look sharp and you will see cairns along the way. The terrain is rather difficult and you must go across some gullies. At 0.40 miles you reach Bee Canyon, a good sized ravine. In the spring this can carry lots of water and you must rock hop to cross it. This is an easy place to lose the trail so look carefully for the cairns.

You reach an old barbed wire fence at 0.50 miles. Follow along it for a short distance to the 0.55 miles point, where you come to a fork. Take the left fork (northeast), going uphill. The trail is level from here to the 0.83 mile point and then it descends. At 1.17 miles you will join a trail coming in from your right (west). Take the left fork here.

You are now on a flank of Munds Canyon and the trail becomes easy to follow. Up to this point you have been following a tortuous detour to avoid private land and only now have reached the true Thompson's Ladder Trail. The trail now becomes a very steep climb. At 1.75 miles the trail winds northwesterly around a point and goes up Bee Canyon. When water is running from the top you will see big waterfalls.

You will reach a false top at 2.8 miles. It is a great viewpoint. The trail continues to the 3.0 mile point, which is the true top. There you will find a trail marker reading, "Thompson's Ladder, Trail #14, Roundup Tank 2, Munds Park 4.5." The top itself is not interesting, being a bare mesa, but you can walk along the rim there to get superb views.

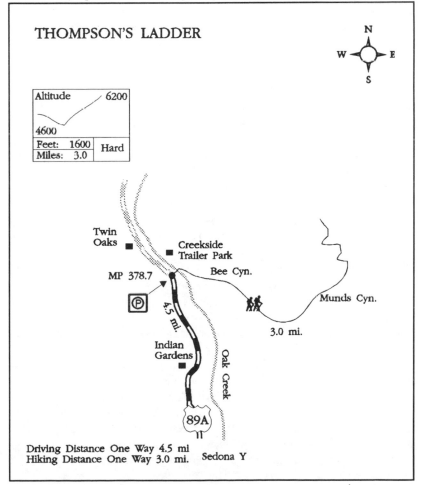

THOMPSON'S LADDER

N
W ← → E
S

Altitude 6200

4600

Feet: 1600   Hard
Miles: 3.0

Twin Oaks

Creekside Trailer Park

MP 378.7

Bee Cyn.

Munds Cyn.

3.0 mi.

4.5 mi.

Indian Gardens

Oak Creek

89A

Driving Distance One Way 4.5 ml
Hiking Distance One Way 3.0 mi.   Sedona Y

TURKEY CREEK TRAIL

General Information
Location Map E3
Sedona USGS Map
Coconino Forest Service Map

Driving Distance One Way: 12.1 miles (Time 30 minutes)
Access Road: High clearance, Last 1.1 miles rough dirt road
Hiking Distance One Way: 3.0 miles (Time 2.0 hours)
How Strenuous: Moderate
Features: Rock formations, Views

NUTSHELL: Located 12.1 miles southwest of Sedona, behind the Verde Valley School, this moderate hike has you climb 1000 feet in about a mile through interesting redrocks to the top of House Mountain.

DIRECTIONS:
From the Sedona Y Go:
    South on Highway 179 (toward Phoenix) for 7.5 miles (MP 306.1), to the Verde Valley School Road. Turn right onto Verde Valley School Road. The first 3.0 miles of this road are paved. Follow it to the 11.0 mile point where you will see a sign marking the **Turkey Creek Trail**. Just beyond the sign you will see FR 9216B, a dirt road to your left. Turn onto FR 9216B. This road can be very rough; it doesn't seem to get any maintenance. We were able to go in about a mile in our Tercel but there were some bad spots. At 11.6 miles you will reach a fork where a lath marks FR 9892 to the right. Don't take that fork; go left. At 12.0 miles you will come to another fork. Here there is a lath marker to the left, FR 9895. Go right instead on an unmarked dirt road. The roads are confusing in this area and there are no markers for the trail. In December 1991 when we took this hike the road became impassable after the 12.1 mile point, so we parked and walked the road a mile to the trailhead. The trail itself is 2.0 miles long one way from Turkey Creek Tank.

TRAILHEAD: At Turkey Creek Tank. It is marked with a rusty sign.

DESCRIPTION: Access to this fine hike is baffling. It is a marked and maintained trail and there is a road marker announcing the trail on the Verde Valley School Road. So the hiker would think that there would be a convenient well-marked road to the trailhead. Quite the contrary. When we first took this hike in early 1988 we were able to drive to the trailhead. In 1990 when we tried it again the road was blocked by an unnamed State Park. This third time, in late 1991, the park was still there but its access gates were locked. We could see a trail symbol sign through the gates, but there was no way to get to the trail through the fence. Finally by trial and error we were able to find the way to the trailhead, as described.

When you get near Turkey Creek Tank you will recognize its presence because it is encircled by cottonwood trees. It is a pleasant oasis, though it goes dry in summer. The hiking trail starts at its farthest edge and goes along a former jeep road, winding through some fine redrocks. It changes to a footpath in about half a mile.

Soon after this you begin to climb House Mountain. The path is fairly steep but the footing is good. It is an old stock trail. It zigzags to a saddle on the top, where you are on the rim of an extinct volcanic crater, a rather shallow one. From that point you can take the trail down into the bowl of the crater, though there isn't much to see there. We prefer to bushwhack along the rim to the north for the fine views of Sedona, which are magnificent from there. The mountain's high point is to the north, a basalt tower worth scaling.

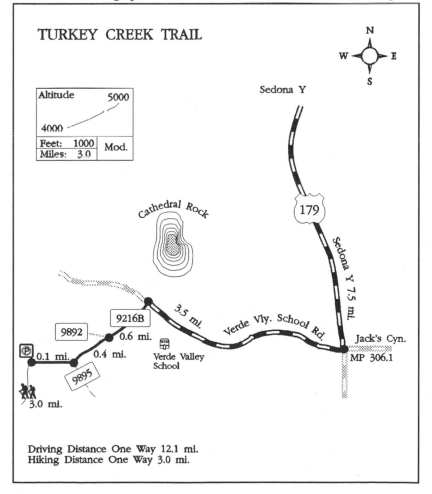

TURKEY CREEK TRAIL

N
W — E
S

Sedona Y

Altitude 5000

4000

Feet: 1000   Mod.
Miles: 3.0

Cathedral Rock

179

Sedona Y 7.5 mi.

9216B
0.6 mi.

3.5 mi.

Verde Vly. School Rd.

9892

0.1 mi.   0.4 mi.

Verde Valley School

Jack's Cyn.

MP 306.1

9895

3.0 mi.

Driving Distance One Way 12.1 mi.
Hiking Distance One Way 3.0 mi.

TWIN BUTTES

General Information
Location Map E5
Sedona USGS Map
Coconino Forest Service Map

Driving Distance One Way: 2.0 miles (Time 10 minutes)
Access Road: All cars, All paved
Hiking Distance One Way: 1.5 miles (Time 1.25 hours)
How Strenuous: Hard
Features: Views

NUTSHELL: The Twin Buttes formation is located a couple of miles south of the Sedona Y. The famous Chapel of the Holy Cross was built near its south face. It is a hard haul to the top of the north face over an unmaintained trail but once there you will enjoy superb views.

DIRECTIONS:
From the Sedona Y Go:
    South on Highway 179 (toward Phoenix) for a distance of 1.4 miles (MP 312.1) to Morgan Road. Turn left onto Morgan Road and follow it to the 2.0 mile point, where there is a cattle guard and the paving ends. Park just on the other side of the cattle guard.

TRAILHEAD: You will see no trail signs. Walk the road, which is FR 179F.

DESCRIPTION: At the cattle guard you will see a sign indicating a "Trail Walk-through." We have tried this and see no earthly reason for its existence. It is much better to walk right down the middle of the road.
    This road is used by the jeep tours that abound in Sedona and you are likely to meet some of them on this hike in good weather. They act as if they own the road, and in a certain sense they do, as they have a maintenance agreement for it with the Forest Service.
    At 0.26 miles turn right, going up on a red sandstone ledge. The jeeps go up there to thrill the dudes, so the trail is easy to follow. You stay on the lower part of the ledge and walk across it, where the dirt road resumes.
    At 0.34 miles go to the right on a sunken road. This will lead you to a sinkhole called the **Devil's Dining Room** at 0.42 miles. At this site, you will come out into a small clearing where you will see a line of boulders and a barbed wire fence. These mark the sinkhole.
    This sinkhole isn't nearly as big as **Devil's Kitchen** but it is impressive. Sinkholes develop when underground cavities undermine a ledge

of rock to the point where it collapses into the void. Some geologists speculate that this sinkhole and Devil's Kitchen were both caused by the same underground river that removed the supporting subsoil from both places.

Behind the sinkhole is a hill. You will see a path going up this hill. This is the path you want to follow. At 0.65 miles you will come out onto a redrock ledge. In a little over 100 feet you will see a trail going left marked by cairns. Take this trail.

At 1.0 miles you will come out onto a saddle, which is a point on the **Battlement Mesa** hike. Just as you top out, look for a trail going left, uphill, marked by cairns. This is the trail you want. Moderately steep up to now, the trail gets much steeper. Your target is the big saddle in the Twin Buttes to your left, and you have a half mile of hard hiking to get there.

Once you top out, we think you will not regret your effort. The view is spectacular. One of the best. From the saddle you have a panoramic sweep from north to south. To the south you look down on the Chapel.

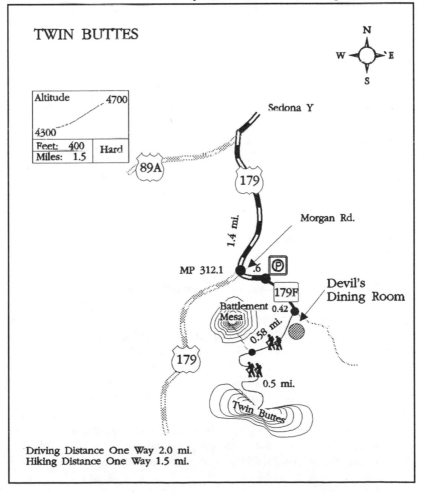

TWIN BUTTES

Altitude 4700
4300
Feet: 400 Hard
Miles: 1.5

Sedona Y

89A

179

1.4 mi.

Morgan Rd.

MP 312.1 .6

179F

Devil's Dining Room

Battlement 0.42
Mesa

0.58 mi.

179

0.5 mi.

Twin Buttes

Driving Distance One Way 2.0 mi.
Hiking Distance One Way 1.5 mi.

TWIN PILLARS

General Information
Location Map E3
Sedona USGS Map
Coconino Forest Service Map

Driving Distance One Way: 12.1 miles (Time 30 minutes)
Access Road: High clearance, Last 1.1 miles rough dirt road
Hiking Distance One Way: 0.5 miles (Time 45 minutes)
How Strenuous: Moderate
Features: Rock formations, Views

NUTSHELL: Located 12.1 miles southwest of Sedona, behind the Verde Valley School, this moderate hike has you climb through interesting redrocks to the top of a ridge overlooking the school.

DIRECTIONS:
From the Sedona Y Go:
        South on Highway 179 (toward Phoenix) for a distance of 7.5 miles (MP 306.1), to the Verde Valley School Road. Turn right onto Verde Valley School Road. The first 3.0 miles of this road are paved. Follow it to the 11.0 mile point where you will see a sign marking the **Turkey Creek Trail**. Just beyond the sign you will see FR 9216B, a dirt road to your left. Turn onto FR 9216B. This road can be very rough; it doesn't seem to get any maintenance. We were able to go in about a mile in our Tercel but there were some bad spots. At 11.6 miles you will reach a fork where a lath marks FR 9892 to the right. Don't take that fork; go left. At 12.0 miles you will come to another fork. Here there is a lath marker to the left, FR 9895. Go left, taking FR 9895 to its end, at 12.1 miles.

TRAILHEAD: Not marked. The trail begins where the road ends.

DESCRIPTION: The access road for this hike is the same up to a point as that for the **Turkey Creek Trail**, which is a very good hike. The roads, once you turn off the Verde Valley School Road, can be very rough, so a high clearance vehicle is recommended.
        As you follow the driving instructions above you will notice that you are heading toward a big butte. The road ends almost at the base of the butte and from there this unsigned but well-defined trail goes up the butte.
        We took this hike not long after a rain and saw many hoof prints on the trail. We would guess that the trail was created as a horse path for the kids at the Verde Valley School, which is on the other (east) side of the butte. It

makes a good hiking trail.

Though the trail was not marked, we had no trouble following it. We built a few cairns along the way for those who follow us. The path winds around in such a fashion that it makes good use of the terrain to climb the butte gradually. It is not very steep. As you climb you will rise high enough to get good views of some pretty country.

At the top you come out onto a saddle. The Twin Pillars for which we named the hike are to your right (south). We could find no name for this place on any map, so we christened it after these prominent redrock pillars. From the saddle you look down onto the school, which has a beautiful setting. You will also have excellent views of Cathedral Rock, a famous Sedona formation.

The trail turns to the left and goes toward a high solitary butte, ending at its base. From there it is possible to scramble completely around the butte for the good views to the north, adding another quarter of a mile to the trip.

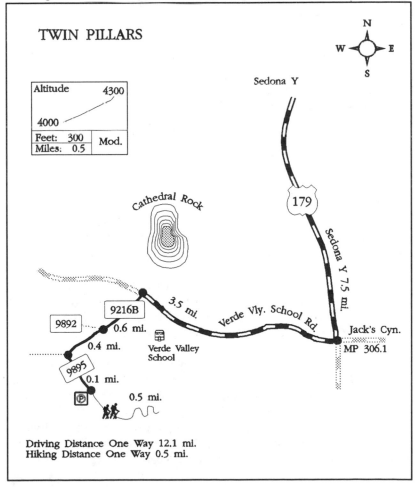

VAN DEREN CABIN

General Information
Location Map C4
Wilson Mt. USGS Map
Coconino Forest Service Map

Driving Distance One Way: 7.6 miles (Time 30 minutes)
Access Road: High clearance car preferable, Last 2.4 miles rough dirt road
Hiking Distance One Way: 0.30 miles (Time 15 minutes)
How Strenuous: Easy
Features: Historic cabin, Views

NUTSHELL: This is a short easy hike to a historic cabin located off the road to Vultee Arch, 7.6 miles northwest of Sedona.

DIRECTIONS:
From the Sedona Y Go:
Southwest on Highway 89A (toward Cottonwood) a distance of 3.2 miles (MP 371) to the Dry Creek Road. Turn right on Dry Creek Road, also known as FR 152C, and follow it to the 5.2 mile point where FR 152 branches to the right. Take FR 152. You will see a sign for Vultee Arch on this road. Follow the road to the 7.6 miles point, where you will see a road to your left marked FR 9917. Turn left on 9917 and park as soon as you can.

TRAILHEAD: There are no trail signs. Walk the road, FR 9917.

DESCRIPTION: Jeep tours regularly come here and drive FR 9917 all the way to the cabin. However, we recommend that you park just off the main road and walk to the cabin because the road is uneven and rough and this is a book of hikes.
At 0.16 miles you will come to the place where the road fords Dry Creek. If the water is high you might want to wait for another day. Upstream there is a broad redrock ledge that has been cut by the action of the creek into charming sculptures. It is well worth a short detour to walk along it and enjoy the shapes.
When you cross the creek the road goes to the top of the bank on the other side. The road forks there. Take the left fork and follow it to its end. From there you will see the cabin. The old homestead was composed of several acres. The Forest Service purchased the cabin site only and devotes it to public use, while the remainder of the old ranch is private property. The private property has been enclosed by a fence that is garlanded with No Trespassing signs. Don't worry about these, because access to the cabin site is guaranteed.

The cabin was built by a pioneer named Earl Van Deren in the 1890s. He built the first unit by recycling a cabin he found on nearby Brins Mesa. This is the part located nearest to the new fence It looks terribly rustic and small to our eyes but was considered a decent living place in its day. Several years later Earl fell in love but his fiancee refused to marry him until he expanded the cabin. He added the second unit, connected the two with a roof forming a breezeway, satisfying his fiancee, and they married.

Earl ranched and made some money as a movie extra. In the 1940s he bought some acreage in what turned out later to be uptown Sedona, where there is a Van Deren Road honoring him. He gradually sold most of the uptown land for a tidy profit.

At the back of the cabin site, just beyond the corner of the new fence, you can see a couple of inclined redrock walls and a pile of old boards. These are the remains of Earl's root cellar. Legend says that the cellar was used by a bootlegger after Earl moved to town and that the bootlegger was murdered.

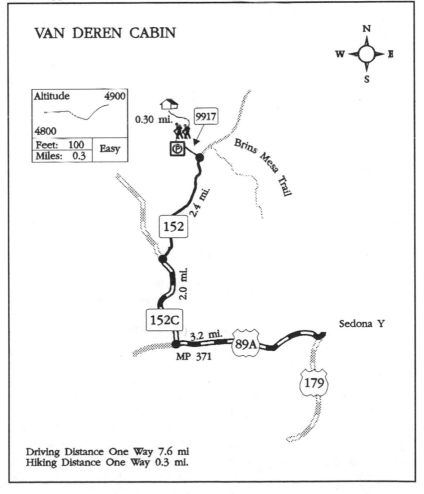

VAN DEREN CABIN

Altitude 4900
4800
Feet: 100 Easy
Miles: 0.3

0.30 mi. 9917

Brins Mesa Trail

2.4 mi.

152

2.0 mi.

152C

3.2 mi.
MP 371 89A

Sedona Y

179

Driving Distance One Way 7.6 mi
Hiking Distance One Way 0.3 mi.

VULTEE ARCH

General Information
Location Map C4
Loy Butte and Wilson Mt. USGS Maps
Coconino Forest Service Map

Driving Distance One Way: 9.6 miles (Time 45 minutes)
Access Road: High clearance best, Last 4.4 miles unpaved
Hiking Distance One Way: 1.6 miles (Time 1 hour)
How Strenuous: Moderate
Features: Arch, Historic marker, Scenic canyon

NUTSHELL: Located 9.6 miles north of Sedona, this hike takes you to a natural arch and a commemorative plaque in a beautiful box canyon. **A personal favorite**.

DIRECTIONS:
From the Sedona Y Go:
 Southwest on Highway 89A (toward Cottonwood) a distance of 3.2 miles (MP 371) to the Dry Creek Road. Turn right on Dry Creek Road, also known as FR 152C, and follow it to the 5.2 mile point where FR 152 branches to the right. Take FR 152. You will see a sign for Vultee Arch on this road. Follow the road to its end, at 9.6 miles. There is a parking area there. Pull in and park.

TRAILHEAD: This is a marked and maintained trail. You will see a rusty sign at the parking place reading, "Vultee Arch #22."

DESCRIPTION: FR 152 can be a very rough road. Sometimes the first mile is graded but it is seldom graded after that. There are many places on the road where the soil has washed away from the surface leaving sharp projecting rocks that compete for the honor of tearing out your oil pan. In other places exposed ledges make for very rough encounters and must be crawled over.
 The hiking trail is sandy and gives nice soft footing. The trail climbs as it progresses, passing through several life zones, which leads to interesting changes in the vegetation surrounding the trail. When you begin the trail you are in a forest of Arizona cypress. After that you will go through oak and pine and finally you will find Douglas fir. The route is shaded the entire way, which makes it a good choice in hot weather.
 The trail crosses a creekbed several times, so don't try to hike it when a lot of water is running in the creek. The creek is dry except for a few weeks in the spring, generally in March and April or after a hard summer rain.

At 1.4 miles you will reach the junction of this trail and the **Sterling Pass Trail**, which forks to the right.

At the end of the trail you will break out into a clearing in a box canyon and the trail will climb onto redrock ledges. You will see the arch against a far wall of the box canyon. There is a trail leading to it that you can easily pick up. It is possible to walk right up to the arch and even to climb on top of it.

The historical plaque is cast in bronze and fastened to the face of a redrock ledge, the second ledge above you as you enter the box canyon. The plaque commemorates the airplane crash that killed Gerald Vultee, an aviation pioneer, and his wife in 1938. They did not crash here, but on nearby East Pocket, when they were caught in a storm at night. Had he been flying one of today's planes with modern instruments, he probably would have brought it in safely.

This is a dandy hike and is deservedly popular, meaning that you are likely to run into other hikers when you take this trail.

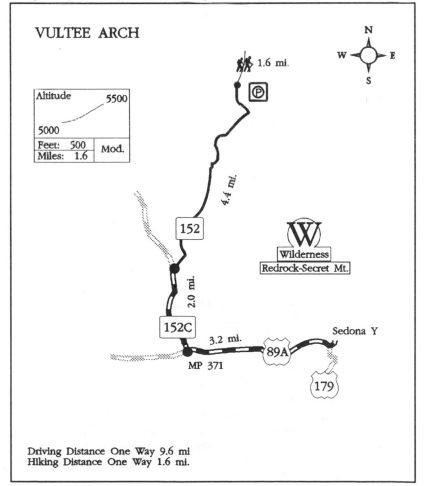

WALKER BASIN TRAIL

General Information
Location Map G6
Walker Mtn. USGS Map
Coconino Forest Service Map

Driving Distance One Way: 31.8 miles (Time 1.25 hours)
Access Road: All cars, Last 17.1 miles good dirt road
Hiking Distance One Way: 8.0 miles (Time 4.5 hours)
How Strenuous: Hard
Features: Views

NUTSHELL: This trail runs from a point 6200 feet high on the Mogollon Rim to the bottom, a 2000 foot drop in 8.0 miles.

DIRECTIONS:
From the Sedona Y Go:
        South on Highway 179 (toward Phoenix) for 14.7 miles, to the I-17 Interchange. Go underneath onto the dirt road, FR 618 and follow it. At the 19.7 mile point you will see a sign for the Walker Basin Trail and a road going left. Pass by. At the 24.5 mile point, you will take a road left, FR 214, "Cedar Flat." FR 214 takes you to the top of the Mogollon Rim, a 2000 foot climb. You will come to the high point at about 30.0 miles, then go downhill. Just past a cattle guard, at the 31.8 mile point, you will see a dirt road to your left (west) marked 214B. Pull in and park. Do not try to drive 214B.

TRAILHEAD: There is a sign where you park.

DESCRIPTION: This is a hard hike. We recommend doing this hike with two cars, in which case it is still pretty strenuous, but is an enjoyable experience instead of an ordeal. The way to do this is to take two cars in to the lower trailhead, at the 19.7 mile point on FR 618, mentioned above. You can drive in about 0.9 miles, to the parking place. Leave one car there and take the other to the top.
        There is one trick at the top, and an important one. After you have hiked about 0.1 miles, you will come to a gate. Go *inside* the gate. There is a path outside as well, but it is not your trail. The gate is not signed, so be sure to follow these instructions.
        The first leg of the hike is on a mesa top. The "cedars" (junipers) have been cleared, giving fine views in all directions, particularly to the north and west, where you see the San Francisco Peaks and the Sedona color country. At 1.75 miles you come to a drop-off where you descend to a lower bench. As you

drop, you will see a pond down to your right. This is Walker Basin.

You reach the pond at 2.5 miles, where the trail gets a little tricky, not well marked. Up to now it has been a jeep road, but here it becomes a footpath only. Walk around the right shoulder of the pond, about one quarter around, and take the trail to the right, at the end of the fence. You will see cairns and also limbs cut from trees. The path goes north from the pond.

From here you climb to the 3.28 mile point, then walk across a fairly level stretch. At 4.18 miles you come upon a mysterious trailless sign, "Jacobs Tank 1/4 mi." At 4.75 miles you come to another drop-off, where you have great views west. As you wind down from here, the views to the south open, to the Verde Valley.

At 5.4 miles you reach the final drop-off where you enter an area of beautiful sandstone ledges with impressive sights both near at hand and far away. You reach the bottom at 7.25 miles and walk across level country to get back to your waiting car at 8.0 miles.

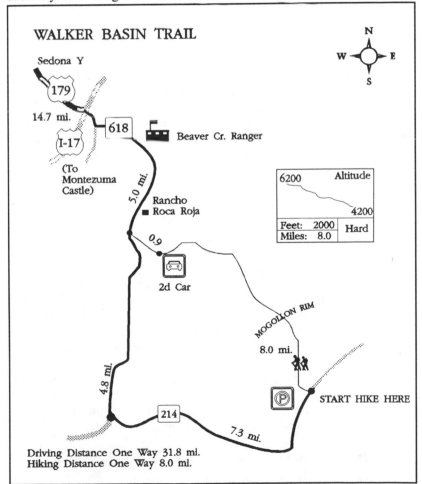

WALKER BASIN TRAIL

WEIR TRAIL

General Information
Location Map G6
Apache Maid and Casner Butte USGS Maps
Coconino Forest Service Map

Driving Distance One Way: 17.2 miles (Time 30 minutes)
Access Road: All cars, Last 2.5 miles good dirt road
Hiking Distance One Way: 2.5 miles (Time 90 minutes)
How Strenuous: Moderate
Features: Views, Creek

NUTSHELL: This trail follows the course of Wet Beaver Creek, some 17.2 miles southeast of Sedona. Then it goes down to the creek to a pool formed by a weir.

DIRECTIONS:
From the Sedona Y Go:
    South on Highway 179 (toward Phoenix) for 14.7 miles, to the I-17 Interchange. Instead of going onto I-17, go underneath it onto the dirt road. At 15.2 miles, you will come to a junction. The right fork goes to Montezuma Castle. Take the left fork (FR 618). It is a good dirt road. At 16.9 miles you are almost to the Beaver Creek Ranger Station. You will see a sign showing a left turn for the Bell Crossing Trail. Take this road. At 17.2 miles you will reach the parking area for the trailhead.

TRAILHEAD: This is a marked and maintained trail. There is a sign at the parking lot for the **Bell Crossing Trail**. Take this trail.

DESCRIPTION: From the trailhead the trail goes up the canyon along the course of Wet Beaver Creek, sometimes near it, sometimes away from it, but always following its path. There is also a Dry Beaver Creek in the area. "Wet" means that the creek you will follow on this hike flows year around. Even when you are not near the creek you can hear water running, a pleasant sound in desert country. The waterway is lined with typical riparian vegetation, tall sycamores and cottonwoods.
    As you look up the canyon you see a flank of the Mogollon Rim, a giant uplift running across Arizona and New Mexico. The top of the rim marks the southern boundary of the Colorado Plateau. The base of the rim is the northern boundary of the Sonoran Desert. This is a significant conjunction of land features.
    The trail is broad and easy to walk, as it was a road. You will cross

through an active cattle ranch. Don't be startled if you run into some cows. As you walk along the trail pay attention to the canyon walls. You will note that they contain the same redrock as in Sedona in the lower layers but that the top is covered with a thick cap of lava. If it weren't for that top layer of hard rock, this country would be just as eroded and colorful as Sedona.

At about 0.60 miles look for a large boulder on the left side of the trail. On the side that faces away from you are a number of interesting petroglyphs. At the 2.0 mile point you will reach the **Apache Maid Trail, #15** branching to the left. Soon after this fork you will find a signboard. Just beyond the signboard is a trail going off to the right, down to the water. This is the Weir Trail, your objective. It is 0.50 miles from the fork to the water.

A weir is a low dam used to regulate the flow of water. You will see the weir, complete with a gaging station that is used to measure water depth and runoff. When the water is high, the pool formed by the weir is a good swimming hole. Upstream from the pool is an interesting cable car.

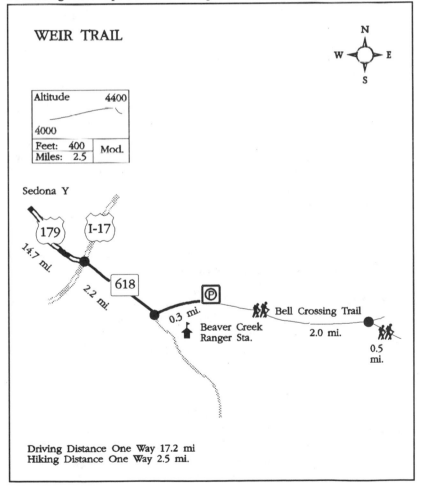

WEST CLEAR CREEK TRAIL

General Information
Location Map G6
Buckhorn Mtn., Walker Mtn. USGS Maps
Coconino Forest Service Map

Driving Distance One Way: 29.5 miles (Time 1 hour)
Access Road: All cars, Last 14.8 miles good dirt road
Hiking Distance One Way: 1.0 miles (Time 30 minutes)
How Strenuous: Easy
Features: Historic ranch, Permanent creek, Wide easy trail, Views

NUTSHELL: This easy trail starts from the West Clear Creek Campground 29.5 miles south of Sedona and takes you through an interesting old ranch to a lovely creek in a deep scenic canyon.

DIRECTIONS:
From the Sedona Y Go:
     South on Highway 179 (toward Phoenix) for 14.7 miles, to the I-17 Interchange. Instead of going onto I-17, go underneath it onto the dirt road. At 15.2 miles, you will come to a junction. Take the left fork (FR 618), toward Beaver Creek Ranger Station. Several minor roads branch off FR 618, but it is always the main one. Follow FR 618 to the 24.5 mile point, where you will see a dirt road branching left, to Cedar Flat. Keep going south on FR 618. At 26.5 miles you will come to a road to the left (FR 215) to the West Clear Creek Campground. Turn left on FR 215 and go to the 29.5 mile point, all the way to the end of the road. Parking for the trail is located there and signed.

TRAILHEAD: At the parking area you will see trail signs for the West Clear Creek Trail #17, and the **Blodgett Basin Trail.**

DESCRIPTION: When we visited this trail in March 1992, it was still routed up the side of a hill to avoid crossing the old Bull Pen Ranch. (This trail is also called the Bull Pen Trail.) The ranch is now public property, so, for an easy enjoyable hike, ignore the official trail and just walk the ranch road. The first part of the road is lovely, as it is quite close to the creek and passes through a lush riparian forest. Farther on it moves away from Clear Creek and opens up into typical scrub and cactus habitat.
     At 0.66 miles you will come out into an open field, where you see a memorable sight that sticks in the mind of every visitor to this place, a rock house with cactus growing on its roof. When you inspect this small structure, which is about 20 x 12 feet, you will see that the builders heaped dirt on the

roof, an old trick in the Southwest. Prickly pears got established in this dirt and have grown there for years. Behind the rock house, on the north side of the canyon, there is a hill composed of exposed red sandstone adding a welcome touch of color to the landscape. The ranch site is very beautiful.

You will continue along the road to the 1.0 mile point where the fields end and the road dips down to the creek. There you will find some redrock ledges just above the water that seem to have been placed there by nature as places to sit and take the sun and watch the creek gurgle by.

When the water is low enough, you can wade across the creek here and hike upstream on the opposite bank for another mile with relative ease. Beyond that point the hike gets pretty tough. There is a place at about 3.0 miles where the trail lifts out of the canyon on the north wall, requiring a strenuous 2000 foot climb to a point on FR 214 about 1.2 miles above the Blodgett Basin trail terminus.

For an easy day hike we recommend stopping at the 1.0 mile point.

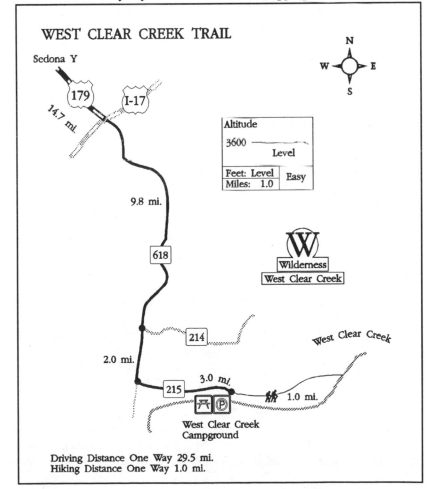

WEST CLEAR CREEK TRAIL

Sedona Y

179

I-17

14.7 mi.

N
W E
S

Altitude
3600
Level
Feet: Level
Miles: 1.0
Easy

9.8 mi.

618

W
Wilderness
West Clear Creek

214

West Clear Creek

2.0 mi.

215   3.0 mi.

1.0 mi.

West Clear Creek
Campground

Driving Distance One Way 29.5 mi.
Hiking Distance One Way 1.0 mi.

WEST FORK

General Information
Location Map B5
Dutton Hill and Munds Park USGS Maps
Coconino Forest Service Map

Driving Distance One Way: 10.3 miles (Time 20 minutes)
Access Road: All cars, All paved
Hiking Distance One Way: 3.00 miles (Time 90 minutes)
How Strenuous: Moderate
Features: Gorgeous canyon with stream

NUTSHELL: One of the best and most popular hikes in Arizona. The trailhead is located 10.3 miles north of Sedona. **A personal favorite**.

DIRECTIONS:
From the Sedona Y Go:
    North on Highway 89A (toward Flagstaff) for a distance of 10.3 miles (MP 384.5.) There is no designated parking area. Park where you can.

TRAILHEAD: On the west (left) side of the road you will see a rusty sign reading, "West Fork #108." The trail goes downhill.

DESCRIPTION: There is no official parking area for this hike. Cars park all along the shoulders of the highway. You can drive up about a quarter of a mile and park off the road at the Call of the Canyon. It will be downhill to your left.
    You will probably see a multitude of people hiking the West Fork trail. There are several homes in the trailhead area and some of their driveways look like the entry to the trail. You will see a wooden barricade marking the West Fork Trail, with the trailhead sign.
    You walk down an old driveway that was built to provide access to Mayhews Lodge. You cross the creek, which usually has a makeshift bridge. This is a good time to check conditions. If the water is high, then you should take this hike another day unless you are prepared to do a lot of wading, because the West Fork Trail meanders across the stream a dozen times.
    Once across the creek, you come upon the site of Mayhews Lodge, built as a hunting and fishing lodge in the early 1900s. Zane Grey immortalized it in his novel, *The Call of the Canyon*. The owners tried to raise as much of their own food as they could. You can see areas where they had orchards and vegetable gardens and you will see the remains of their chicken coop set into a shallow cave. The path forks at the entrance to the lodge. The left fork

goes around the ruins, while the right fork goes through them, under an ivy covered arch. The Forest Service bought the lodge two decades ago only to have it burn shortly afterward.

As you enter the West Fork canyon you become immediately aware of the charm of this place, with the gentle stream flowing through a lush habitat framed by tremendous and colorful canyon walls.

The path follows along and over the streambed. At the crossings you will usually find stepping stones that allow you to get across without getting wet. Some people prefer to wear old tennies and wade. You will find distance markers every half mile.

The canyon is narrow, so you are often right next to the cliffs. The stream has undercut them in many places, creating interesting overhangs. You really feel the majesty of the canyon on this hike, for the cliffs dwarf you.

The canyon is 12.0 miles long. We have you stop at 3.0 miles, a moderate distance that allows you to see some of the finest parts of the canyon.

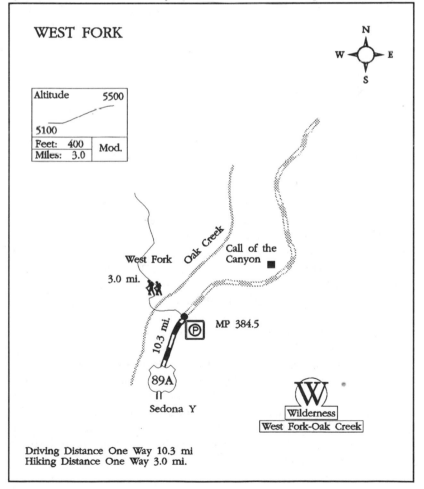

WEST FORK

Altitude 5500

5100

| Feet: | 400 | Mod. |
| Miles: | 3.0 | |

West Fork 3.0 mi.

Oak Creek

Call of the Canyon

MP 384.5

89A

Sedona Y

Wilderness
West Fork-Oak Creek

Driving Distance One Way 10.3 mi
Hiking Distance One Way 3.0 mi.

WILSON CANYON

General Information
Location Map D5
Munds Park USGS Map
Coconino Forest Service Map

Driving Distance One Way: 1.1 miles (Time 5 minutes)
Access Road: All cars, All paved
Hiking Distance One Way: 1.5 miles (Time 1 hour)
How Strenuous: Moderate
Features: Views

NUTSHELL: Just 1.1 miles north of Sedona, Wilson Canyon is spanned by Midgley Bridge. You can take a short easy stroll along the rim of the canyon or a longer hike up the canyon.

DIRECTIONS:
From the Sedona Y Go:
North on Highway 89A (toward Flagstaff) for a distance of 1.1 miles (MP 375.9). Go just across Midgley Bridge and turn left into the parking area.

TRAILHEAD: You will see a rusty sign at the parking lot. It reads, "Wilson Canyon #49."

DESCRIPTION: You will see the parking area just across the bridge. This is a very popular spot and you may not find a parking place open. If not, go up the road a bit. There are several wide shoulders for parking.
　　The trailhead is as easy as pie to locate. Just walk toward the picnic tables at the end of the parking lot. There you will find the Wilson Monument, a bronze plaque set in stone, and two rusty signs. The sign to the left marks Wilson Canyon #49 and is the one you want for this hike. The other sign marks an uphill trail, Wilson Mountain #10, which we call **Wilson Mountain South**.
　　The Wilson Canyon hike is little more than a leisurely stroll for the first 0.25 miles. This may be as much of a hike as some readers want.
　　Up to the 0.25 mile point, the trail is as broad and flat as a roadway. It was a road. Turn around and look at Midgley Bridge and imagine what the road would have been without it. Drivers had to make a sharp turn and go up the canyon to a point where it narrowed and a bridge could readily be installed, cross over the canyon, then go back out and make another sharp turn. Old-timers tell us that the sharp unexpected turns were very dangerous. You will see the old bridge placements at the head of Wilson Canyon. This is the place to stop for the short hike.

For the longer hike, you keep walking up the canyon. Sometimes a stream runs in it. The trail meanders from bank to bank There are many intersecting paths, but it is easy to stay on course if you keep paralleling the canyon. At about 0.5 miles you will see a footpath going uphill to your left. This is part of the **Old Jim Thompson Road**. A few yards beyond that you will see an alternate branch of the Old Jim Thompson Road coming down to intersect your path.

The trail is a gradual uphill climb, quite gentle. In a few places the trail will seem to scramble up a steep bank and go to the top. Ignore these side trails and keep following the canyon.

The canyon encloses you so that you can't see much outside it. At about 1.5 miles you will reach a place where a side trail goes uphill to the right. This goes out of the canyon to a viewpoint and is the place to quit.

Beyond this point the canyon becomes impassable, choked with brush and rock. Time to quit.

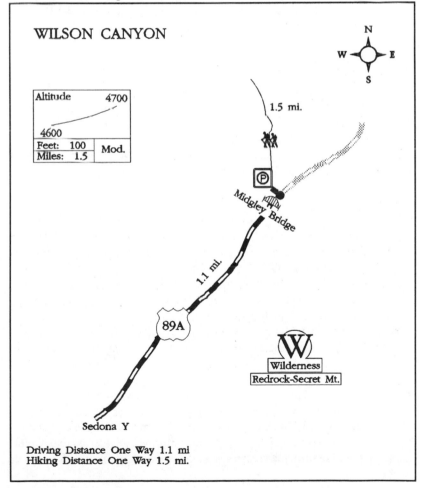

WILSON MOUNTAIN NORTH

General Information
Location Map C5
Munds Park and Wilson Mt. USGS Maps
Coconino Forest Service Map

Driving Distance One Way: 5.3 miles (Time 10 minutes)
Access Road: All cars, All paved
Hiking Distance One Way: 3.4 miles (Time 4.0 hours)
How Strenuous: Hard
Features: Views

NUTSHELL: Located just north of Sedona, Wilson is the highest mountain in the area. This trail, originating at Encinoso Picnic Area, climbs Wilson's north face.

DIRECTIONS:
From the Sedona Y Go:
North on Highway 89A (toward Flagstaff) for a distance of 5.3 miles (MP 379.5), where you will see the Encinoso Picnic Area to your left. Park in the Encinoso parking lot.

TRAILHEAD: From the parking lot, walk up the canyon on the shoulder of the road about 100 yards. There you will see a trail sign reading, "Wilson Mt. #123" with the trail heading uphill.

DESCRIPTION: The trail climbs to the top of a small ridge at about 0.25 miles, where you have a good vantage point to look across the canyon at the cliffs of the east wall. During spring runoff and after hard rains, the Encinoso Waterfall appears there and this is one of the best places from which to see it.

From this ridge the trail climbs gently for another 0.75 miles along a refreshing, wooded side canyon through a lovely mixed forest of pine, fir, spruce, oak and maple. The streambed here seldom carries any water, but when it does, it is delightful. Best bet for this is in April and May.

At 1.0 miles, the serious work begins. Here the canyon pinches in and the trail begins a steep climb up the north face of Wilson. If you want an easy hike, the 1.0 mile point is the place to stop. The ascent beyond the 1.0 mile point is treacherous if the trail is slick with mud or snow. When dry, it is only strenuous. You will climb 1300 feet in 0.5 miles.

After this hard haul, you top out on a flat flank of Wilson called First Bench. You will have great views to the north from here. Across Oak Creek Canyon you will see a major tributary, Munds Canyon, which empties into Oak

Creek at Indian Gardens.

Keep walking south along First Bench. At the 2.0 mile point, at the edge of First Bench, you will intersect the Wilson Mt. South Trail coming up from Midgley Bridge. The junction is well marked with cairns. Take a look off the rim from here; it's great! You may want to quit here.

From this trail junction, you can go to the top of the mountain. See the **Wilson Mountain South** article for details. You will have to hike 0.60 miles to Tool Shed, at the top of the mountain, climbing 800 feet, then hike a level trail 0.80 miles to the North Rim viewpoint, 3.4 miles total one way from Encinoso. This hike is 0.60 miles longer than the Wilson Mountain South Trail because of the walk across First Bench from north to south.

An interesting way to do this hike is with a 2-car shuttle, parking one car at Midgley Bridge and the other at Encinoso. Go up from Midgley Bridge on the South Trail and then come back on the North Trail, doing both on one long hard day.

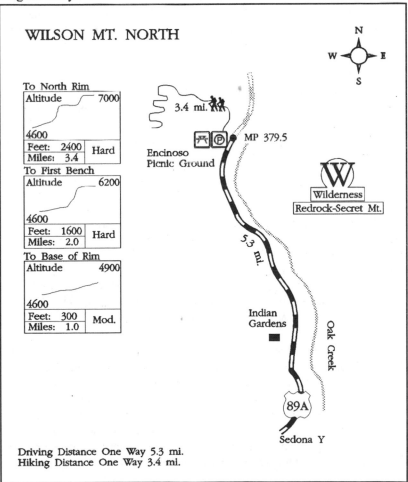

WILSON MT. NORTH

N
W ↔ E
S

To North Rim
Altitude	7000
4600	
Feet: 2400	Hard
Miles: 3.4	

To First Bench
Altitude	6200
4600	
Feet: 1600	Hard
Miles: 2.0	

To Base of Rim
Altitude	4900
4600	
Feet: 300	Mod.
Miles: 1.0	

3.4 mi.

Encinoso
Picnic Ground

MP 379.5

W
Wilderness
Redrock-Secret Mt.

5.3 mi.

Indian
Gardens

Oak Creek

89A

Sedona Y

Driving Distance One Way 5.3 mi.
Hiking Distance One Way 3.4 mi.

WILSON MOUNTAIN SOUTH

General Information
Location Map D5
Munds Park and Wilson Mt. USGS Maps
Coconino Forest Service Map

Driving Distance One Way: 1.1 miles (Time 5 minutes)
Access Road: All cars, All paved
Hiking Distance One Way: 2.8 miles (Time 3.5 hours)
How Strenuous: Hard
Features: Views

NUTSHELL: This popular hike starts at Midgley Bridge, 1.1 miles north of Sedona, and goes up Wilson Mountain to the highest point in the Sedona area, then goes across the mountain top to a fabulous lookout point on the north rim.

DIRECTIONS:
From the Sedona Y Go:
        North on Highway 89A (toward Flagstaff) for a distance of 1.1 miles (MP 375.9). Go just across Midgley Bridge and turn left into the parking area.

TRAILHEAD: You will see a rusty sign at the parking lot. It reads, "Wilson Mt. #10."

DESCRIPTION: The trailhead is easy to locate. Just walk toward the picnic tables. There you will find a bronze plaque set in stone, and two trail signs. The sign to the left is **Wilson Canyon**, #49. The other, uphill, is Wilson Mountain #10, which we call **Wilson Mountain South** in this book, and is the trail you want to take.
        This hike is divided into three phases, each with a different feel:
        Midgley Bridge to First Bench, 1.4 miles, a 1700 foot climb;
        First Bench to Tool Shed, 0.60 miles, an 800 foot climb;
        Tool Shed to North Rim, 0.80 miles, fairly level.

        Midgley Bridge to First Bench: You climb quickly, rising on a hill. Ahead of you on the skyline you will see the saddle that is your destination. Along the way you have constantly enjoyable views of the formations of Wilson Mountain. You are in a high desert landscape, with juniper, manzanita and cactus. As you rise higher, you get into an area with little shade where you switchback to the top. This stretch would be murder on a hot sunny day. Finally you break over the top of First Bench, a long plateau running the length of the east side of the mountain. The views from here are very fine, though the bench itself is pretty drab and featureless.

First Bench to the Tool Shed: Take the path going left, toward the high cliffs. You will soon climb above First Bench and get into a heavy forest of pine and oak. This has a decidedly alpine feeling compared to the desert you have just been through. After a 500 foot climb you will come onto the top, where the land is pretty level, then make a modest 300 foot climb to the Tool Shed, where fire fighting tools are stored. The main trail goes ahead here, with a side trail to the left.

Tool Shed to North Rim: This is a delightful walk through a cool forest on nearly level ground, very easy compared to the first two phases of the hike. You are walking out to the mountain's north edge. When you come to a pond on the east side of the trail, you are almost at the end. Keep walking and you will come out onto a cliff face where you are struck with a soul-stirring view, absolutely one of the finest in the region.

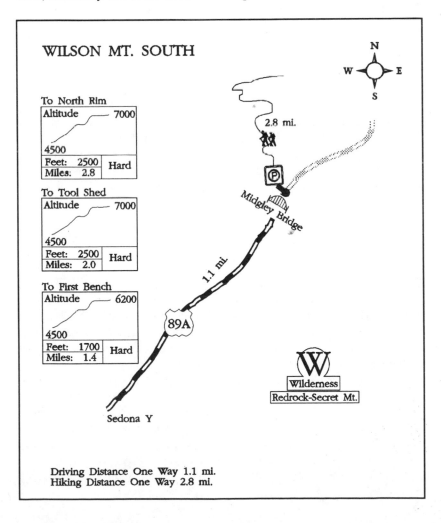

WINDMILL MOUNTAIN

General Information
Location Map E2
Page Springs USGS Map
Coconino Forest Service Map

Driving Distance One Way: 9.5 miles (Time 30 minutes)
Access Road: All vehicles, Last 1.3 miles rough dirt road
Hiking Distance One Way: 1.0 miles (Time 45 minutes)
How Strenuous: Moderate
Features: Views

NUTSHELL: This sprawling mountain 9.5 miles southwest of Sedona is rather drab but is a platform for great views.

DIRECTIONS:
From the Sedona Y Go:
Southwest on Highway 89A (toward Cottonwood) for a distance of 8.2 miles (MP 365.9) to a place where you will see a dirt road, FR 9573C, going off to your right through a gate in a barbed wire fence. Go through the gate and follow FR 9573C. At 8.3 miles, an unmarked road forks right. Ignore it. At 8.7 miles FR 9573 branches to the left. Ignore it. At 8.9 miles there is a fork. Take the right turn and begin to circle around the mountain headed north. At 9.3 miles you will be on the north side and you will see a big power line. Turn left on FR 9573P. Drive up to the power line and park at 9.5 miles.

TRAILHEAD: There are no signs. You will see a trail going uphill along the power line. Take that trail.

DESCRIPTION: As you drive to the trailhead, there are many roads in the area due to the wood cutting which was allowed there recently. The cutters went off in all directions, leaving tracks that sometimes look like roads but are not; so follow the map carefully. If you keep in mind that your destination is to curl around the north face of Windmill Mountain in counterclockwise direction, you will be able to pick out the correct path.

From the parking place a jeep road goes up along the line for about 0.60 miles, then it ends where the line dips down into a valley. From this point the way to the top of the mountain is obvious. You just bushwhack there. There is no trail and none is needed. The country is open and it is easy to see the way. The footing is not good. There is a lot of rock. Also cactus. In fact, this place is a veritable cactus garden, so watch your step.

You will come out on the north rim of the mountain, from where you will get great views of beautiful redrock country. You will see **The Cocks-comb, Doe Mountain, Bear Mountain** and **Loy Butte** very clearly. From where you will be standing, the rim of Windmill Mountain curves like a reverse C, with the opening to the east. It is plain to see that you are on a shield volcano like its brethren **Schuerman Mountain** and **House Mountain**.

Suit yourself in deciding how far you want to hike on the mountaintop. Most hikers will want to make the whole circuit around the top. As you work west you will get views of **Casner Mountain, Black Mountain** and the Sycamore Pass country and you are high enough to enjoy grand panoramas of it all. The views to the south are dull.

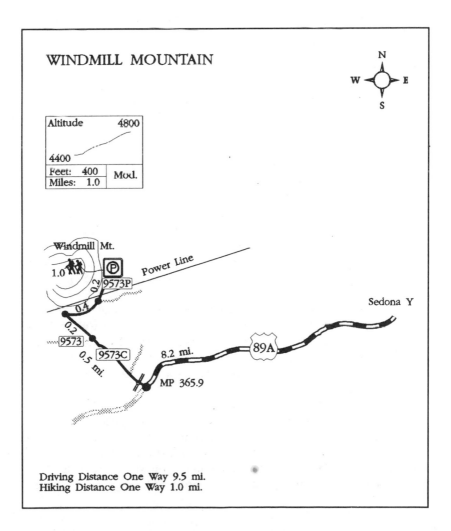

WOODS CANYON TRAIL

General Information
Location Map G5
Munds Mt. and Sedona USGS Maps
Coconino Forest Service Map

Driving Distance One Way: 8.7 Miles (Time 15 minutes)
Access Road: All cars, Paved except last 0.10 miles
Hiking Distance One Way: 3.25 Miles (Time 90 minutes)
How Strenuous: Moderate
Features: Views

NUTSHELL: South of the Sedona Y 8.7 miles, this trail follows Woods Canyon, through which Dry Beaver Creek flows.

DIRECTIONS:
From the Sedona Y Go:
　　South on Highway 179 (toward Phoenix) for 8.6 miles (MP 304.8) to an unmarked dirt road to your left. Turn left on the road, follow it for 0.10 miles and then park.

TRAILHEAD: Right at the highway you will see a gate and a rusty sign reading, "Woods Canyon #93."

DESCRIPTION: The gate is unlocked. Go through it. We recommend that you park just beyond the gate. You can drive farther but the road conditions are dicey especially if the road is wet. We have driven in as far as a mile but do not recommend this unless you are sure you and your vehicle can handle it. If you park near the highway as we recommend then this is a 3.25 mile hike each way.
　　To follow the trail just walk along the main jeep road. At 2.0 miles from the highway you will come to a fence. Just beyond the fence you will find a rusty sign marked, "#93 Hot Loop." This is the place where the **Hot Loop Trail** branches off to the left, going uphill. It looks like a road. The Woods Canyon trail forks to the right here and turns into a footpath descending to the bottom of the canyon.
　　We recommend going to about the 3.25 mile point on the Woods Canyon Trail, where the trail goes onto a sloping redrock shelf above the water.
　　Dry Beaver Creek usually is dry, living up to its name. During the spring thaw it can carry a lot of water and we have seen it at times when it was wild and woolly. This hike is more interesting when water is running. Your best chance of hiking it when water is running is in March or April. There is

another stream nearby called Wet Beaver Creek, which runs year around.

Woods Canyon goes all the way to Interstate-17 just south of the Pinewood Country Club in the Munds Park area. When you are driving on Interstate-17 you will see a sign for an exit marked "Fox Ranch" where the highway bridges Woods Canyon. For many years until 1991 this sign read "Woods Canyon." Hard to tell why the highway department changed it, but they did. Woods Canyon and Munds Canyon, which is located to the north, are major lateral canyons that cut into Oak Creek Canyon. You can see why Interstate-17 is located where it is: it crosses these canyons at their heads, where they are narrow. Even so, the highway department built high bridges at both places. These canyons were a major obstacle between Sedona and Flagstaff in the old days and detouring around them added miles to the trip.

The developed part of the trail ends at the 4.0 mile point, but we think the best stopping place is at 3.25 miles. To hike the entire length of the canyon would mean going a rough 11.0 miles and is not recommended.

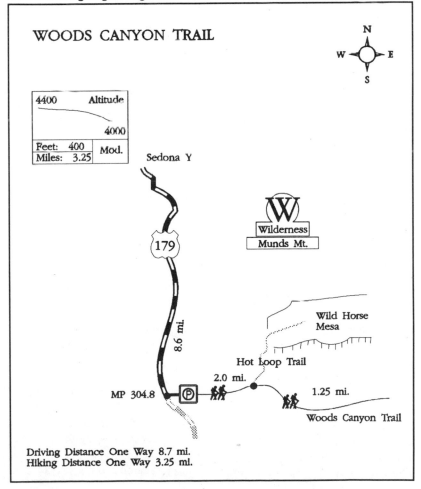

WOODS CANYON TRAIL

N
W — E
S

4400	Altitude
	4000

Feet: 400	Mod.
Miles: 3.25	

Sedona Y

179

Wilderness
Munds Mt.

Wild Horse
Mesa

8.6 mi.

Hot Loop Trail

2.0 mi.

MP 304.8

1.25 mi.

Woods Canyon Trail

Driving Distance One Way 8.7 mi.
Hiking Distance One Way 3.25 mi.

INDEX

A

AB Young 10
Airport Hill Vortex 12
Allens Bend 14
Angel Falls 16
Apache Fire 18
Apache Maid 20
Arches:

Damfino Canyon 88
Devils Bridge 90
Fay Canyon 104
Soldier Pass Arches 204
Vultee Arch 232

B

Battlement Mesa 22
Bear Mt. 24
Bear Sign 26
Beaverhead 28
Bell Crossing 30
Bell Rock 32
Black Mt. 34
Black Mt. Mystery House 36
Blodgett Basin 38
Boynton Canyon 40
Boynton Spires 42
Briant Canyon 44
Brins Mesa East 46
Brins Mesa West 48
Brown House Canyon 50

C

Capitol Butte 52
Carroll Canyon 54
Casner Canyon North 56
Casner Canyon South 58
Casner Mountain South 60
Cathedral Ridge 62
Cathedral Rock, Back O' Bnd. 64
Cathedral Rock, VV School 66
Chicken Point 68
Chimney Rock 70

Chinup 72
Cibola Mittens 74
Cockscomb 76
Coffee Pot Trail 78
Cookstove 80
Courthouse Butte 82
Cow Pies 84
Coyote Ridge 86

D

Damfino Canyon 88
Devils Bridge 90
Devils Dining Room 92
Devils Kitchen 94
Doe Mt. 96
Dogie Trail 98
Dry Creek 100

E-F-G

Eagles' Nest 102
Fay Canyon 104
Frye Wash 106

H

HS Canyon 108
Harding Spring 110
Hermit Ridge 112
Hot Loop 114
House Mt. 116

I-J-K

Indian Ruins:

Allens Bend 14
Boynton Canyon 40
Fay Canyon 104
Lost Canyon 130
Lost Cyn. Ruins 132
Loy Butte 136
Loy Canyon 138
Mescal Mountain 144
Mushroom Rock 154
Oak Creek/Verde 156
Red Canyon 178
Sacred Mountain 184

Steamboat Rock 208
Sugarloaf Black Mt. 214

Jacks Canyon 118
Kisva Trail 120
Kushmans Cone 122

L
Little Horse 124
Little Park Heights 126
Long Canyon 128
Lost Canyon 130
Lost Canyon Ruins 132
Lost Wilson Mt. 134
Loy Butte 136
Loy Canyon 138

M
Marg's Draw 140
Merry-Go-Round 142
Mescal Mt. 144
Mitten Ridge 146
Mooney Trail 148
Mountain Bike Rides 8-9
Munds Mt. North 150
Munds Mt. South 152
Mushroom Rock 154

N-O-P-Q
Oak Creek/Verde Conf. 156
Oak Creek Vista 158
Old Highway 79 160
Old Jim Thompson Rd. 162
Old Schnebly Hill Rd. 164
Parsons Trail 166
Personal Favorites:
    Boynton Canyon 40
    Cow Pies 84
    Doe Mountain 96
    Fay Canyon 104
    HS Canyon 108
    Long Canyon 128
    Lost Canyon 130
    Vultee Arch 232

West Fork 240
Pink Sand Canyon 168
Pumphouse Wash 170
Purtymun Trail 172

R
Rattlesnake Cyn. 174
Rattlesnake Ridge 176
Red Canyon Ruins 178
Red Tank Draw 180
Robbers Roost 182

S
Sacred Mt. 184
Schnebly Hill Buttes 186
Schnebly to Marg's 188
Schuerman Mt. 190
Secret Canyon 192
Shooting Range East 194
Shooting Range West 196
Slide Rock 198
Smoke Trail 200
Snoopy Rock 202
Soldier Pass Arches 204
Soldier Pass Trail 206
Steamboat Rock 208
Sterling Pass 210
Submarine Rock 212
Sugarloaf Black Mt. 214
Sugarloaf in Sedona 216

T-U
Telephone 218
Thomas Point 220
Thompson's Ladder 222
Turkey Creek 224
Twin Buttes 226
Twin Pillars 228

V-W-X-Y-Z
Van Deren Cabin 230
Vortexes:
    Explained 255
    Airport Hill Vortex 12

Bell Rock 32
Boynton Canyon 40
Boynton Spires 42
Cathedral Rock, Back O' Bynd. 64
Cathedral Rock, VV School 66
Cow Pies 84
Mitten Ridge 146
Vultee Arch 232
Walker Basin 234
Waterfalls:
Angel Falls 16
Brins Mesa East 46
Cookstove 80
Rattlesnake Canyon 174
Thompson's Ladder 222
Wilson Mt. North 244
Weir Trail 236
West Clear Creek 238
West Fork 240
Wilson Canyon 242
Wilson Mt. North 244
Wilson Mt. South 246
Windmill Mt. 248
Woods Canyon 250

VORTEXES

Many persons claiming to be authorities have spoken about the Sedona Vortexes. Some of these people make very specific claims: that a particular Vortex is male, female, electric, magnetic, Yin, Yang, etc. These authorities don't always agree with each other.

We think it is a mistake to go to a Vortex expecting to find an anticipated experience. If you do, you may set up a self-fulfillment trap, where you deceive yourself into thinking that you have found what you were *told* you would find, rather than having your own authentic experience. We recommend that you approach a Vortex openly, seeking no prescribed result.

The Vortexes are not hard to reach. You could easily visit all of them in a single day if you choose. Approach each one as a reverent seeker, open to what is there for you. Be quiet and unobtrusive so that you do not disturb others who are at the sites.

Experiences at the Vortexes range from negative, to neutral to cosmic. Each site is a place of beauty, worth visiting for aesthetic reasons; so your time will not be wasted even if you don't have a life-altering reaction. See the Index, pages 253-54, for Vortexes that we recommend.

SCENIC DRIVES
Airport Hill
This is a very easy, short drive. The road is paved all the way. It takes you past one of the Sedona Vortex spots to the top of the hill where the Sedona Airport is located, an excellent viewpoint from which to see Sedona and some of its famous landmarks. When you get to the top, turn left and go toward the cross. You will find a fine lookout point there. See **Airport Hill Vortex**, page 12.
Boynton Canyon
If your time is limited and you want to see some of the redrock backcountry, this is a nice, short drive over paved roads. See **Boynton Canyon**, page 40.
Loy Butte
You will drive over ten miles of good unpaved roads through some unspoiled country, allowing you to get away from town and see some great redrocks. At the end of the trip you will be within an easy walk from the best Indian ruin in the area. See **Loy Butte**, page 136.
Oak Creek Vista:
By taking this drive you will travel the length of Oak Creek Canyon, a beautiful scenic area. At the end of the drive you will be at a high point from which you can see the canyon, take a nature walk and learn about the area. See **Oak Creek Vista**, page 158.
Schnebly Hill Road
This is a favorite six mile drive that takes you through some beautiful country to the top of a hill from where you can enjoy sweeping views. The road is paved the first 1.3 miles. The unpaved portion can be travelled by any car unless it is wet and slippery. See **Munds Mt. North**, page 150.

RULES OF THE TRAIL

Artifacts: Leave potsherds, arrowheads and other artifacts where you find them.

Bikes: Stay on roads and trails. You cannot ride your bike inside a Wilderness Area. Some people will go into a legal area on a road and then sneak from it onto a wilderness trail. These scofflaws cause road and trail closures. Abuse it and lose it.

Cabins: Northern Arizona's climate is hard on cabins and they are scarce. Treat the few remaining ones gently. Don't climb on them, pry boards off or go digging for buried treasure.

Caves: Though caves appear indestructible, they are actually quite fragile. Whatever happens in them stays, as they are not self-cleaning. No graffiti, no smoking, no fires. Don't urinate or defecate in them or leave glass that might break. No firearms or fireworks.

Dogs: If you take your dog along on a hike, it should be on a leash.

Garbage: Pack it in, pack it out.

Rock Art: Don't touch it. Skin oils cause deterioration. Professionals don't even apply chalk in order to photograph rock art these days.

Ruins: Just look, don't touch. Preserve them. Don't pothunt, climb walls or do anything else that might harm a ruin. Help them survive.

Springs: Springs are vital to the survival of wildlife. Camp no closer than 200 feet. Don't do anything that could pollute a spring like bathing in it or throwing objects in it. Never use one for a latrine. As for yourself, even the purest looking water may contain harmful microbes. Today, the fear of giardia makes the wise er cautious about drinking untreated water.

ls: Stay on trails. They have been designed not only to provide access but bypass areas that can be harmed by people walking on them. Don't cut acks. It is disheartening to see how fast a trail can be destroyed by se.

Areas: These are special places. The goal is to leave them for future use and enjoyment as a wilderness. Here the hiker is chanized travel is permitted within them, not even bicycles. ear very rugged, they are in fact quite fragile environments. Leave no trace. They are a gift.